The day the johnboat went **up** the mountain

The day the johnboat went **up** the mountain

**Stories from my twenty years in
South Carolina maritime archaeology**

Carl Naylor

The University of South Carolina Press

© 2010 University of South Carolina

Published by the University of South Carolina Press
Columbia, South Carolina 29208

www.sc.edu/uscpress

Manufactured in the United States of America

19 18 17 16 15 14 13 12 11 10
10 9 8 7 6 5 4 3 2 1

Library of Congress Cataloging-in-Publication Data

Naylor, Carl.
  The day the johnboat went up the mountain : stories from my
twenty years in South Carolina maritime archaeology / Carl Naylor.
     p. cm.
  Includes bibliographical references and index.
  ISBN 978-1-57003-868-6 (cloth : alk. paper)
  1. South Carolina—Antiquities. 2. South Carolina—History, Local.
3. Excavations (Archaeology)—South Carolina. 4. Historic sites—South
Carolina. 5. Shipwrecks—South Carolina—History. 6. Underwater
archaeology—South Carolina. 7. Coastal archaeology—South Carolina.
8. Naylor, Carl. 9. Archaeologists—South Carolina—Biography. 10.
University of South Carolina. Institute of Archeology and
Anthropology—Biography. I. Title.
  F271.N39 2010
  917.57'04—dc22

                          2009029585

This book was printed on Glatfelter Natures, a recycled paper with
30 percent postconsumer waste content.

For Frank and Dorathy

Contents

Illustrations

Acknowledgments

Maritime archaeology is a team effort. The stories told here result from the combined efforts of the members of the Maritime Research Division at the South Carolina Institute of Archaeology and Anthropology. In addition to their endeavors in the field, their hard work in finding funds, researching records, recording sites, writing reports, and drawing illustrations made this book possible.

My biggest thanks go to Joe Beatty, archaeological technician, expert diver, and good friend, for being a central character in this book. His participation provided many of the lighter moments we have enjoyed over the years, and his reading of chapter drafts proved invaluable in filling gaps in my increasingly unreliable memory.

My gratitude goes to Chris Amer, state underwater archaeologist and head of the Maritime Research Division, and Jim Spirek, deputy state underwater archaeologist, for allowing me access to their files on the archaeological projects discussed here and for their assistance with photographs and artwork. I also thank Lora Holland, maritime archaeologist, for bringing passion to her job and friendship to mine.

I would like to thank the Benton clan—Terry, Jane, Hana, Arthur, Mickie, Sandie, Joan, and especially Maura—for their encouragement and for being friends who are like family, only a lot less annoying.

And to all the professional archaeologists, enlightened volunteers, and expert divers with whom I have had the pleasure of working over the years, I express my heartfelt appreciation.

Twenty Years and Counting

On a blustery fall day in 1986, I walked into Buddy Line Divers in Mount Pleasant, where I was a staff instructor, and went straight to the shop's bulletin board. Looking at the scuba course sign-up sheet, I noticed that few names appeared on the lists for my upcoming scuba courses. If I were to juggle the scheduled classes, I might be able to put together one, maybe two, full classes. Maybe. Winter is not a popular time to take scuba lessons, even if South Carolina has mild weather. Perhaps people just have other things on their minds at that time of year. Like the holidays. Things will pick up in January, I told myself, when a new wave of Jacques Cousteau wannabes would be coming into the shop, clutching as if they were lottery tickets the scuba course gift certificates they had received for Christmas.

Then, next to the sign-up sheet, I noticed an announcement I had not seen before. It was from the South Carolina Institute of Archaeology and Anthropology at the University of South Carolina. I knew little about these people other than that they were the outfit that issued the hobby diver license that allowed me to collect old bottles, fossilized shark's teeth, and other stuff from the rivers in the state. The notice said the institute's Underwater Archaeology Division planned to excavate a shipwreck in the Cooper River near Moncks Corner. They were looking to hire two divers for the six-week project to take place that October and November. Aha, I thought, a potential job. Even though temporary, it was a way to help make it through a winter that in many ways promised bleakness.

I looked at the class sign-up sheets and back at the job announcement. I actually liked teaching winter classes. Since I had fewer classes, I was able to get to know the students better, and it meant checkout dives in Florida, staying at dive resorts, diving some excellent sites—all paid for. And this institute project would mean diving long hours in the

1

dark Cooper River in October and November. Not the best time, weather-wise, to be on or in the river. On the other hand, the dive shop paid by the student. The institute paid by the week.

So I applied for the job and was asked to come to Columbia for an interview. After meeting and talking with Alan Albright, head of the Underwater Archaeology Division, and Mark Newell, I got the job. This was the first excavation of the Little Landing Wreck. At the end of the project, I collected my paycheck, thanked Albright and Newell, and said goodbye to everyone, thinking I would never see these people again. Several months later, however, I received a call from Newell, who said that the institute was starting a new program to be located in Charleston and that there was a slot for a full-time diver. He asked if I was inter-ested. I had to think about this. I loved teaching scuba diving and the freedom the job allowed. But the job with the institute offered two things I could not resist—interesting work and a steady paycheck. I took the job. So began my career in underwater archaeology.

The South Carolina Institute of Archaeology and Anthropology (re-ferred to hereafter as SCIAA or the institute) had its beginnings in 1963 when the South Carolina General Assembly created the South Caro-lina Department of Archeology. The department's mandate was to con-serve and preserve the archaeological heritage of the state—a tall order. In 1968 the governor transferred the department to the University of South Carolina and renamed it the Institute of Archeology and Anthro-pology. In 1984 the name was changed to the South Carolina Institute of Archaeology and Anthropology. In addition to adding an additional *a* to the word *archaeology,* the new name was intended to reflect the insti-tute's dual role as a research arm of the university and as a state agency. The curating of state artifacts, archaeological site information manage-ment, and artifact conservation come under its mandate as a state agency. As curator of state artifacts the institute is responsible to the state for the storage and care of archaeological collections in South Carolina. These collections originate from both land and underwater archaeological investigations conducted by institute staff as well as by other agencies and private archaeological companies. The institute also maintains the South Carolina Statewide Archaeological Site Inventory, containing the official files of all recorded archaeological sites in the state. In addition the institute is responsible for the conservation of all artifacts accepted.

The new program for which I was hired in 1987 was the Underwater Antiquities Management Program (UAMP). Our offices were aboard the nuclear ship *Savannah,* which at that time was moored at Patriots Point Naval and Maritime Museum in Mount Pleasant. The purpose of the program was to monitor construction and development that might affect archaeological or paleontological sites in state waters. This included the construction of docks, piers, wharves, boat ramps, marinas, dikes, revetments, and highway bridges as well as the dredging of waterways by private individuals or state and federal agencies. During the tenure of this short-lived program, we reviewed hundreds of dock construction requests. One of the actions that resulted from this review was the mitigation of a proposed dock on Hobcaw Creek whose planned location would have put pilings through the remains of an early-nineteenth-century wooden sailing vessel. With a simple change in the construction of the walkway leading to the dock, a valuable archaeological resource was saved. We also conducted surveys prior to the construction of new bridges for Highway 52 over the Black River near Kingstree, for Highway 39 over the Saluda River, and for the Cross Island Expressway Bridge over Broad Creek on Hilton Head Island. In July 1989 UAMP was abolished, and I was transferred to the institute's Underwater Archaeology Division, headed at this time by Christopher Amer. Shortly thereafter the museum's lease on the *Savannah* expired, and the ship was returned to the federal government and taken from Patriots Point. So we moved our offices into a trailer at the Fort Johnson Marine Resources Center on James Island. My primary duty there was to work with the newly created Sport Diver Archaeological Management Program (SDAMP) under Lynn Harris.

One of the Underwater Archaeology Division's mandates is to administer the state's Underwater Antiquities Act, which makes the division the custodian of all the archaeological sites in state waters—more than eight hundred sites! SDAMP was specifically concerned with the role of sport divers under the Antiquities Act. In addition to offering an educational program, SDAMP monitors the more than three hundred licensed sport divers who recover artifacts and fossils from state waters. In 2003 the Underwater Archaeology Division changed its name to the Maritime Research Division.

People I meet tell me that I have an interesting job. Who wouldn't find the archaeology of South Carolina interesting, especially since our state is blessed with such a rich and varied past? Prehistoric archaeological sites such as the Allendale Chert Quarry site are telling us not only how Native American peoples lived and subsisted in ancient times, but are also providing evidence that humans existed in South Carolina far earlier than anyone suspected. The discovery and recovery of the Confederate submarine *H. L. Hunley* has rekindled worldwide interest in this important aspect of the Civil War. And should we discover the remains of *Le Prince*, the French corsair that was lost in Port Royal Sound in 1577, or of Lucas Vázquez de Ayllón's *Capitana*, which foundered and was lost in 1526, possibly near the entrance to Winyah Bay, we would indeed be involved with groundbreaking maritime archaeology. *Le Prince* would be the first sixteenth-century French vessel found in North America, and Ayllón's *Capitana* would be one of the earliest Spanish ships found in North America.

The institute's Maritime Research Division has played a role in all of these projects and many more. Each archaeological site is different. Each promises different glimpses into the past. Each provides a different set of conditions and problems requiring diverse and innovative approaches. More important, each has brought me into contact with a wide variety of South Carolinians—private citizens who have provided invaluable assistance to the cause of maritime archaeology in this state. I have also had the honor of working with some of the best archaeologists in the country. You will meet many of these people in this book.

Calling these stories memoirs or recollections is misleading. The contents of this book go far beyond my recollections, combining them with the technical archaeological data and other historical research relative to each chapter. These sources are delineated in the bibliography.

Readers may note that archaeology projects are frequently inconclusive. We often end a project with more questions than when we started. Such is the nature of archaeology, particularly maritime archaeology. Scientific knowledge is cumulative. So it is with archaeology. Archaeology projects are pieces of a larger puzzle. The stories in this book do not begin or end a specific phase or era in maritime archaeology in South Carolina. They are merely single episodes in a continuing story. Like archaeology projects, they are pieces of a larger puzzle, part of a never-ending story.

Little did I know, as I read the bulletin board notice that day at Buddy Line Divers and contemplated a temporary job with the institute, that twenty years later I would still be part of the state's underwater archaeology team. I originally took the job because it promised to be interesting and provide a steady paycheck. The job sure has been interesting, as I hope the following stories relate, and it has provided a steady—if somewhat thin—paycheck.

The Lewisfield—No, Two Cannon—No, Little Landing Wreck Site

It was October 1985, and sport divers Bobby Snowden, Steve Thornhill, and Don Ard were on the bottom of the Cooper River off Lewisfield Plantation. The three had read stories of Revolutionary War vessels being burned and sunk at the plantation and decided to look for their remains. Snowden was exploring the murky water near the old plantation landing when suddenly one of the hoses of his scuba gear snagged an unseen object. Imagine his excitement when the object turned out to be a small iron cannon protruding from the bottom sediments. Snowden alerted Thornhill and Ard to the artifact he stumbled upon, and the three divers began examining the cannon. Digging around and under their find, they discovered a second cannon—a smaller swivel gun—buried beneath the first one. With renewed enthusiasm they continued their search of the river bottom, and it wasn't long before they spotted ballast rock and then the charred stem post of a vessel sticking out of the mud. Could this be one of the vessels they had read about? To the three divers, the presence of the cannons said yes.

Lewisfield Plantation, located just below Moncks Corner on the west branch of the Cooper River, became the property of Sedgewick Lewis in 1767. Known as Little Landing at the time of sale, it had originally been part of Sir John Colleton's Fairlawn Barony. In 1774 Lewis gave the property to his daughter Sarah on her marriage to Keating Simons. A year later Simons, an ardent patriot, enlisted in a militia regiment and had the misfortune of being in Charleston when the city fell to the British in 1780. Paroled by the British to his Cooper River plantation, he might have seen the end of his rebel activities except for the British army's constant use of Lewisfield as a landing place.

In July 1781, as the story goes, South Carolina militia colonel Wade Hampton and his men were traveling from Goose Creek to rejoin the main American army located in Berkeley County. As they neared Moncks Corner, the patriot leader left his troops to visit Molsie Simons, Keating's youngest sister. Arriving at Lewisfield, Colonel Hampton found the plantation swarming with British redcoats, specifically about one hundred soldiers of the Nineteenth Regiment of Foot under Lieutenant Colonel James Coates. According to the American account, the British soldiers were loading loot taken in raids on nearby plantations onto boats at the plantation's landing. The British account differs. They claimed they were loading the boats with wounded British soldiers for transport down to Charleston. In all likelihood the British were indeed preparing to transport their wounded in the boats—along with a cargo of plundered belongings. In any case Colonel Hampton returned with his troops and attacked the British, capturing seventy-eight prisoners and burning the boats.

Further mention of the burned vessels is absent from the historic records, and any evidence of their possible fate remained unknown until that October day in 1985.

The three sport divers, Snowden, Thornhill, and Ard, had no training in underwater archaeology. Bobby Snowden drove a truck for the Georgia Pacific plant in Russellville, Steve Thornhill was a maintenance supervisor at the same plant, and Don Ard worked at the Federal Mogul Company in Summerville as a production supervisor. Nevertheless they knew that what they had found was historically significant, and they knew the right thing to do was to notify SCIAA of their finds. The three divers called Alan Albright, then head of the Underwater Archaeology Division at the institute, and the two cannons were brought to Columbia for examination.

The first cannon measured slightly less than five feet (59.74 inches, to be exact) in total length. At the end of the eighteenth century, however, cannon lengths were measured from the end of the breech to the muzzle. For this piece this measurement was four feet, six inches—precisely the specified length for an iron British naval three-pounder of the early to middle eighteenth century. Its designation as a "three-pounder" meant it shot a lead ball weighing three pounds. And it was still loaded. Inside the barrel was a paper envelope of powder, rope wadding, a canvas shrapnel bag containing eight pieces of scrap iron, a cast-iron shot, and more rope wadding. Archaeologists discovered an identical canvas shrapnel bag on the American privateer *Defence,* which sank in Stockton Harbor, Maine, in 1779.

The swivel gun, so named because it was mounted on a ship's railing with the ability to pivot up and down and turn 360 degrees, measured

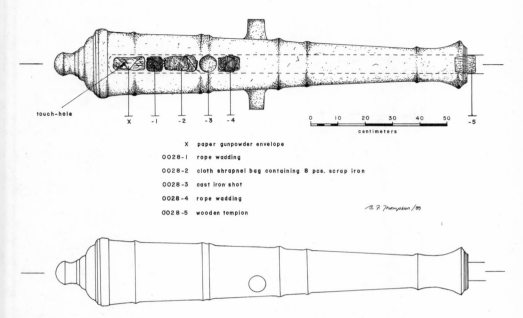

X   paper gunpowder envelope

0028-1   rope wadding

0028-2   cloth shrapnel bag containing 8 pcs. scrap iron

0028-3   cast iron shot

0028-4   rope wadding

0028-5   wooden tompion

Drawing of three-pounder cannon showing placement of wadding, shrapnel, and cast-iron shot. The cannon led three sport divers to the discovery of a possible Revolutionary War gunboat. SCIAA illustration by Bruce F. Thompson

a hair under three feet in total length and was bored for a half-pound shot. While too small to do any damage to a ship, swivel guns were effective at short range in clearing an enemy's decks of personnel, especially when loaded with grapeshot or other antipersonnel shot. Removed from this gun's barrel were five iron shot and scraps of wadding rope. Muzzle-loading swivels such as this one became popular in the first part of the eighteenth century. Ships of the Royal Navy, as well as any other armed vessel that could get hold of them, used swivel guns with great success until 1815. The one found by the divers is similar to one recovered by archaeologists from the gondola *Philadelphia,* sunk in Lake Champlain in 1776.

After hearing the divers' story, Albright sent Underwater Division staff members Joe Beatty and David Brewer to make a reconnaissance of the area in December 1985. While scouting the surrounding area by boat, they spied another wreck. Several hundred yards down from Lewisfield, the remains of a wooden vessel were plainly visible in the shallow water

LLI/0029

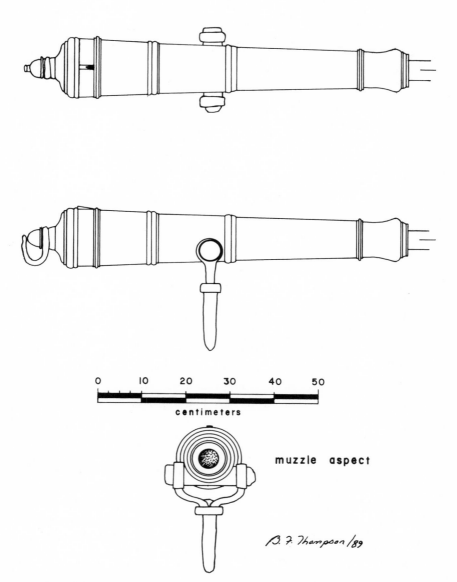

0   10   20   30   40   50

centimeters

muzzle aspect

B. F. Thompson/89

Drawing of the swivel gun, so named because it was mounted on a ship's railing and had the ability to pivot up and down and turn 360 degrees, found off Lewisfield Plantation in the Cooper River. SCIAA illustration by Bruce F. Thompson

near the edge of the river. The wreck showed obvious signs of burning. Could this be another of the boats burned by Colonel Hampton? Albright was intrigued, but, he realized, first things first: the wreck found off Lewisfield Plantation.

Alan Albright had made a name for himself excavating shipwrecks in Bermuda for the Smithsonian. He came to SCIAA in 1973, taking over the newly formed Underwater Archaeology Division. A thin, wiry man, he was full of energy and passion despite being in his sixties. He had a gaunt, sun-tanned face accentuated by wire-rimmed glasses and a neatly groomed gray mustache that looked as if it were trimmed using a ruler.

On January 23, 1986, a press conference was held at SCIAA's conservation facility on the University of South Carolina's main campus in Columbia to announce the finding of the Lewisfield shipwreck. "The find is of major importance for the state," Albright said in a press release announcing the press conference. "This is the first time that the undisturbed remains of a Revolutionary War vessel have been found in South Carolina."

Albright approached state senator Rembert C. Dennis, who at that time was not only a powerful South Carolina legislator but also the owner of Lewisfield Plantation, for state funding to excavate what by then was being called the "Lewisfield Wreck." Senator Dennis came up with the funding, a little more than one hundred thousand dollars, but had one request—that the wreck not be called the Lewisfield Wreck. His reason was understandable. He did not want attention drawn to his plantation or to the wreck site. Albright accepted the money and quickly renamed the site the Two Cannon Wreck.

The Two Cannon Wreck project began in November 1986. Albright's team included archaeologists Carl Steen from the University of South Carolina and Howard Weaver of Appalachian State University. The rest of the team consisted of Tony Magliacane and Greg Seminoff, whose duties included acting as surface staff and diver tenders, and divers Mark Newell, Joe Beatty, Peggy Brooks, and me. To save money Albright arranged for us to stay at the Berkeley Yacht Club. While this may sound grand, in actuality the yacht club was little more than a bar-restaurant (emphasis on bar), a boat ramp, and a few boats in various stages of becoming wrecks themselves. In addition Albright borrowed several large eight-man squad tents from the South Carolina National Guard for us to live in. We pitched the tents behind the bar-restaurant, next to the parking lot and the fish cleaning station. For showers we unhooked the garden hose from the fish cleaning station. We then alternated soaping up and rinsing in the cold water. This was my first archaeological project.

Author, in Kirby-Morgan band mask, prepares for shift on Little Landing 1 wreck site; assisting are Tony Magliacane, left, and Howard Weaver. SCIAA photograph

After several nights of screeching tires leaving the parking lot after midnight and cold showers while standing on a pile of fish scales, I began to wonder whether all archaeological projects were like this one.

We spent four weeks excavating the wreck. Our entourage included two twenty-four-foot pontoon boats, a sixteen-foot johnboat, and a twenty-foot McKee. We also had an eight-by-sixteen-foot barge on which we placed an air compressor to run the airlift. This was a good idea, as the compressor was the size of a World War II jeep and loud enough to be heard two counties away. Using all the air hose on hand, we anchored the barge as far away from the other boats as possible.

To provide communication with the divers, allow for surface-supplied air, and impress anyone who happened to see us in action, we dived with Kirby-Morgan KMB-10 band masks. This was the first time I had used band masks and surface-supplied air, although when I interviewed for the job I had assured Albright that I had tons of experience with this type of diving gear. As it turned out, the hardest part of using a band mask was learning how to equalize the pressure in your ears. Those of you who are divers know that as a diver descends the ambient pressure increases, creating an imbalance of pressure in one's ears. By pinching off the nose with one's fingers and gently blowing out, pushing air through the eustachian tubes, the pressure inside the ear equalizes with that outside. This is not possible with a band mask, however, since there is no way to pinch off one's nose with one's fingers. To equalize using a band mask, the diver pushes in a knob on the front of the mask. This moves a rubber-coated metal plate away from the front of the mask and under the diver's nose. Then, mashing the nose down on the plate, thereby sealing off the nostrils, the diver can equalize the ears.

The band masks provided diver-to-diver as well as diver-to-surface communication. This proved invaluable for the entire project, but never more so than at the beginning while we were setting up the grid over the wreck. Underwater archaeologists like to set up grids; the more unwieldy the grid the better. In theory once a grid is set up over a wreck, floats on two of its corners are surveyed in to the nearest geodetic marker on land. With the grid divided into squares, key points along a wreck's timbers and any artifacts can be mapped by taking measurements to them from three corners of the square. This provides a three-dimensional location for each point measured. Since the grid is tied into the nearest geodetic marker, moreover, each timber's and each artifact's precise location is recorded in relation to the rest of the known world.

Before we could put the grid down over the wreck, we spent a day or two removing debris, waterlogged trees mostly, from the site. On the first day, I tried to beat my dive partner into the water and begin my descent first. I wanted to give myself some extra time to master this new way of equalizing with the band mask. As I descended, I experienced varying amounts of success. My nose would slide off the rubber plate, or I would misjudge and my nose would push it away. I would then have to reach up and mash the knob in again. Several times I had to go back to the surface, relieve the built-up pressure in my ears, and start all over. A test of my equalizing skills came soon enough. After clearing debris the next chore was taking the pieces of the grid down to the bottom to assemble there. The first time the topside crew handed me a piece to take down, I realized I needed three hands. As I cradled one corner of the square piece in my arms, I struggled to reach the inflator hose on my buoyancy compensator jacket with my left hand. Normally I would let air out so that I could descend. In this case, however, the weight of the grid had me sinking to the bottom like a depth charge. If I could add some more air, I might be able to slow my descent. Just before I could grab the inflator, my ears began telling me they needed equalizing—now! Still cradling the grid, I reached up with my right hand and pushed the knob on the front of the band mask. As soon as the plate was under my nose I mashed down, hoping it wouldn't slip off or push the plate away. Determined not to let go of the grid despite what was happening, I went back to holding the grid in my hands. I never mashed so hard in my life. Luckily my first attempt was successful. Whew! As I continued to sink, the pressure soon began building back up. I hoped my next attempt would be as successful as the first. Failure meant a stretched eardrum, at best. A punctured eardrum also came to mind as a possibility. The second attempt was only partially successful, and the pressure in my ears soon turned to pain. Just as I was about to let go of the grid and get back to the surface, I crashed into the bottom. Setting the grid down, I began to ascend. Without the extra weight, I was too light. Again I reached for my inflator hose. Dumping air out of my jacket, I managed to stop the ascent. Coming up also relieved the pressure in my ears and ended the pain. I let some more air out of my jacket and slowly drifted down to the bottom, mashing my nose onto the rubber pad all the way. I picked up the piece of grid and took it to the assembly area, no one on the surface knowing what had happened.

The three-inch angle-aluminum grid we set up over the wreck measured fifteen feet by thirty and was subdivided into three-foot squares. Setting it up underwater required careful planning, a certain amount of rehearsal topside, and diver-to-diver communications once on the bottom, especially in the murky waters where visibility is often measured in inches. The first team of divers setting up the grid consisted of Joe Beatty and Peggy Brooks. As they pieced the grid together underwater in near-zero visibility, their ability to talk to each other proved essential.

Joe: Where does this go?
Peggy: Give me your hand. It goes in here.
Joe: Here?
Peggy: Um, yes. Now push it in.
Joe: Is it going in?
Peggy: Yes, keep pushing.
(*Joe grunting.*)
Peggy: C'mon, Joe, push harder.
(*Joe grunting more.*)
Peggy: You're almost there. Keep pushing.
(*Joe grunting even more.*)

It was at this point that listening to the diver-to-diver conversations became a favorite pastime of the topside personnel. After the merciless teasing they received by the topside crew, though, Joe and Peggy seemed less talkative while underwater. Joe was particularly wary of grunting while going about his work.

The Kirby-Morgan band masks also allowed for surface-supplied air to the divers. Using 310-cubic-foot air bottles mounted on the pontoon boat, the divers could stay down, in theory, for days without surfacing to change air tanks. While we didn't stay down for days, we did get into a routine of working four-hour shifts underwater. Four hours is an incredibly long time to work underwater, especially in November and December. It wasn't long before the second and third shifts, prior to donning the masks, spent a considerable amount of time cleaning them out while observing the previous divers for signs of sniffles, congestion, coughing, sneezing, runny nose, or anything that might be construed as an indication of something contagious, infectious, or transmittable.

We began the excavation at the stem post and worked toward the vessel's stern, moving ballast and airlifting mud, sand, leaves, and bricks as we went. The wreck was oriented bow to shore and rested not far from the old plantation wharf. While the exposed stem post found by Snowden, Thornhill, and Ard stuck up out of the bottom, we quickly realized the rest of the vessel sloped down into the bottom sediments at an angle of about thirty degrees. As we worked toward the stern, the vessel sunk deeper and deeper. By the time we reached the stern, we were working more than six feet below the river bottom.

To remove the mud and sand covering the wreck, we used an airlift. The airlift consisted, in our case, of a four-inch-diameter aluminum tube about ten feet long. A flexible hose was attached to the top end. This led to the surface, where any artifacts coming up the airlift could be screened out. About six inches from the bottom of the airlift, a garden hose was attached that allowed pumped air to enter the tube. The principle was simple. As the air rose in the tube, the air bubbles expanded, creating suction on the bottom end. This suction could, and did, suck gloves off our hands, and any object that could fit in the tube rocketed to the surface. The airlift worked beautifully except when we came across pockets of broken brick. If the diver wasn't quick enough to gather these by hand, they too would shoot up the tube, where they often jammed in the flexible hose. Other things, especially leaves, would then accumulate around the jammed brick, completely blocking the hose. When this happened, the portion of the hose below the blockage would quickly fill with air, making the airlift too buoyant for the diver to control. This meant the diver had to make a quick decision—either let go of the airlift and let it shoot to the surface like a Polaris missile or hold on and ride to the surface with it. Neither choice guaranteed a satisfactory outcome. Once the topside crew saw what was happening, they would immediately shut off the air supply to the airlift. If the diver had let go of the airlift, he or she then faced the possibility of the airlift crashing down on his or her head. If the diver rode it to the surface, then he or she faced the possibility of crashing back down with it. This could have adverse consequences not only for the airlift operator but also for the other diver still on the bottom.

As we vacuumed up the overburden using the airlift and got closer and closer to the buried timbers, we became more careful with the airlift. A contest of sorts developed among the divers. You got points for uncovering artifacts without moving them from their resting places so they could be mapped in, and you lost points if you let an artifact go up the airlift to be culled out by topside personnel in the screen boat, thereby losing its precise locational information. Archaeologists place heavy emphasis on locational information. They can learn more from an artifact that is in situ (in its original resting place) than they can from one that has been moved. And we found a good number of artifacts, including glass and ceramic shards, gunflints, a bar shot, a button, and a cartridge case.

During the third week of the excavation, Joe Beatty uncovered what we first thought was the remnants of a mast. The exposed portion showed burning, and it was about halfway down the anticipated length of the vessel, just where the mast would have been stepped. Excavating it further, we realized it was the remains not of a mast but of a bilge pump. What remained was just under two feet long and about two feet in circumference. The bottom tapered to form a square end that fit perfectly in a hole in the ceiling (inner) hull planking, allowing it to reach down into the bilge. Fashioned from a pine log, it had a two-inch hole drilled through its center. Bilge pumps on vessels this size were uncommon but not unheard of. On a vessel the size of the Two Cannon Wreck, it would have worked very much like a hand-cranked well pump.

Later that same day, as Joe continued airlifting down the keelson, he reported that the frames were beginning to slant toward the keelson, rather than being perpendicular. If this were true, it meant that they were what is called "cant frames," indicating the end of the vessel. Albright was skeptical. Considering the existence of a bilge pump and the depth of hold it implied, he assumed the vessel would be in the fifty- to sixty-foot range. In his field notes he wrote: "Joe thinks he has found the end of the keelson," and "Does not make sense—vessel might now be only 35 feet in length." We continued excavating until we had the entire remains of the stern exposed. Albright remained unconvinced. Despite doctor's orders forbidding him from diving, he donned scuba gear and

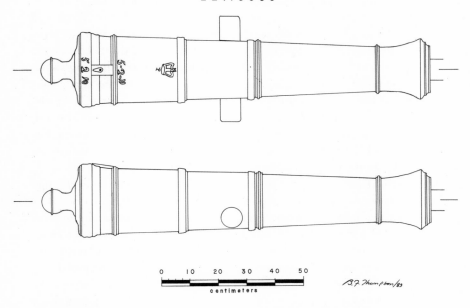

Drawing of third cannon, with British markings, found by the divers.
SCIAA illustration by Bruce F. Thompson

went down to see for himself. Sure enough, Joe had found the stern of the vessel.

Finding the end of the wreck seemed to take the steam out of the project. Sickness, equipment failures, and constant slumping of the mud and sand back onto the wreck plagued the fourth and final week of the project. First we had problems with the airlift. Then the motor on the McKee went out. The slumping meant we had to spend two hours each morning dredging material that had covered the wreck during the night. In addition several of the divers displayed signs of sore throats and fevers. Albright wrote in his field notes, "Crew is getting tired and so am I." On Wednesday of the last week, we decided to retrieve the grid and break camp. As we worked, there were few of us who didn't show signs of some ailment. Again I wondered if all archaeological projects were like this one.

Subsequent to our survey of the Two Cannon Wreck, the three divers who found the wreck, Bobby Snowden, Steve Thornhill, and Don Ard, returned to the site and found a third cannon. They reported that they located the cannon about ten feet east of the wreck. It seems incredible to me that we had missed it during our four weeks of mucking around the site. Nevertheless this created somewhat of a dilemma. What was at first the Lewisfield Wreck and then the Two Cannon Wreck suddenly found itself with three cannons. Should we change the name to the Three Cannon Wreck? Fearful that a fourth cannon was lurking somewhere near the wreck just waiting to be found, the name was wisely changed to the Little Landing Wreck after the original name for Lewisfield Plantation. Actually it became the Little Landing 1 Wreck, or simply "LL1." The wooden wreck downriver from Lewisfield, discovered by Joe Beatty and David Brewer during their reconnaissance of the area in 1985, was dubbed Little Landing 2, or "LL2."

This third cannon found by the divers, another three-pounder, had British markings, consisting of a crown with the letter *P* beneath it. The *P* meant the gun was proofed. Engraved just above the vent astragal was the preproof weight, "5-2-11" (627 pounds). Below the vent the postproof weight, "5-2-10" (626 pounds), was engraved. Like the other two cannons, this one was also loaded. This class of gun dates to circa 1770.

We returned to the site in November 1988. Since the previous visit, Alan Albright had left the institute, and the Underwater Archaeology Division was now under the direction of Christopher Amer. Amer, a native Canadian, had received his master's degree in nautical archaeology from Texas A&M University. Before coming to South Carolina, he excavated wrecks of Basque whalers in Red Bay, Canada. Other members of the team were Bruce Thompson, Joe Beatty, graduate student Jim Errante, David Beard, Peggy Brooks, and me.

The primary purpose of our visit was to map the bottom contour of the cove where LL1 rested. With a Lietz theodolite transit, we set up survey lanes five meters (16.25 feet) apart over the LL1 site, using range markers on either side of the river. We ran these lanes in a pontoon boat, recording depths at precise intervals using a Lowrance X-16 computer sonar. This produced a fairly accurate contour map of the river bottom in the vicinity of the wreck. The map showed that the wreck was lying in a trench running parallel to the shore. The average depth of the trench was twenty feet. The bank of sand, mud, and silt forming the channel side of the trench rose to less than ten feet from the surface.

We went back in December to begin excavations of both the LL1 and LL2 sites with the same personnel as the November survey, with the addition of SCIAA staff archaeologist Tommy Charles. From the beginning bad weather, illness, and equipment failure plagued us as it had during the last week of the 1986 project. After two days the decision was made to postpone the project until the following year.

We returned at the end of March 1989. The entire crew from the previous December was on hand, with the addition of graduate student Ashley Chapman. This time the weather was good, everyone stayed well, and the equipment worked properly. We spent eleven days excavating and recording both LL1 and LL2.

The LL2 wreck was the primary focus of the project, since this was the first chance we had to study the site. We found it covered with weeds. As we uncovered the wooden timbers, we began measuring them. Every imaginable measurement of each timber was taken—all in metric. I have since learned the ease and precision afforded by metric measurements, but at the time I thought it strange that we were taking metric measurements of timbers that had been formed by a shipwright to specific dimensions of feet and inches.

What we found was the remains of a vessel just under 48 feet in length and 17 feet 6 inches at its widest point. A single mast step notched the keelson about a quarter of the way from the bow. The depth of hold turned out to be 4 feet 3 inches, giving the vessel a displacement of between twenty and twenty-four tons. The keel measured 40 feet 8 inches long and averaged 8¼ inches wide and 17¾ inches deep. We sent wood samples to Clemson University, where Carol Buhion of the forestry department analyzed the keel, keelson, and outer and inner planking as being made of southern pine. The rest of the structural timbers (such as frames and the stem post) were live oak. The use of these woods suggests the vessel was of local manufacture. Square, wrought-iron nails, iron bolts, and treenails of southern pine fastened the timbers and planking together. The construction of LL2 reveals a strongly built boat, crafted with an attention to detail. This is indicated by the fact that the shipwright beveled the top of the keelson—an extra measure to prevent splitting. The hull lines suggest a flat-bottomed vessel, with a wide, beamy midships (well suited for carrying either wounded soldiers, loot, or both).

We also were able to record the Little Landing 1 wreck with more detail than had been possible during the 1986 excavation. The vessel found by Snowden, Thornhill, and Ard appears to have been single-masted and double-ended. Its overall length was 31 feet 7 inches. Amidships the vessel was flat and broad (its maximum beam was 10 feet), indicating a craft built for carrying cargo. Its hull was certainly capable of carrying the cannon found nearby. Charring on the timbers indicates the vessel suffered severe burning.

It was during this part of the project that I discovered underwater archaeologists are gadget freaks, perhaps more so than other folk. It's the

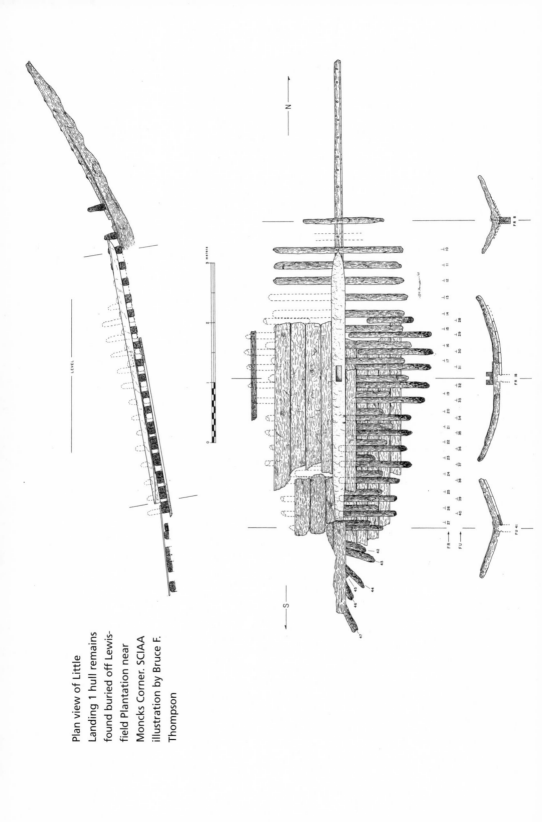

Plan view of Little Landing 1 hull remains found buried off Lewisfield Plantation near Moncks Corner. SCIAA illustration by Bruce F. Thompson

nature of the business. There are the scuba gadgets—regulators, buoyancy compensators, lights, compasses, depth gauges, air gauges, and those dive computers that tell you your maximum depth, present depth, bottom time, remaining air, decompression stop times, and the number of shopping days left before Christmas. There are the boat gadgets—depth finders, GPS units, chartplotters, VHF radios, and the all-important bilge pumps. And there are the archaeology gadgets—all those airlifts, water dredges, pumps, grids—and now that remote sensing has become standard in underwater archaeology, the magnetometers, side-scan sonars, sub-bottom profilers, and their related paraphernalia. Underwater archaeology is an equipment-intensive science. For this project we brought along a new gadget: the Helle broadcaster model 3510 underwater public address system.

This new addition to our equipment inventory consisted of a control box with a microphone and a submersible speaker. Since we no longer were using the KMB-10 band masks, and therefore had no surface-to-diver communication, we purchased the system to allow topside personnel to recall divers quickly. No matter how far the diver got away from the dive boat, the voice coming through the water was always loud and clear. At first this was somewhat disconcerting. We would be working along when suddenly an all-encompassing voice would speak to us. As a result we soon dubbed the device the V-O-G—Voice of God.

During the first days of the project, the divers were constantly bombarded with "Testing, one, two, three," and other inane phrases. And of course the topside crew had to try out the built-in siren and screech features. One day, as I was taking measurements on LL1, a completely new use for the contraption was discovered. Suddenly in addition to my own bubbles, I began hearing music all around me. I realized that I was hearing an underwater version of a mandolin solo. Jim Errante, one of the graduate students on the project and a proficient guitar and mandolin player, decided to place the topside microphone between his knees so that it was "keyed" and serenade us with his mandolin. He thought our underwater shift would go faster with some music. It worked. Jim soon discovered that all subsequent shifts wanted to be entertained as well. He played his guitar for us also, but the mandolin sounded the best coming through the water as we went about our tasks at the bottom of the Cooper River. Jim's primary duty became playing his music over the V.O.G. I don't think he minded, although I thought I saw bandages on the tips of his fingers by the end of the project.

In 1991 we heard reports that unknown divers were attempting to dig up the LL1 site, hoping to find artifacts on or near the wreck. Because of these reports, we visited the site for three days in July and August of that year. Sure enough there were clear signs that there had been digging around the wreck. To prevent any further digging by divers and any possible harm to the wreck, we purchased a roll of chain-link fence. After filling the hole dug over the wreck by the divers, we spread three lengths of fencing over the site, piling sandbags on top to hold it down. We then spent two days dredging sand and silt back over the whole affair.

So are these vessels (LL1 and LL2) the British vessels burned by Wade Hampton at Lewisfield?

While the presence of the three cannons, all from the right time period, would support the idea that LL1 was indeed one of those vessels, the fact that they were found on the river bottom, and not buried with the wreck, keeps us from using them as positive evidence. Ceramics found on the wreck included pearlware and delft. Pearlware, a type of lead-glazed earthenware manufactured in England, first came to America as early as 1775. Delft, a tin-enameled-glazed earthenware, was made in England as early as the mid–sixteenth century and is still made today. Most of the glass shards were too small or too burned to be of any use; three pieces were large enough to identify, however. All three are pieces of English, dark green glass wine bottles. Two of the bottle shards date from 1760 to 1790, the other from 1770 to 1785. The two gunflints we found are French, having a rounded heel as opposed to the British square heel. French gunflints were more popular than the British ones throughout the colonial period and were even favored by British soldiers until the turn of the nineteenth century. The button is a brass coat button of a type popular from 1726 to 1776. The iron bar shot is a dumbbell-shaped projectile, ten inches long, weighing just over six pounds. When fired, a bar shot rotates end over end, snagging ropes, tearing sails, and splintering spars. It can also have an unpleasant effect on any human that happens to be in its flight path. An identical bar shot was recovered from the French vessel *Machault*, which had shipwrecked in 1760. Other than the cannons, perhaps the most interesting artifact found on the wreck was the cartridge box. It is typical of those used by the British army throughout this period. Recovered in almost pristine condition, the cartridge container consists of a leather case holding a rectangular wood block drilled for twenty-six cartridges arranged in three staggered rows. Six of the slots still held lead balls and paper cartridges. The lead balls were the proper size to be used in the standard British firearm of the middle to late eighteenth century—the Brown Bess. These artifacts provide serious evidence that this vessel may indeed be one of Hampton's vessels. Armed British vessels often plied the Cooper River during the American Revolution, however, and were a common sight at Lewisfield landing. Any one of them could have deposited the artifacts.

How about LL2? Did it somehow drift downriver after being set on fire to deposit itself at its present location? It is possible. The construction of the boat says it could be from the Revolutionary War period. The vessel does show signs of burning that would be consistent with the story of Wade Hampton's skirmish at Lewisfield. The truth is that fire has been and still is one of the most prominent causes of ship disasters. Unfortunately we found no artifacts associated with the LL2 site: no ceramics, no bottles, no gunflints, no buttons, no cartridge case, nor anything else to fix the date of the wreck more precisely or to reveal any military association.

We haven't returned to the site in years and presently have no plans to do so. It is doubtful further excavations would reveal any new evidence. Perhaps we will never know for sure whether these two wrecks are the remains of the vessels captured and burned by Col. Wade Hampton in 1781. This is a disappointing conclusion to the story, but archaeological projects are like that.

Mud Sucks

As I struggled through the chest-deep mud that filled the old Santee Canal after nearly 150 years of neglect, I realized the past reveals its secrets reluctantly. They often hide in the most awful places. This revelation came as no sudden epiphany. It came after days in the thick muck, probing for the remains of canal boats and lock structures. It came after repeatedly falling face first into the ooze as a stuck leg suddenly came free. It came after becoming too exhausted from struggling through the deeper mud and having to be pulled out by rope. It came after . . . well, you get the picture.

When we began the Santee Canal Project in November 1987, we had no idea the mud would prove to be such a formidable foe. For one thing it slowed our work. Immensely. Tasks that should have taken minutes took hours to accomplish. With a tight budget, this presented a major problem. For another we were accustomed to working in open water. The debris and mud blocking the old canal was a new environment for us. Some of our established archaeological techniques worked. Others did not. Moreover we often worked completely submerged in the ooze. At the end of most days, we emerged from the canal dog tired and gritty, with mud stuffed, crammed, and caked in every orifice and crevice. The canal project taught us one of the great lessons of maritime archaeology: mud sucks.

The Santee Canal, which connected the Santee River with the upper reaches of the Cooper River, opened in 1800. Its claim to fame is in being America's first summit canal, meaning a canal that uses locks to go up in elevation and then back down to another body of water. In addition it was a true marvel of engineering, taking thousands of workers seven years to complete its 20.42-mile length.

The canal was intended to open up the interior of South Carolina to the port of Charleston. The products of upcountry farms and plantations, cotton and other goods, brought down the Congaree, Broad, Saluda, and Wateree rivers into the Santee would have a shortcut to Charleston. Conversely the imported commodities from abroad would have an easier path into South Carolina's hinterland.

Imagine the relief William Buford felt as he maneuvered his small cargo vessel out of the flow of the Santee River at White Oak Plantation and entered the Santee Canal in May 1801. Buford, who owned a plantation on the banks of the Broad River some ninety miles above Columbia, was bringing his crops to market in a boat built at his plantation. No information as to the size or method of propulsion of Buford's boat is available. We know, however, that his boat was less than sixty feet in length, ten feet in width, and drew less than four feet of water. We know this because that was the maximum interior size of the canal's ten single and two double locks.

No doubt Buford looked forward to a leisurely two-day journey through the canal. Not only had he successfully managed the falls and sandbars along his journey, but with the new canal connecting the Santee River with the Cooper River, he no longer faced the shoals and breakers at the mouth of the Santee or the forty or so miles of open ocean between the Santee and Charleston Harbor.

Less than one hundred feet after leaving the river, Buford came to the first lock. With the momentum built up from the river flow, he could easily maneuver his boat into the lock. Behind him the lockkeeper closed the lock gate. When closed, the gates angled slightly inward toward the lock. Above Buford a roadway sixteen feet wide crossed the lock, providing shade for Buford and his crew. The lockkeeper then moved to the upper gates and began working a crank that opened sluices built into the gates, releasing water into the lock. As the water rose, pressure pushed against the lower gates, providing the force to keep them shut. When the water in the lock reached the height of the water above the lock, a rise of five feet, the pressure against the upper gates eased, and the lockkeeper easily opened them. On the draw paths that bordered the canal, black workers hooked teams of either horses or mules to Buford's vessel. These teams effortlessly pulled the boat from the lock, starting it on its journey through the numerous lowcountry plantations that bordered the length of the canal. Less than a half mile later, Buford came to a second lock, which would raise his boat another ten feet. Here, next to the lock, was the house of the toll receiver. Again a bridge passed over the lock, as one did over every lock on the canal. After collecting the fee for passage, the toll receiver also probably reminded Buford of the rules of the canal. Buford could not load or unload cargo anywhere but at the public landings. He could stop no-where but at the public landings, and if his boat was delayed and not able to reach one of the public landings before dark, he was to stop at the next lock and stay there under the watchful eye of the lockkeeper.

Leaving the second lock, Buford passed a dry basin off to the side of the canal. Built to hold two boats undergoing repair, the basin measured 30 by 60 feet. Then came a stretch of level ground that turned into a low, swampy area. The open swamp soon closed in around his boat as he passed a tree line, and the canal became walled by woods of pine, sweet gum, oak, and hickory. About a mile past lock number two, the woods were replaced by open fields. A half mile ahead he saw lock number three, the first of the canal's two double locks. To his left he saw the residence of Samuel Porcher. On the right was the lockkeeper's house. Passing through the double locks took an hour, raising his boat another 19 feet. He was now 34 feet above the level of the Santee River and 69 feet above the Cooper River. Beyond the lock he could see that the canal and towpaths passed beneath the Eutaw Road bridge. Next to the bridge was the St. Stephen basin. Built to allow boats to spend the night or to load or unload cargo, the basin measured 100 by 150 feet. He also could see a 25-by-60-foot brick warehouse near the Eutaw Road. Nearby was the canal company's work yard, which included several workshops, the residence and gardens of the canal's director, and the overseer's house. He was now in the five-mile-long summit canal and as high as he would go. Ahead of him he had another double lock, six more single locks, and two tide locks to pass through, lowering him into Biggin Creek and the Cooper River at Stoney Landing. In between he would pass rice fields, pastures with grazing cows, and long stretches of woods. He would go by large reservoirs holding water to keep the canal filled and skirt numerous swamps with their large cypress trees.

After the two-day trip through the canal, Buford came to Stoney Landing. Here canal barges were transferring their cargo into the schooners that would take the produce to Charleston and vice versa. If Buford's boat carried a sail, it was here he would rerig his mast and sails before the trip down the Cooper.

Ending the canal at Stoney Landing was a logical decision. Being at the head of navigation for the Cooper River and possessing high bluffs, Stoney Landing had been a natural landing site for boat traffic as the early European settlers began moving inland. Sir Peter Colleton, one of the Lords Proprietors, was granted twelve thousand acres at the head of the Cooper River, including the area of Stoney Landing, in 1678. This property stayed in the Colleton family for about 140 years. During the

American Revolution, the British built a redoubt on the property and turned the Colleton home into a fort and later a magazine. When they left in 1781, they burned the Colleton home and the structures associated with the Colleton plantation.

Construction of the canal began in 1793. Talk of connecting the Santee River with the Cooper had started much earlier, in fact twenty years earlier, in 1773. But a small matter of a revolutionary war delayed further discussion until 1785, when a meeting was held in Charleston to discuss the matter again. Governor Moultrie presided over the meeting. The next year, in 1786, the South Carolina General Assembly passed an act forming a company to open inland navigation between the Santee and Cooper rivers. Members of this new corporation were some of the big names of the day, including Moultrie, John and Edward Rutledge, Judge John Grimké, Theodore Gaillard, Thomas Sumter, Francis Marion, Benjamin Waring, John Vanderhorst, Aaron Loocock, Ralph Izard, Commodore Alexander Gillon, William Bull, Nathaniel Russell, Philip Gadsden, and Henry Laurens Jr.

Many proposed courses for a canal were offered, including five from mapmaker Henry Mouzon. One report states that as many as thirty-eight different plans were studied. One was selected, and Col. John Christian Senf, a Swedish engineer, was hired as project engineer. Senf had come to America with General Burgoyne's Hessian troops, falling into American hands with the British loss at Saratoga. Henry Laurens brought Senf to South Carolina, where he served as an engineer with the South Carolina militia and as the state's chief engineer.

Senf began work on the canal in 1793 with ten workers. By the end of the year, there were one thousand employed on the project. Senf rented slaves from the local plantations to build his workforce. He also had a number of white workers in his employ. These included physicians, master carpenters, master bricklayers, overseers, cooks, wagon drivers, butchers, and various tradesmen. In 1794 a total of eight hundred whites and blacks were employed on the canal. In 1795 and 1796, there were seven hundred. Maintaining such a large workforce was not without its problems. Summer fevers devastated the workers. In his final report, Senf noted that during the construction of the canal "twenty-four white persons died at the Canal by Fevers." Senf made no mention of how many slaves died of fever.

For its twenty-mile length, the canal was to be thirty-two feet wide at the surface and twenty feet on the bottom. The depth of water was to be four and a half feet. Towpaths ten feet wide bordered either side of the canal. Construction of the canal meant a massive earth-moving effort. This was manual labor, using picks and shovels. Just as laborious was the driving of pilings. Pilings were pushed into the earth as far as possible. A rammer called a "tup" was then used to drive them. The tup was a square device, three feet long, with a base of fourteen inches, weighing two hundred pounds. Four laborers lifted it using handles on each of the sides. Once over the piling, the tup was slammed down, driving the piling into the earth. This was repeated until the piling reached the desired depth.

On Monday, May 19, 1800, Colonel Senf reported that the canal was ready to commence operation. The total cost of building it was $750,000. The first vessel through the canal entered in July 1800. Thus began an important era in the history of transportation in South Carolina as cargoes of rice, naval stores, and cotton passed through the canal. In 1809 canal stockholders received a dividend of $12.50 per share. In 1828 the dividend rose to $40 per share.

Nevertheless the canal was plagued with problems. The lack of water to fill the upper levels of the canal was just one. It closed periodically for lack of water. A protracted drought closed the canal from 1817 to 1819. Another problem was keeping it cleaned of debris. In 1804 the canal closed in September to clear it of obstructions. Each year thereafter the months of July, August, and September were devoted to cleaning out the canal.

Sometime about 1820 John H. Dawson of Charleston bought Stoney Landing at auction for $2,500. The canal experienced one of its high points in 1830, when 1,720 boats passed through. Nevertheless the operation continued to suffer from a multitude of problems. Droughts continued. The need to clear the canal of snags continued. Finally it was the ever-expanding railroad system, which opened up the South Carolina interior in the 1840s, that brought on the end of the canal. It closed sometime about 1850.

The Stoney Landing property subsequently passed through a series of owners. In 1856 St. Julien Ravenel bought the 935-acre plantation. Shortly thereafter Ravenel began mining and processing limestone from the bluff adjacent to Biggin Creek. The limestone was processed into quicklime, mortar, cement, and niter, a necessary ingredient in gunpowder. During the Civil War, the gunpowder went to supply Confederate forces.

Stoney Landing played another important role during the war as the construction site for three Confederate ships. The most important of these was the CSS *David,* one of those newfangled Confederate semi-submersibles. On the night of October 5, 1863, the Confederate warship slipped past the Union picket boats and attacked the USS *New Iron-sides*. The *David* successfully exploded its torpedo against the hull of the *New Ironsides*, though owing to bad placement of the charge, it failed to sink the Union warship.

In 1910 the property passed into the hands of the Dennis family. The Tailrace Canal was cut through the property in 1940 in conjunction with the construction of the Pinopolis Dam. The resulting Lake Moultrie inundated much of the Santee Canal, leaving only small portions exposed. One of these was on the north end where it connected with the Santee River. The other was the south end where the canal entered Biggin Creek and the Cooper River at Stoney Landing. In 1982 the old Santee Canal was listed on the National Register of Historic Places. Senator Rembert Dennis sold Stoney Landing and two hundred surrounding acres to the state in 1984 with the understanding that the property would become a state park. Not long after the sale, the South Carolina Public Service Authority (Santee Cooper) and the South Carolina Department of Parks, Recreation, and Tourism (PRT) were charged with the park's development and operation.

Planning for the proposed park included an archaeological investigation of the property. This is how the Institute of Archaeology and Anthropology became involved. In early 1986 Santee Cooper contracted with SCIAA for a two-week field survey of the property. SCIAA archaeologists Tommy Charles and James O. Mills performed the land portion of the survey. The survey investigated fourteen sites in all, including two underwater sites discovered during an initial reconnaissance of the area.

Three of the land sites indicated prehistoric occupation only. Three sites consisted of both prehistoric and historic components. Charles and Mills found these six sites along the top of the bluffs that mark the western edge of the proposed park. The prehistoric artifacts recovered from these six sites, mostly pottery shards, indicate a Native American presence during the Middle Woodland period, which lasted from 200 B.C. to about the time of Christ. These dates are consistent with other nearby Native American sites. The historic components of three sites consisted of artifacts, mostly ceramics dating from 1780 to 1900. The archaeologists found no evidence of any structures on the six sites.

Four sites were associated with the industrial use of the land, specifically the limestone mining and processing in the mid–nineteenth century. These sites included the remnants of a limekiln, two cisterns, an iron sluice, foundations for buildings or sheds, and mining areas. One site, given the artifacts found (including a windlass, chain links, a pintle plate, metal straps and spikes, iron rings, and tin sheet fragments), was probably the building site for the *David* and the two other Confederate boats.

The main house was recorded as a site, as were the bluffs behind the house, which had been used as a trash dump. When the survey was conducted, two structures existed on the house site. The archaeologists wanted to determine whether the main house was the original home on the site or a replacement. Construction details showed that the house was built about 1850 and was indeed the first house on the site. The other structure is the William Dawson house. Moved to the site in the 1950s to replace an earlier structure that burned, the house lies south-west of the main house. William Dawson was caretaker of the property in the mid-1900s. The trash disposal site extends for sixty meters across the top of the bluff between main house and Biggin Creek. Pottery shards from the dump yielded a mean ceramic date of about 1840, yet it was obvious the site was used into the twentieth century. Included in the artifacts found were lightbulbs, aerosol cans, a car muffler and seat belt, a garden hose, and one 1928 South Carolina license plate.

A portion of the trash dump extended into Biggin Creek and was recorded as a separate site. Owing to this and the two vessels spotted by the land archaeologists, the institute's Underwater Archaeology Division was called in, specifically Alan Albright, Joe Beatty, Ashley Chapman, and Mark Newell. They conducted a one-day investigation of the dump site and the two vessels.

Investigating the dump site, the underwater team found four distinct concentrations of artifacts in the waters of Biggin Creek, indicating four separate time periods. One pile dated to the eighteenth century, one to the early to middle nineteenth century, one to the late nineteenth century, and one to the twentieth century.

One of the vessels was a wooden flatboat (barge) measuring forty feet by sixteen feet. The exterior consisted of pine planking, two inches by ten inches. Deck planking measured one inch by twelve. Iron drift pins and wire nails used as structural fasteners indicate that the flatboat was built in the early twentieth century. The vessel is of the type used in the construction of the Pinopolis Dam and Tailrace Canal. The other vessel spotted by Charles and Mills in Biggin Creek turned out to be a wooden ship-built vessel. About thirty feet of the vessel was visible in the creek's tannic waters. Its forward end disappeared into the creek bank. The exposed portion consisted of the keel, frames, keelson, and remnants of a sternpost. A single mast step was observed about sixteen feet from the stern. Since single-masted vessels had their mast a good ways forward of midships, the placement of the mast step indicates the vessel may have had two masts. The archaeologists named the craft the Biggin Creek Vessel and tentatively dated it to the mid–nineteenth century.

By the time Charles and Mills issued their report, Santee Cooper was formulating plans for the proposed park. Part of those plans called for dredging a portion of the canal in the park area. The intent was to give the public the feel of what the canal would have been like during its operation and to open up the canal to canoers. This necessitated a full archaeological survey of the canal. On October 10, 1987, Santee Cooper and PRT signed a contract with SCIAA's Underwater Antiquities Management Program (UAMP) to perform this survey.

A month later, on November 9, UAMP staff members Mark Newell, Jodie Simmons, Peggy Brooks, and I packed our gear and headed for Moncks Corner. We ensconced ourselves at the Berkeley Motel. The motel contained a restaurant that was not only convenient but was open for breakfast. All small towns have a place where the locals gather, where you are likely to run into the mayor in a suit and a farmer in overalls drinking morning coffee at the same table. The Berkeley Motel Restaurant was such a place. For lunch the restaurant turned into the epitome of a southern meat-and-three. A large portion of our per diem meal allowance was spent there.

As we headed down to the canal for our first day of work, we were filled with trepidation. The planned survey of the portion of Santee Canal destined to become a state park was the largest project yet undertaken by UAMP. Moreover the swampy environment threatened to defy our skills and talents. In effect it was us versus the mud.

Our plan was fourfold. First, we were to find and document all cultural remains within the project area. This included almost anything that could have found its way into the canal bed either during its operation or since. Of course we were hoping to find one of the boats built especially for canal use. This would have been a unique find. Second, we were to complete the documentation of the Biggin Creek Vessel. Third, we planned to examine the underwater artifact scatter in Biggin Creek. Fourth, we were to document further the remains of the flatboat in Biggin Creek. Moreover the schedule called for us to accomplish this in twenty working days. *Daunting* is the word that comes to mind.

Our first chore was to survey the canal for cultural remains. This required a magnetometer to locate any ferrous metal under all that mud, silt, debris, and fill dirt. We leased a Geometrics 866 proton magnetometer with an integral paper strip chart from Harvey Lynch, Inc., of Houston to accomplish the task. For power we rigged two car batteries.

We decided to divide the canal into four sections. Area A ran from Highway 343 (the road from Highway 52 to what was then the Dock Restaurant) to about the midpoint of the property, where an access had been cut at a right angle over to a culvert connected to the Tailrace Canal. While this area of the old canal ran for 1,030 meters, the average width of the waterway was 17 meters, giving us a total area of about 17,500 square meters (or about 4.3 acres) to survey in this one section. Area B was a partially dry area that ran from the end of Area A south to Biggin Creek. This portion of the old canal had been filled with dredge spoil that had slumped down from the large embankment that ran between the Tailrace Canal (the origin of the spoil) and the old canal. This added another 1.7 acres to our survey area. The Biggin Creek Vessel and area around it were designated Area C. The river bottom around the trash piles at the mouth of Biggin Creek and the flatboat examined earlier by the underwater team were designated Area D.

We began in Area A. In this section the canal took on the characteristics of a small tidal creek. Water from the Tailrace Canal and Cooper River entered the canal through the culvert. At high tide the water depth in the canal (on top of the three to four feet of mud) ranged from about one foot at the north end to about four feet at the bottom end where the culvert connected the water bodies. To survey the area, we rigged the magnetometer head to the end of an eight-foot-long piece of angle aluminum. We thrust the mag end out the front of the boat, like an aluminum bowsprit, clamping the other end to the johnboat's bow. Once this was rigged, we oared and poled the johnboat down the mud-filled canal, starting at the upper end. We soon found the error in our method. While there was enough water to float our johnboat at high tide, about midway to low tide all the water was gone from the canal, returning to the Tailrace Canal through the culvert at the southern end of Area A. Needless to say, we could not paddle through the mud, although a few times, as the water left the canal faster than we could get back to our launch area, we had to get out and push the boat and ourselves through the muck. This cut our available work time drastically.

To lengthen our workday, we needed to slow the flow of water from the canal. We decided to rig a flapper valve over the culvert. This would keep the water in the canal longer, we thought, letting us extend our magnetometer surveying each day. Using a piece of plywood, some poles, and rope, we made a flapper and tied it over the culvert on the canal side. In theory the incoming tide opened the flapper, allowing the water into the canal. When the water started out, the water pressure closed the flapper, keeping the water in the canal. Our contraption worked well for three days, then deteriorated to the point where it was useless. We blamed the failure on the stresses of the strong water flow. The idea that our engineering and construction abilities were lacking was not considered. We went back to surveying at high tide. The mud had won this round.

Nevertheless we recorded seven magnetic anomalies in Area A. In addition, while conducting the survey, we spotted the sternpost of a small vessel sticking up out of the mud on the east side of the canal just north of the culvert.

Two of the seven anomalies, located about 150 meters down from the north end of what remains of the canal, were within the confines of what we identified as one of the canal's locks from features on the canal bank. Another 100 meters south, where a small creek entered the canal, the magnetometer recorded a large anomaly spreading over some 30 square meters. Still farther south of the canal lock, about 300 meters, were two anomalies—a small one on one side of the canal and a large one on the other. Finally two other anomalies, one small and one large, were recorded. The large one was located near the southern end of the canal, just north of the culvert. To mark each site, we jabbed wooden poles into the canal mud. Now came the chore of ground truthing the magnetometer hits to identify the source.

Our methodology (a big archaeological term meaning "plan of attack") consisted of probing into the mud with the wooden poles we used as markers. If this proved unsuccessful, we donned our wet suits and got down into the canal bed, gingerly sweeping around with our feet for the object in the mud. In places sand covered our target objects, making our foot probing impossible. We then slipped on our scuba gear and dug in the sand with our hands or, in hard-packed sand, with our water dredge.

The first time we pushed our way through the waist-deep mud in the canal around the markers, we discovered grooves in the canal floor. These grooves were made more than two hundred years ago by the picks of hundreds of slaves as they carved the canal out of the hard marl. These laborers had a quota of two cubic yards of material to move per day. Perhaps they would have been happy to have mud to excavate rather than the rock-hard marl. The grooves reminded us that our difficulties with the mud were nothing to those endured by the slaves.

After the first day of ground truthing, we realized we had to add a step to our methodology. At the end of the day, we could not simply pack up our gear and return to the motel. Far too much mud covered us for us to get into our vehicle or enter our motel rooms. Instead we walked down to the Tailrace Canal near the Dock Restaurant. First, we waded into the water and rinsed as much mud as possible off our wet suits. This accomplished, we peeled off our suits, pulling them inside out to clean out the several pounds of mud that had found its way inside. Then we turned our attention to ourselves, sluicing the mud out of our armpits, ears, necks, and other crevices. We attracted more than one strange look from early dinner customers at the nearby seafood restaurant. After washing off as much of the mud as possible, we walked, dripping, barefoot, and carrying our wet suits, back to our vehicle and the motel. We put this part of our workday in the category of public relations, that is, we didn't want to tick off the motel management by trashing our rooms with mud every afternoon.

The first two anomalies, the ones inside the canal lock, we were unable to find, as they were covered by slump from the canal banks. We refrained from dredging these two unknown magnetometer hits since we did not want to disturb any of the lock structure, but their locations, on either side of the lock and near opposite ends, indicated metal hinge parts for the lock gates.

The large anomaly one hundred meters south of the lock was easy to locate, as was the large anomaly further south. These two items turned out to be two of the wooden lock gates, supposedly from the nearby canal lock. We dredged enough of the mud and sand covering the gates to determine that our magnetometer had recorded the thick wrought-iron reinforcing bands holding the corners of the gates together and a sliding iron plate that acted as a sluice gate in one corner. With time being short, we moved on without fully excavating and recording the gates.

The small anomaly across from the second lock gate turned out to be a jumble of wire, perhaps the remains of a small fish trap. The other small anomaly was an unidentifiable wooden construct consisting of longitudinal planks and one curved cross member. Nails, spikes, and iron dowels held the wooden pieces together.

Searching for the cultural remains with our feet was successful in locating most of the magnetic anomalies. The seventh anomaly eluded us, however. The strength of the magnetometer reading (469.2 gammas) indicated a large object. By comparison a metal boat trailer we found in Station Creek off Port Royal Sound registered 358.1 gammas. We probed with a wooden pole. We struck nothing. We got into the canal and probed with our feet. Again we found nothing. There was a small mound of sand, perhaps one foot high and two feet across, at the location, but we dismissed it as the site of our anomaly. We assumed that

Archaeologist Jodie Simmons after failed attempt to walk on mud in old Santee Canal. SCIAA photograph

an anomaly with such a large signature could not hide in such a small mound of sand. After searching everywhere else, though, we returned to the sand mound. In the center of the mound, at the very bottom, we found a fist-sized chunk of metal. A clear break indicated that it was part of a larger object, making it hard to identify. Despite being small, it was heavy, weighing about four and one-half pounds. We discovered another attribute when the metal object kept attaching itself to any ferrous metal it met. Once attached to some metal object, our metal weight belt buckles or steel air tanks, it was nearly impossible to pry off. We determined the object was a piece of an electric motor magnet.

One day archaeologist Jodie Simmons decided he was tired of struggling through the chest-deep mud to get from one section of the canal to another. He had a solution. He was going to walk on top of it. The theory was that if he spread out his weight over a bigger area he would be able to stand on top of the mud without sinking to his waist. So he tied two pieces of plywood to the soles of his dive boots. Each piece of plywood was oval, eighteen inches in length and about twelve inches wide. The first time Jodie tried his new mud shoes his descent into the mud was slowed little, if at all. In fact, instead of sinking straight down, the plywood pieces skittered sideways as they cut down into the mud, causing Jodie to fall backward onto his butt. Undaunted by his first attempt, he tried again. This time he fell forward onto his face. Never a quitter, he repeated his attempts several more times. At last he gave up. A discussion among the onlookers ensued. The theory was correct but the math was off just slightly, we decided. The plywood would have to be much larger. Spreading his weight was the right idea. He just needed more spreading. We figured that one complete four-by-eight sheet of plywood would do the trick—one on each foot.

Our attention then turned to the sternpost we saw near the south end of Area A. Probing the area, we discovered a vessel resting parallel to the east bank of the canal. A fallen tree covered the wreck. After sawing the tree into segments and removing it, we could take some basic measurements. The vessel turned out to be fifty-five feet nine inches long and nine feet ten inches wide—the right size to fit through the canal locks. We excavated a portion of the bow area, revealing clear evidence of burning. Probing the interior of the hull indicated a double-ended vessel of light construction.

The remaining area of the canal, Area B or the "dry" area, consisted of two marshy areas divided by a central area of standing water—that is, swamp. In the marshy areas, one person (usually me) carried the magnetometer while Jodie Simmons worked the strip chart and Peggy Brooks wrangled the magnetometer cable through the woods. We first set up the strip chart at the extent of the cable into the survey area. I then carried the magnetometer head, following the marked centerline of the old canal, to the extent of the cable. This was repeated ten feet on each side of the centerline. We then moved the strip chart down the canal again to the extent of the cable and repeated the process. In addition to the magnetometer head, a hundred or so feet of cable, and the strip-chart unit, several car batteries that powered the magnetometer had to be carried through the area as well. In the central, wet portion, we dragged and pushed the johnboat through the dry portions to the central area and rerigged the magnetometer out the bow on angle aluminum, and we repeated the procedures we used in Area A. Several days of carrying the magnetometer through the marshy woods and rowing it up and down the wet portion of Area B resulted in the discovery of no magnetic anomalies.

Meanwhile Chris Amer, Bruce Thompson, and Billy Judd had joined our team. At the time Chris was the new head of SCIAA's Underwater Archaeology Division. Bruce Thompson was an underwater archaeologist from Texas A&M University who became SCIAA's conservator in 1988. Billy Judd was a SCIAA research affiliate and an expert on barge construction. Chris, Bruce, and Mark Newell were there to record the Biggin Creek Vessel (Area C). Billy had the Biggin Creek Flatboat (Area D).

Chris, Bruce, and Mark spent two days recording the Biggin Creek Vessel. Their task was to make a more detailed analysis of the vessel than had been accomplished the previous year. Since their time was limited, they were unable to excavate the bow section of the vessel, which extended into the creek bank, leaving them only the exposed 30 feet of the vessel to study. Nevertheless fourteen sets of frames were visible. These frames measured about 5 inches square and were spaced 18 inches apart. The 1-inch-thick outer hull planking ranged in width from 11 inches to 14½ inches. Square iron nails and wooden treenails attached the planking to the frames. The vessel's keel tapered from 7 inches to 5 inches at the stern and was 15 inches deep near the mast step. About 19 feet of the keelson was visible. The measuring tape showed it to be uniformly 7 inches wide, but tapered in depth from 10½ inches at the mast step to 7 inches at the stern. Iron bolts and treenails attached the keelson to the frames and keel. Two lodging knees, indicating the vessel was decked, were still attached to the hull. Before finishing its work, the team took fourteen wood samples from the wreck.

From the observations, Chris determined the vessel was a double-ended, flat-bottomed workboat. He estimated the vessel to be from 46 feet to 65 feet in length and about 16 feet in width, which precluded it from being a canal boat. The keel and keelson were made of southern yellow pine. The frames were made of southern yellow pine, spruce, and white oak. Since the derelict vessel would have blocked Biggin Creek, it is evident it was abandoned sometime after the closing of the canal in the 1850s. Chris speculated that the vessel might have been associated with the lime mining and processing activities that took place at Stoney Landing from around 1853 until after the Civil War.

As mentioned earlier, the Biggin Creek Flatboat measured 40 feet long and 16 feet wide. Its sides measured 3 feet 5 inches deep. Billy found that the barge was decked with 1½-inch planks running across the barge at the top of the gunnels. Five deck supports ran longitudinally. Billy also discovered that the sides, bow, stern, and possibly bottom of the flatboat were double planked, with tar paper or roofing felt sandwiched in between. This may indicate that as the barge aged it began to leak. Instead of caulking the seams, the owner placed the tar paper over the outside of the hull and planked it over. This was consistent with our earlier conclusion that the flatboat might have been used in the construction of the Pinopolis Dam and Tailrace Canal.

The other feature in Area D were the trash piles examined in 1986. Our original thinking was that further excavation of the dump site might reveal horizontal and vertical contextual association of artifacts—in other words what was dumped when and where in relation to the other items. After reexamining the earlier findings, however, Jodie Simmons determined that no clear stratigraphy in the trash piles existed. The swift currents through the canal evidently scattered and mixed the artifacts into an unenlightening jumble. Jodie decided that further excavation of the site would be pointless.

With just a few days left of our allotted twenty days, we realized we needed to wrap up our efforts. Plans called for the park contractor to drain the canal and remove most of the mud using heavy machinery. This meant we needed to provide some protection for the artifacts we had discovered and partially exposed. For this we used some heavy machinery of our own, in the form of a backhoe. First, the backhoe dug a trench about three feet from each of the remains, which included the two lock gates, the two vessels, and the unknown wooden construction. We then covered each area over the item with a thick layer of burlap sacking. Over this we spread large sheets of black plastic film, pinning these in the trenches with stakes and granite rock. Stakes were driven around each site to warn the construction equipment operators of the locations. We then returned to our offices.

We considered the project a success. We had discovered and partially recorded the canal's terminal tide lock, the remains of a vessel that may well be an elusive canal boat, two of the lock's gates, and another unknown wooden construct. We added to our previous knowledge of the Biggin Creek Vessel and the Biggin Creek Flatboat. And we provided some protection for these sites from possible harm during the coming canal park construction. Not bad for just twenty days of work. We figured we had won our struggle with the mud.

In May 1988, because of our discoveries in the park portion of the canal, the South Carolina State Historic Preservation Office entered into an agreement with Santee Cooper for further archaeological work in the proposed park area. This agreement stipulated that SCIAA do that work.

So on June 1, 1988, we packed our bags, loaded our equipment, and headed back to the Berkeley Motel. I wondered if they would be glad to see us. Despite our best efforts in the Tailrace Canal, a good amount of canal mud managed to find its way into the motel rooms, particularly our showers. Our dripping wet suits draped over balcony railings had not been a pretty sight, either. Nevertheless they greeted us cordially, saying they were glad to see us. The fact that our rooms were on the very backside of the motel this time did not go unnoticed, however.

We had several tasks to accomplish. We had eight weeks to accomplish them. We wanted a better look at the canal lock and the two lock gates. We were determined to identify the wooden construct. In addition we had to provide these items and the small vessel found at the south end of Area A with protection from the elements and park construction.

As we headed for the canal on the first day back, we decided to walk the old pathways that led along the side of the canal for the length of Area A. We were curious to see what if anything had changed during our six-month absence. Several things popped out. First, we immediately noticed the contractor had cut several roads through the woods surrounding the canal. We also noticed the water and mud had not been removed as we expected. This didn't mean the contractor had not been busy. He had installed a well-point system north of the canal lock, just south of Highway 343, lowering the water level just enough to get a large backhoe into the canal. This backhoe was in the process of filling huge ore trucks with the watery mud from the canal. We continued down the canal. The second thing we noticed, after passing the canal lock, was that our fears of not having marked the two lock gates and other sites well enough were, except in one case, unfounded.

The locations of the relics could not have been more obvious. The marsh gas had built up under their black plastic coverings and, aided by the hot June sun, expanded the airtight protective sheeting like hot air balloons. My dictionary says methane, the primary ingredient of marsh gas, is odorless. Perhaps so, but *something* about it is anything but odorless. Bursting pockets of marsh gas as we pushed through the built-up silt and leaves in the canal during the project often created the impression that the mud was an entirely different type of brown, mushy "soil." Guess who had the job of slithering into the still-mud-filled canal and slitting the black plastic, allowing the balloons to deflate as the foul gas gushed out into my face. Protecting the canal's large artifacts would take more thought.

The contractor told us that the work in the area north of the canal lock would be done in a few days, and work would then commence in the area below the lock. At first the contractor's plan was to load the mud into large ore trucks and haul it off to a local landfill. This plan was soon abandoned when much of the soupy mud slopped over onto the roads of Moncks Corner before it could ever reach its intended destination. This did not make Moncks Corner officials overly happy. The contractor then began dumping the mud on the hillside between the old canal and the Tailrace Canal. We decided the best thing we could do would be to re-mark the areas around our sites in the area below the canal lock. While we did this, the contractor moved to the area where we were working and set up a well point there. Again the water was lowered somewhat, but it was not removed altogether. Nevertheless the process of removing the mud continued. We decided to cease our operations while the contractor struggled with the water and mud.

A month later it was apparent that the contractor had mounted a losing battle with the water in the old canal. He had lowered the mud to about a half foot, but this had been replaced by water.

This changed our plans. Okay, we told ourselves, the water was still there. We could deal with that. Actually this could turn out to be a good thing. We no longer had to worry about the boat and lock gates drying out from not being submerged in water. With the water still in the canal, it would also be easier to remove the hundreds of cubic yards of mud from the canal lock site.

When we turned our attention to the south lock gate, we were saddened to find it destroyed. Bashed to bits. Stomped to splinters. We thought we had marked the site clearly enough. Apparently we had not. After being loaded the large ore trucks drove down the canal bed to one of the exit points. Our marker poles had been mowed down on one of these passes. Without the markers the trucks began driving over the lock gate. Repeatedly. The damage was total.

We were relieved to find that the north lock gate, located about one hundred meters south of the canal lock, had fared better. After removing our temporary coverings, we water-jetted most of the mud overlaying the gate. Close to the artifact, we used trowels to remove the remaining mud by hand. With the mud removed, water filled in and covered the gate at high tide. At low tide the gate was partially exposed to air. We decided that after recording the gate we would move it out into the canal, where water would cover it at all tide stages. Also, lifting it up to move it would make it easier to record. We then measured, drew, and photographed every feature of the gate. The gate consisted of two large side posts connected by four cross members, giving it an overall width of 9 feet 6 inches. The bottom cross member joined the bottom ends of the side posts. The top cross member connected the side posts about three-quarters of the way up the posts. The two other cross members were equally spaced between the top and bottom cross members. The upper ends of the side posts would have been fitted into the gate's balance beam. All members of the gate were made of cypress and joined by mortise and tenon. The side posts measured 10 feet and 11 feet 6 inches in length. The difference in their lengths allowed the gate to hang vertically from the downward-angling balance beam. The side posts averaged 10 inches by 7 1/2 inches. The top and bottom cross members measured roughly 8 inches by 7 1/2 inches. The two middle ones averaged 6 inches by 6 inches. Metal straps 2 1/2 inches wide and a half inch thick reinforced the middle cross members.

A small upright post was located between the bottom cross member and the one above and 22 1/2 inches in from the outside side post. A frame around the resulting square hole held the gate's sluice, which could be lifted to allow water to flow into or out of the lock. Except for the sluice, cypress planking covered the outside of the gate. These boards were of random widths, ranging from 11 inches to 16 inches, and were butted against each other to form a watertight, or as close as possible, covering.

When we were finished recording the gate, we wrapped it in geofabric and buried in on the bottom of the canal. Geofabric is a woven monofilament fabric designed for erosion control. Manufactured by Exxon Corporation, the fabric allows water to pass through it but not soil or sand. It is used primarily along highway and waterway embankments. To keep the gate in place, we nailed the edges of the geofabric into the bottom of the canal using hundred-penny galvanized nails.

The unidentified wooden anomaly we discovered on our first project turned out to be the flat transom of a small boat. This became apparent after removing the overburden of mud, leaves, and debris and raising the wooden construct to the surface. Constructed of three planks held together by iron spikes, the transom measured 7 feet 4 inches by 2 feet 6 inches. After examining the transom, a thought struck us. Could the rest of the vessel be somewhere nearby? Sure enough, some 15 feet north of the transom we found the remains of a small vessel. These remains consisted of a keelson and hull planking sticking out of the bank. No keel was present. Instead the vessel had a king plank, essentially an outer hull plank, indicating a small boat intended for use in shoal waters. Because only a small portion of the vessel was exposed, it was impossible even to guess at its actual length and width. We placed the transom with the rest of the vessel and dredged a blanket of mud over the remains. Over this we placed geofabric, again nailing the edges into the canal bottom.

Next our attention focused on the canal lock. Our first chore was to remove the tons of mud that had filled in the structure over the years. For this we turned to a tried-and-true underwater archaeology tool—the water induction dredge. Like an airlift, the water dredge creates a suction used to remove sand, mud, small rocks, leaves, and even bricks from a site. Unlike an airlift that uses air to create the suction, a water dredge uses pressurized water. A pump jets a stream of water down a hose from the surface into the dredge head about a foot behind the mouth. Shooting the water up the effluent hose creates suction at the mouth. By adjusting the pump's throttle, either a gentle suction can be generated to sift sand carefully off a shipwreck or a suction several times stronger than an airlift can dig down through layers of hard-packed sand, mud, and shell to locate a buried anomaly.

With the failure of the contractor to remove the water from the canal, we had plenty of water to use the dredge. But where should we put all the mud? We had no large ore trucks to haul it away. We couldn't pump it onto the bank of the canal. We decided the best (and most expedient) methodology would be to pump the mud several hundred feet down the canal to the culvert area, where the tidal flow would flush it into the Tailrace Canal. We had never pumped our dredge effluent that far before, though. Undaunted, we bought two dozen 12-foot sections of 6-inch PVC pipe, several Y-sections of PVC pipe, and a supply of flexible rubber connectors. We connected the sections together with the connectors, inserting Y-sections along the way to form a pipeline 220 feet long. On the front of this, we attached a length of flexible hose and our 4-inch dredge head. We realized that just the pressure from the dredge head pump would not be enough to push the mud the entire length of our PVC pipeline. To increase the flow, we attached additional pumps to force water into the pipeline at the Y-sections. We also relied heavily on gravity. We elevated the pipeline on floating fifty-five-gallon drums, adding water to the barrels in increasing amounts the further the pipeline extended away from the dredge head. This gave a downward slope to the pipeline, facilitating the flow of mud. At the end of the pipeline, we rigged a floating screen to catch artifacts. We soon realized that while the rubber connectors gave the pipeline needed flexibility, it also gave it the ability to sag. In places where the sags occurred, gravity was negated and mud and sand would pool, clogging the pipe and stopping our dredging activities. To solve this problem, we assigned one crew member to walk the pipeline continuously, lifting the sags to prevent clogging. As it turned out, we excavated an estimated 450 cubic yards of mud through the pipeline in the record time (for us) of ten days.

With the mud removed, we recorded the canal lock features. The lock consists of four wall structures, one at each corner of the lock. These structures supported the lock gates and were made of brick. Between opposite lock walls, wooden floors laid on the bottom of the canal provided a watertight base for the gates. These floors were constructed by laying timbers across the canal at right angles to the banks. Planking was then laid over the beams and fastened with treenails and iron spikes.

We found abundant evidence that the lock was the victim of apparently deliberate destruction. One wall was completely torn down, the bricks scattered over the bottom of the lock and canal. How many of the bricks were gone was impossible to determine. One wall was intact except for the absence of the quoin stones, which were missing. These stones, which act as swivel points for the lock gates, weighed several hundred pounds each.

To complete our work, we needed to cover the small vessel found at the south end of Area A. First we used a water jet to dig a trench around the vessel. After laying geofabric over the vessel, we nailed the edges to the bottom of the canal; we did the same with the transom boat and lock gate.

The Santee Canal Park opened to the public on April 24, 1989. A brick entrance resembling a canal lock leads visitors into the interpretive center, which overlooks Biggin Creek. A scale model of a canal lock and a three-eighths scale model of the CSS *David* are on display in the open area around the center's theater, where a short film tells the story of the Santee Canal. Four miles of boardwalks and trails guide visitors along the canal and the Tailrace Canal, passing by remnants of the old limestone mining operations in the industrial area above Biggin Creek. Historic and prehistoric artifacts from the area are displayed in the Berkeley County Museum, which is also in the park.

So how did we do in our battle with the mud? Did we win the Santee Canal "Mud Bowl"? Looking back, it was probably a draw. Our efforts were greatly hampered by the muck. We encountered endless difficulties caused by the ever-present ooze. On the other hand, we accomplished much. We managed to discover and record several unique artifacts, including a possible canal boat and a canal lock from America's first summit canal. Most important of all, we learned one of the great lessons of underwater archaeology: mud sucks (and smells). But it's no match for a good water dredge.

The Day the Johnboat
Went up the Mountain

We arrived at the Mulberry mound and village archaeological site on the Wateree River with our fourteen-foot johnboat, our four-wheel-drive Suburban, our Dodge Carry Van, and all the dive gear, scuba tanks, water pumps, dredge hoses, artifact screens, and dredges heads we could fit into the boat and two vehicles. We spent several days waist deep in the cool waters of Big Pine Tree Creek, oohing and aahing every time someone came up with a large piece of Native American pottery despite the fact that these pieces littered the creek like rocks in a mountain stream. We also put on our scuba gear and dove out in the river, increasing the growing mountain of pottery fragments we were recovering. The work was exhilarating and exhausting. The sun was hot and overbearing. A lingering drought had the river at record low water levels, and while this was advantageous for finding artifacts, it did present unexpected problems. Nevertheless it was a typical project for SCIAA's underwater archaeology team—except for the day the johnboat went up the mountain.

The Mulberry site sits on a high bluff overlooking the junction of Big Pine Tree Creek with the Wateree River, just downriver from Camden in Kershaw County. Occupied between about A.D. 1300 and about 1700, Mulberry is the largest of eight Mississippian mound sites along an eighteen-mile stretch of the Wateree valley. This makes the place important in itself. What's more, experts now believe the Mulberry site was the location of Cofitachequi, a major ceremonial center and capital for the Native Americans of the region.

This is a new placement for Cofitachequi. Until recently many historians and archaeologists thought Cofitachequi was located on the Savannah River below Augusta at a site known as Silver Bluff. Others believed it was on the Congaree River near present-day Columbia. However, recent archaeological discoveries, newly translated historic accounts, and a more precise interpretation of previous documents have provided a more accurate location. This new information places Cofi-tachequi firmly atop the Mulberry mound site.

None other than Hernando de Soto visited Cofitachequi in 1540 on his journey throughout the Southeast in search of gold. He undoubt-edly was pleased to discover that a woman ruled the lush river valley. The natives he encountered in what is now Florida and Georgia told him of a rich chiefdom ruled by a woman. To the Spaniards "rich" meant gold. Or so they hoped. When they asked where this place was located, the natives pointed to the northeast. After weeks of fording rivers swollen with spring rains, nearly running out of food for his men and horses, and finding that his native guides were totally lost, de Soto reached the Wateree River across from Cofitachequi.

Carried on a litter borne by her subjects, a high-ranking woman came out to greet de Soto. Some accounts say she was the chieftainess of Cofitachequi, some the niece of the chieftainess. In either case the woman crossed the river in a canoe with a covered awning, sitting on a bed of cushions. Upon meeting the Spanish explorer, she presented him with a pearl necklace, and his soldiers received gifts of food, skins, and blankets. With six hundred heavily armed Spanish soldiers at his com-mand, de Soto unsurprisingly found the inhabitants of Cofitachequi outwardly friendly and cooperative. The Spanish stayed in the village for two weeks, foraging the area for food. Before leaving the village, de Soto and some of his men entered the local temple and found chests containing the remains of former chiefs as well as chests and baskets filled with freshwater pearls. They also found rosaries with crosses and several Spanish axes they attributed to the brief Lucas Vázquez de Ayl-lón excursion near Georgetown in 1526. But no gold.

To soothe their disappointment, they eyed the pearls. The natives prized the freshwater pearls found in the rivers and apparently spent a great deal of time and effort gathering them for use as decoration, as ceremonial offerings, and in burials. When de Soto and his soldiers departed, they took with them the chieftainess as hostage and guide, as well as two hundred pounds of pearls from the ceremonial temple.

As they traveled inland, they found that the region ruled by the chief-tainess was extensive. The chroniclers of the expedition noted that her authority was absolute in the villages they visited for the nearly one hun-dred miles she accompanied the explorers. She escaped from the Span-ish, presumably at the limit of her influence, and returned to her village.

Spanish explorer Juan Pardo and a contingent of 125 soldiers visited Cofitachequi in 1566, twenty-six years after de Soto. Pardo was on a quest to find an overland route from the Atlantic coast to Mexico. When he reached the Appalachians, however, he found them inhospitably covered with snow and turned back. At Cofitachequi he ordered the natives to build houses reserved for the Spaniards and cribs for storing food. He returned there in 1568, building a fort and leaving it manned by a contingent of 30 soldiers. Faced with such a small garrison, the natives soon slaughtered the soldiers and destroyed the fort.

The inhabitants of Cofitachequi were typical Mississippian-period Native Americans. This advanced people is generally associated with an increased emphasis on farming, the development of larger villages, and a more complex social organization.

Their social organization was characterized by hereditary ranking and centralized leadership. They centered their existence around the cooperative, large-scale cultivation of corn, supplemented with a variety of wild plants, including grapes, sunflowers, squash, gourds, blackberries, blueberries, wild sweet potatoes, and beans. They hunted deer, turkey, and other small animals. They fished the river and gathered nuts, especially hickory and walnuts. They traded pottery, copper, seashells, mica, and galena with nearby and distant villages.

They lived in wattle and daub houses that were either round, square, or rectangular. They made these structures by setting wooden poles into the ground. Then they wove reeds (wattle) horizontally through the poles in a basketlike fashion. They covered this framework with a mixture of clay or mud and grass (daub), sealing the walls. They made the roofs by placing reeds or sheets of bark over a stick framework.

They also built mounds. They built large mounds, sometimes several hundred feet across, used as ceremonial temple mounds with public buildings or residences for the elite constructed on top. They built small mounds, often with structures used for burials. Archaeological evidence suggests they built the mounds in stages, with additional layers added every twenty to twenty-five years on average, perhaps upon the succession of each new chieftain or chieftainess.

The arrival of Europeans in the New World signaled the end of the Mississippian culture. In 1670 Henry Woodward traveled inland from the newly founded Charles Town to Cofitachequi. He found the region ruled by an "emperor" commanding more than a thousand bowmen. Whether through dwindling resources, new diseases brought by the Europeans, or a combination of factors, the chiefdom of Cofitachequi soon disappeared. When John Lawson toured the area in 1701, just thirty-one years after Woodward, he found Cofitachequi abandoned and a new group of people known as the Congaree occupying the region.

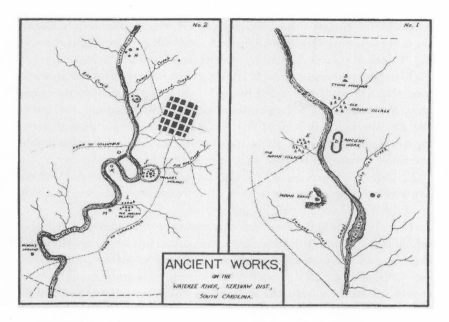

Dr. William Blanding's 1848 map of Native American mound and village areas around Camden. Taylor's Mounds, now known as the Mulberry mound site, are believed to be the site of Cofitachequi, the center of a vast Mississippian-period chiefdom. From E. G. Squier and E. H. Davis, *Ancient Monuments of the Mississippi Valley* (Washington, D.C.: Smithsonian Institution, 1847), 105

William Blanding, a Camden physician and amateur archaeologist, visited the area in 1806. His account provides us with the first "modern" view of the mound site. He describes it as a group of eleven mounds, two large and nine small, surrounded by a low embankment. Even then the destruction of the site was evident. One of the large mounds was already eroding into the river, and years of cultivation had much reduced the others. The fields were cultivated with cotton at that time. Yet the largest mound was still twelve to fifteen feet high.

In 1891 Henry Reynolds of the Smithsonian Institution undertook the first archaeological excavation of the site. By then the large mound had further eroded into the river and was only ten feet high. It was still quite large, measuring 154 feet by 115 feet. Only three of the small mounds, now only two feet high, remained. They found no trace of the low embankment that Blanding describes as surrounding the mounds.

Inevitably the obliteration of the mound site continued. When A. R. Kelly of the University of Georgia, in conjunction with the Charleston

Museum, investigated the Mulberry site in 1952, he found only half of the large mound and one small mound, now only one foot high, remaining. Traces of a second small mound were still visible.

Twenty-one years later, in 1973, Dr. Leland Ferguson, then an institute archaeologist, conducted limited testing at the site. At this time only the remains of the large mound and one small mound were present. Despite Ferguson's short visit, he realized the importance of gaining as much information about the site and its inhabitants as possible before all remains of the site were gone.

So from 1979 through 1982 and again in 1985 and 1990, the University of South Carolina's Department of Anthropology conducted a series of summer field schools at the site.

The 1985 field school was perhaps the most interesting, providing a valuable insight into the activities of the natives of Cofitachequi. At the beginning of the season, researchers conducted a surface collection of the village area, which is located east of the mounds, away from the river. In one area of the village, the researchers discovered a large concentration of sheets of mica. A methodical excavation of the site revealed three sides of a structure approximately thirteen feet wide by at least thirteen feet long with a hearth almost in its center. Twenty-five postholes delineated three of the structure's walls. Postholes for a fourth side were not found. The excavation also turned up some pottery shards, lithics (mostly in the form of projectile points), and an abundance of mica. In the Southeast large deposits of mica are located in the Appalachian mountain region of North Carolina. The natives of Cofitachequi most likely acquired it through trade, signifying a certain importance given to the material. Field school participants unearthed several hand-sized sheets of mica, along with several worked pieces, including two drilled pieces and one heart-shaped piece. Presumably the worked pieces were on the way to becoming buttons for the cloaks of high-status individuals. The excavated structure was probably the home/workshop of a skilled worker who made the buttons and other mica objects for Cofitachequi's elite.

As often happens in science, a chance occurrence sometimes leads to a major discovery. Just such a thing happened one day during the 1985 field school. As members of the field crew were cooling their feet in the waters of Big Pine Tree Creek, one of the students, Chris Judge, noticed that large shards of pottery littered the creek bottom. The students recovered enough of the shards to provide a preliminary ceramic sequence for the site and a master's thesis topic for Judge. The previous archaeological excavations at the site produced some ceramic remains, but too few for any real analysis. Blanding conducted some surface collecting of the area in the early nineteenth century, and we can assume amateur "pot hunters" gathered many items exposed by plowing, periodic flooding, and their own digging. For the most part these recoveries are in forgotten private collections and unavailable for study. The Smithsonian excavations of 1891, under Henry Reynolds, were limited in scope, consisting of digging trenches through two of the mounds. The 1952 project under A. R. Kelly and the Charleston Museum was the first real excavation of the site. Unfortunately the group had limited funds and time and discovered few artifacts. Not until the 1985 field school were enough potsherds recovered for any worthwhile analysis.

Prehistoric archaeologists spend endless hours studying ceramic shards. This is due in no small part to the fact that the most abundant artifacts found on prehistoric sites are ceramics. Other types of containers, such as baskets, gourds, and wooden utensils, seldom outlast the ravages of time. Fortunately much can be learned from even small pieces of bowls, jars, and other pottery containers. Were the inhabitants of a certain site using only small ceramic containers and vessels, for instance, indicating a small, highly mobile society centered more on hunting and gathering than on farming? Or did they have large containers, indicating a larger, more settled agricultural society that needed vessels for serving large numbers and for long-term storage of grains and other cultivated foods?

For ceramics to tell a story, two things must be ascertained—age and use. By determining a ceramic object's age and use, archaeologists can discover clues as to how the people who used these objects lived. Prehistoric ceramic containers were used for cooking, serving, and storing food. Mississippian Native Americans also used ceramic vessels for ceremonial and burial rituals. Usage can be determined through the vessel's shape, decoration, and other clues, such as the presence of soot on the outside indicating that it was used for cooking and not strictly for ceremonial usage. Shape is, obviously, the best indication of a ceramic vessel's purpose.

Age is often determined through context, temper, and surface treatment. Context is where the artifact was found in relation to other artifacts. In most cases as archaeologists excavate a site, the newest artifacts are the first encountered. The deeper the digging goes, the older the objects found are. So at any level being able to date one object dates all other objects at that level and provides a comparison for objects either above or below. Other factors come into play if the artifacts are not found in situ, such as the ceramic shards recovered from the river and creek. Then shape, surface treatment, and temper (a substance added to the clay to help in firing) are compared with datable in situ ceramics to determine age. In addition to giving us clues as to how the Native Americans lived at any one time, by comparing how the shape, temper, and surface treatments of ceramic vessels changed over time, we can unearth clues as to how these lifeways changed as well.

The Mississippian Native Americans made their ceramic vessels using the coil method, where the sides of the vessel are built up using thin strips of clay. Once the potter shaped the vessel, the maker often added elaborate surface treatments while the vessel walls were still pliable. These decorative features came in several styles during the Mississippian period, including complicated stamped, incised, punctated, and burnished.

Complicated stamped surface treatment was the most common. A wooden paddle with carved designs on its face created a variety of complex designs when pressed over the outside surface of the vessel. Diamonds, rectangles, squares, curved, and circular designs are the most common result of this technique.

Incised decorations—formed by dragging a sharp object, usually a stick, across the surface—were another popular type of surface decoration during the Mississippian period. The resulting designs vary from parallel lines to curved patterns. Unlike stamped treatments, incising resulted in deep, sharp lines often spaced irregularly on the vessel surface.

Other shards showed punctated surfaces made by jabbing the end of a stick, a shell, a reed, or even fingers into the ceramic surface to make patterned designs. The resulting patterns can be irregular or carefully patterned.

Many pieces had plain surfaces with no surface treatment; on others the potters used smooth stones to burnish the surface. Burnishing results in polished streaks that are usually parallel.

As a result of the discovery of large quantities of ceramic shards, institute archaeologist Chester DePratter, codirector of the 1985 field school, along with SCIAA's Underwater Archaeology Division returned to the Mulberry site in October 1985. The plan was to conduct limited excavations in Big Pine Tree Creek and adjacent areas of the Wateree River.

Chester DePratter is the epitome of an archaeologist. He sports a full beard and slim physique. He presents an aura of both explorer and scholar. He wears Indiana Jones hats, tattered khaki shirts, faded blue jeans, and scruffy high-top work boots. This is on office days. He holds a doctorate in anthropology from the University of Georgia and is one of SCIAA's preeminent prehistoric archaeologists. He also served as

South Carolina's representative on the federal De Soto Expedition Trail Commission from 1987 until 1992. It is partly his reinterpretation of historic accounts that places Cofitachequi at the Mulberry mound site.

Divers spent four days in the creek and river, systematically excavating three areas of the creek and several areas of the river. The quantity of artifacts collected far exceeded those of the previous excavations on land. Much more of the creek and river remained to be studied, however.

In 1988 DePratter took another stab at it. This time SCIAA's underwater archaeology team included Chris Amer, Joe Beatty, Mark Newell, Jodie Simmons, Peggy Brooks, and me.

In addition to further excavations of the creek and adjacent river bottoms, the plan called for a visual survey of the river bottom both upstream and downstream of the bluff. Chester was especially interested in any evidence of the Spanish visits. Both Hernando de Soto and Juan Pardo brought an assortment of trade goods to exchange with the natives they encountered. The de Soto expedition carried "gift kits" containing beads, bells, hatchets, knives, rattles, feathers, and cloth. Pardo distributed hatchets, wedges, chisels, knives, mirrors, cloth, buttons, and beads. Most of these items they gave to chiefs and other important individuals. The natives who acted as guides and interpreters also received gifts.

Moreover Pardo left the soldiers manning the forts a variety of metal tools, including pickaxes, shovels, hoes, spikes, nails, chisels, and drills.

Since so much pottery found its way into the nearby waters, DePratter realized a logical place to look for Spanish artifacts was in the river and creek. Though these artifacts would no longer be in situ, meaning much of the information they could have provided was lost, they could provide vital evidence of Spanish contact with the resident Native Americans and further confirmation that Mulberry was indeed Cofitachequi.

Several days into the project, DePratter decided to leave the cool waters of Big Pine Tree Creek and, along with Chris Amer, Joe Beatty, and me, do the reconnaissance of the river bottom both upstream and downstream from the site. The plan was for Chester and Chris to walk the exposed sand and gravel bars in the river while Joe and I dove the remaining pockets of deep water.

We set off in the johnboat, and this meant trouble from the start. We brought two engines for the boat, both identical 25-horsepower Evinrudes, and one might figure this was wise planning. It never hurts to have a spare motor aboard a boat, even on a river shallow enough in most places to wade across. I remember a conversation at our project-planning meeting, however, in which we discussed equipment needs.

"We need to bring the johnboat," Chris Amer said.

"One of the 'rudes doesn't work too well," Joe replied.

"Which one?" Chris asked.

"Don't know. Can't tell them apart," Joe answered.

So we mounted one of the engines on the transom, slumped the other into the bottom of the boat, and set off. As it turned out, neither engine worked well. Each ran for a short time before its particular malfunction mysteriously shut it down. Strangely enough, when one broke down its partner was ready to go again. Nevertheless this meant yanking the engine off the stern and replacing it with its partner, each weighing 116 pounds. We did this about every ten minutes, repeating the procedure enough to equal a Schwarzenegger-level weight-training session at a gym.

To make matters worse, long stretches of the river were too shallow to use the motors. In these areas it required the four of us to push and pull the johnboat, sometimes as much as fifty yards at a stretch, to the next deep water. Normally this would be no problem with the light johnboat, but the scuba gear, air tanks, and extra engine made the aluminum craft as hard to move as an unconscious rhinoceros.

It was a relief reaching the deep-water areas, where Joe and I could don our scuba gear and scoot along the river bottom. We scrutinized gravel beds, fanned deposits of leaves, and looked under logs, keeping our eyes peeled for any artifacts that might have been scattered by the river's currents. Luckily the water was clear, giving us excellent visibility, and the drought-induced low water meant no strong currents—perfect conditions for finding the remains of our cultural past. Of the items we found, however, the one that caused the most commotion—the one discovery we still talk about today—turned out to be cultural, but not from the past.

After searching under the I-20 bridge, Joe Beatty surprised us all when he came up brandishing a 9-mm Smith & Wesson semiautomatic pistol. We were immediately convinced a kidnapper, a bank robber, or maybe a murderer had ditched the weapon. Our extensive training convinced us that it was not a sixteenth-century Native American or Spanish artifact. We subsequently turned the pistol in to the State Law Enforcement Division. They thanked us but were not interested in whom we thought it had killed, what bank robbery it had been used in, or even which famous person might have been kidnapped with it.

They probably had their own theories.

Joe Beatty holding 9-mm Smith and Wesson semiautomatic pistol found under I-20 bridge near Camden. SCIAA photograph by Christopher Amer

Anyway, after changing engines several dozen times, donning and doffing scuba gear and tanks, pushing and pulling the johnboat across vast stretches of sand, and theorizing about the possible illegal uses of a 9-mm Smith & Wesson semiautomatic pistol, we were exhausted by the time we got back to the mound site. Moreover we still had the chore of getting the johnboat and all the equipment loaded into our vehicles, which of course were on top of the bluff.

Now about this bluff. Despite cavorting with a bunch of Spaniards wearing heavy metal armor during the middle of summer, these natives were no fools. They had picked the site for their village with great care. More like a small, flat mountain, the top of the bluff stood a good fifty feet above the river below, and it was nearly straight up. Just getting up it meant pulling ourselves up a rope tied to a tree at the top, and taking equipment to the top required a leapfrog maneuver. This was achieved by putting the piece of equipment as far above you as you could, pulling yourself ahead of it with the rope while keeping a hold on the equipment, then pulling the equipment ahead of you again and repeating the maneuver as necessary. Much repeating was necessary.

For several days we had been hauling gear up and down this way. The johnboat presented a new challenge—one we hadn't foreseen when we launched the boat that morning at a nearby landing. We realized that taking the boat back to the landing would take a considerable amount of time and personnel, and this would slow the process beyond acceptability. After a strenuous field day, acceptability levels are predictably quite low.

Joe suggested we load all the equipment into the johnboat and hoist the whole shebang up the bluff using the heavy-duty Warn winch on the front of the Dodge Carry Van. The Carry Van, a utility vehicle about the size of a UPS delivery truck, acted as a mobile office, equipment hauler, and changing room. It had the bad habit of not starting unless on perfectly level ground and breaking down at the exact midpoint between two Interstate exits. We considered Joe's suggestion. We knew the winch could handle the weight. We knew it would take no time at all to winch the boat up the bluff. With hot showers and going out for dinner the next items on our agenda, heads nodded approval, tired muscles applauded, and Joe went for the winch control.

Once the johnboat was loaded with all the gear, hooked up to the winch cable, and pointed in the right direction, everyone pulled himself or herself up the rope to the top of the hill. Not that we thought Joe's plan wouldn't work, it was just that we had never done anything like this before, and none of us wanted to become a target for a runaway johnboat, especially one filled with pumps, hoses, dive gear, scuba tanks, artifact screens, and two malfunctioning 25-horsepower Evinrude outboard engines each weighing 116 pounds.

Joe engaged the winch, and slowly the johnboat and its contents crawled up the face of the bluff. Steadily it came, foot by foot, yard by yard, with hardly a groan from the winch motor. We were congratulating ourselves on agreeing to Joe's idea when it happened. Just as the boat neared the top of the slope, we heard the winch take a serious strain. This was followed by what sounded like four or five shots from a .22-caliber rifle coming from where the boat had stopped just below the lip of the bluff.

Rushing to the edge of the bluff, we saw immediately what had caused our plan to go awry. When the bow of the boat reached the lip of the bluff, the angle of the winch cable changed from almost straight up to more horizontal. Since the johnboat couldn't change with it, the bow of the boat simply dug into the side of the bluff. After hauling the equipment out of the boat and muscling it up over the edge of the bluff, we noticed that four or five of the rivets holding the flat bow of the boat to its front platform had popped, and the flat bow had been pulled out into a perfect V. You will be happy to know that the boat has been returned to its original flat bow at no cost to the taxpayers of South Carolina. The dock we accidentally collided head on with did sustain some slight damage. Nothing you would notice. At least not on first glance, and if I remember right, Joe was driving the boat at the time.

In all, by the end of the project, we had retrieved approximately five thousand artifacts, the most abundant of which were pottery pieces, dating from A.D. 1200 to 1700. A mountain of shards sat on the makeshift table at the field station. Back at SCIAA the pottery pieces would undergo washing, cleaning, sorting, labeling, analyzing, and recording. In other words they would become several smaller, but well processed, mountains of shards sitting on a table at the institute.

Several of the ceramic pieces were sufficiently large to be reassembled, giving us a better understanding of vessel forms made at Mulberry. These forms included jars, bowls, and burial urns. The practice of placing the remains of the dead, particularly infants, into ceramic urns is common in many cultures around the world, including Mississippian Native Americans. For the most part, the urns used by these natives in the Southeast are all of the same shape, varying only in size from five to twenty gallons. These are round-bottomed vessels that bow out in the middle and taper in toward the top, with rims that flare out. Most of these vessels are complicated stamped; however, the bowl-shaped tops of these urns are plain. The urns found at the Mulberry site follow these specifications.

A European traveling in the Southeast in 1694 witnessed a ritual urn burial. He noted that the deceased's relatives first wrapped the body in sheets of cane. Then they dug a hole about two feet deep, placed the body, standing up, in the hole, and packed earth around the legs. They then took palm fronds and wrapped the body until it was watertight. After a period of time, long enough to cleanse the bones of all flesh, the remains were unwrapped and put into a basket. This basket was taken into a ceremonial building. When all of the deceased's relatives were gathered around, they brought in the burial urn and built a fire around it. They then cast the bones into the urn. When the fire died out, they buried the urn and remains.

While archaeological evidence reveals that the above procedure was just one of many burial methods, the account gives us a valuable insight into the ceremonial nature of Mississippian Native Americans.

Interestingly at many sites, including the Mulberry site, the urns were ritually "killed" by knocking out their bottoms with a rock. Often buried with the urn is the rock used in the "killing."

From shards collected from Big Pine Tree Creek, we were able to reconstruct a partial bowl used for ceremonial purposes. Incised patterns cover the outside of the bowl. Two flying squirrel effigies were applied to the rim, presumably as handles. While the exact meaning of the flying squirrels is unknown, we do know that flying squirrels played a large part in Native American folktales. Also the outside of the bowl showed no signs of sooting, leading to the conclusion that it was not used for cooking. This reinforces the idea this was a ceremonial bowl.

Several shards retrieved from Big Pine Tree Creek were indicative of extensive trade patterns with neighboring Native Americans. About a dozen shards were identified as having been made in the upper reaches of the Catawba River, some 120 miles from Mulberry. Another group of shards were made in eastern Tennessee and northeast Georgia, some 150 to 190 miles from the Wateree valley.

Other artifacts recovered consisted of stone ax fragments, steatite pipe bowl fragments, projectile points, and a fragment of a marine whelk shell from which a gorget, or ceremonial neckpiece, had been cut. We also recovered two nearly complete ceramic pipes from Big Pine Tree Creek.

We found no Spanish artifacts. Not one bead, bell, hatchet, knife, or rattle from one of Hernando de Soto's gift kits. No hatchets, wedges, chisels, knives, mirrors, buttons, or beads given to the natives by the Juan Pardo expedition, and not a single pickax, shovel, hoe, spike, nail, chisel, or drill left by Pardo with the soldiers manning the ill-fated fort. This in no way diminishes DePratter's belief that Mulberry is the site of Cofitachequi. We know that the natives would have valued the items given to them and not used them in everyday activities that would lead to their loss or disposal. In addition the items could have been widely distributed to outlying villages. The lack of Spanish artifacts only provides us with incentive for more fieldwork on the site. We know that further work in Big Pine Tree Creek and the Wateree River near the bluff could produce Spanish artifacts or additional Native American artifacts, revealing additional pieces in the story of Cofitachequi. Besides, we have since purchased a new engine for the johnboat. So we no longer have to struggle with the two malfunctioning 25-horsepower Evinrude outboard engines. On the other hand, we no longer have the dive truck with the heavy-duty Warn winch to get the johnboat up the mountain.

Hobcaw Shipyard

Shortly after joining the SCIAA staff in 1987, I was assigned the task of researching early shipbuilding in South Carolina. Going through newspaper accounts, ship registers, deed abstracts, wills, estate inventories, and numerous other colonial and early state records, I came across a 1786 plat of a large shipyard. The plat intrigued me. It shows a piece of property on Wackindaw Creek rendered with hand-drawn features. There are three slipways, two long wharves, and a freshwater spring. There is a building denoted as stables; an unlabeled building off to one side of the shipyard, where, presumably, the shipyard slaves lived; and paths leading from one part of the property to another. There is even a main house with a pitched roof and little curlicues of smoke rising from chimneys at either end of the house. Today we know Wackindaw Creek as Hobcaw Creek and the shipyard as the Hobcaw Shipyard.

As I studied the plat, I wondered how much of the site was still intact. Few maritime archaeologists get the chance to examine a colonial shipyard site. Too often the bulldozers of waterfront development have been there first, plowing under these cultural remains in favor of gated communities, waterfront parks, and marinas for million-dollar yachts. So while fine examples of colonial vessels may abound in local waters, their birthplaces sadly are no longer available for study. Questions about shipyard organization and the shipbuilding process go unanswered. Moreover a part of history is lost.

In 1989 the owner of the Hobcaw Creek property sought a permit to build a private dock at the shipyard location. This gave us, as one of the state and federal agencies that review dock permits, the opportunity to conduct a cursory survey of the location of the proposed dock and see what evidence of the shipyard remained. We arranged a visit to the site. The foundation of the main house lay in piles of brick at the end of the avenue of oaks leading from the house to the slipways. Along the

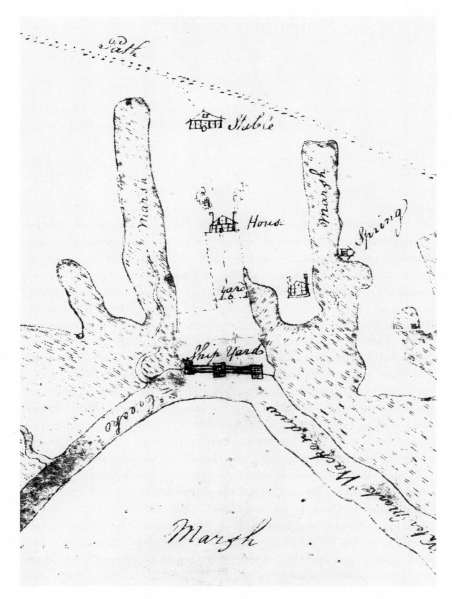

A portion of the 1786 plat showing Hobcaw Shipyard, the avenue of oaks, and the main house with curlicues of smoke. Courtesy South Carolina Department of Archives and History

shoreline we found wood cribbing and pilings from two of the original three shipyard slipways. We think the third slipway lies beneath a concrete boat ramp. On the creek bottom, we found ballast rock, brick, and scattered remnants of ship frames dating to the late eighteenth century. We did not return to the shipyard site until 1992, following its purchase by Pepe and Cyndy Hernandez. In the meantime I continued my research into wooden shipbuilding in South Carolina and at the Hobcaw Shipyard in particular.

As soon as the early Carolina colonists cleared their land and built their homes, they undoubtedly turned back to the sea and constructed watercraft. The rivers and creeks of the Carolina lowcountry provided ready-made highways for the colonists, and they needed a variety of watercraft to carry on the business of establishing a new colony. They needed vessels to visit their neighbors, to trade with the friendly natives who inhabited the region, to carry goods from town to their homes, and (not least of all) to explore their new world. Fortunately any colonist with the tools and knowledge to build a house could build a boat to suit almost any purpose.

In addition a lucrative trade in furs, skins, indigo, rice, lumber, and naval stores with England and the West Indies started Charleston on the road to becoming the third largest city in North America. This required deep-draft oceangoing vessels.

As the colony grew and began to thrive, so did the boat- and shipbuilding industries. The extant colonial ship registers show that between the years 1735 and 1775 South Carolina shipbuilders built more than three hundred oceangoing and coastal cargo vessels, ranging from five to nearly three hundred tons burden.

While not comparable with the shipbuilding activities of the northern colonies, shipbuilding became South Carolina's largest manufacturing industry. Building wooden ships was a labor-intensive activity. Not only did it take a considerable amount of time to build a ship of wood, it took dozens of laborers working in concert to piece it together. In addition to shipwrights, sawyers, and ship carpenters, a wide variety of craftsmen earned their livelihoods, either wholly or in part, through shipbuilding. Lumbermen cut the timber and floated it downriver to the yards. Caulkers sealed the decking and outer hull, pounding in the miles of oakum and pitch. Block makers and rope makers produced the necessary ingredients of the vessel's rigging. Riggers installed it. Sailmakers sewed the yards of canvas into the sails that harvested the wind. Painters painted hulls and interiors. Blacksmiths made the metal fastenings. Woodcarvers shaped the elaborate figureheads that adorned the bows of colonial ships. Coopers made the barrels in which the colony shipped its goods.

Shipyards, both the large commercial yards employing dozens of workers and the small one-man operations, dotted the rivers and creeks near South Carolina's coastal population centers, specifically Charleston, Beaufort, and Georgetown. Moreover the ship registers for the colony list construction sites at other, more remote, locations, including Pon Pon, Dorchester, Bull's Island, Wadmalaw, Combahee, and Pocotaligo.

At the beginning of the last half of the eighteenth century, Charleston's economy was enjoying boon times. Large cargo ships were sailing for England loaded with Carolina rice and indigo every few days. As a result Wackindaw Creek off the Wando River became the colony's largest shipbuilding center, boasting as many as three commercial shipyards. One of these was the one owned by Scottish shipwrights John Rose and James Stewart. In 1753 the two men formed a partnership and bought 340 acres of land on the south side of the creek, bounding northwest on the Wando River, east on the lands of David Maybank, and south on Molasses Creek.

The first mention of the property comes in the records of the secretary of the province of South Carolina when, in 1681, William Craven, 1st Earl of Craven, granted the land to Lt. Col. John Godfrey. Godfrey sold the property a year later to Richard Dearsley, a Barbados merchant. In 1701, according to colonial records, Maj. George Dearsley bought the plantation "together with all buildings, timber, fences, slaves, cattle and stock." Eight years later, in 1709, the Lords Proprietors granted the property to Benjamin Quelch. His son Andrew inherited the property upon his death in 1716. Andrew held onto the land for some time, but in 1748 he mortgaged the property to Thomas Bolton, a Charleston merchant. In October 1753, after Andrew failed to make good on the mortgage, Bolton took possession of the property. Twelve days later Bolton sold the land to Rose and Stewart for their shipyard. Rose became sole owner of the shipyard when Stewart died in 1755. Today this area is a Mount Pleasant subdivision known as Hobcaw Point.

The shipyard soon became the largest in the Hobcaw area, indeed in all of colonial South Carolina. This was owing to two important factors. First, the location was ideal. Wackindaw Creek was close to a ready supply of timber—the hardwoods, most notably live oak, suitable for heavy ship timbers and the soft woods, specifically pine for masts and planking. The creek had plenty of deep water running close up to its banks, and it was well protected from the strong winds that whip across Charleston Harbor. Also it was close enough to Charleston so that obtaining necessary supplies and labor was not the problem it was for more rural shipyards. Second, John Rose and James Stewart were master shipwrights. Stewart had apprenticed at the Woolrich Naval Yard near London, and Rose had learned his trade at the Deptford Naval Yard in southeast London. Known for his small stature and great strength, Rose arrived in Carolina "with a Broad Ax on his shoulder," as his friend Henry Laurens was fond of saying. Both Rose and Stewart were well trained in the construction of large oceangoing ships.

A colonial shipyard in full production must have been a scene of sight and sound. The rhythmic rasping of long two-man saws as they cut pine logs into planking, the chop-chop-chop of the adzes turning oak into the various ship frames, the ringing of caulking tools hammering the oakum between the ship's hull timbers—all must have seemed like some unrehearsed symphony. At the Hobcaw Shipyard, its three slipways multiplied this activity. On one slipway a new ship might be in some stage of building, while at another a vessel might be in repair.

In fact much of the Rose and Stewart shipyard's business in the early years seems to have centered on the repair of ships. Records indicate that several Charleston shipowners sent their vessels to Hobcaw during the shipyard's first ten years for repairs or alterations. One of these was the two-hundred-ton *Cooper River*. In 1757 Rose replaced its hull sheathing, painted the entire vessel, and conducted "a thorough repair from Stem to Stern." The *Cooper River*, a prize taken from the French a year earlier by the British warship *Jamaica*, had been condemned at vice-admiralty court in Charleston and sold to a group of Charleston businessmen that included Henry Laurens. The letters of Laurens show that after Rose completed his repairs, the owners intended to have the ship armed with ten or twelve guns and procure a letter of marque. This was at the height of the French and Indian War, and huge profits were being made in the capture of French merchant ships. Even so, whether the *Cooper River* ever had the guns added or received a letter of marque is not known. During this same time, Rose worked on the ship *Betsey,* replacing its sheathing to cover the damage done to its bottom by worms.

In 1763 John Rose built the 180-ton ship *Heart of Oak*. The *South Carolina Gazette* of May 21 reported, "The fine new ship Heart-of-Oak, commanded by Capt. Henry Gunn, lately built by Mr. John Rose at Hobcaw, came down [to town] two days, completely fitted, and is now taking in her cargo at Messrs. Inglis, Lloyd, & Hall's wharf; 'tis thought she will carry 1100 barrels of rice, be very buoyant, and of an easy draught." An "easy draught" in 1763 could be considerable. Lloyd's Register for 1764 lists the *Heart of Oak* as having a draft of fourteen feet when fully loaded. Rose, as builder and owner, no doubt planned its measurements, including draft, to suit its home port. In 1748 Governor James Glen noted that "Charles-Town Harbour is fit for all Vessels which do not exceed Fifteen Feet Draught."

In fact everything about the *Heart of Oak* seems built for the Charleston trade. South Carolina shipwrights could and did build larger ships. The *Queen Charlotte*, built in 1764, was registered at 280 tons. Another 280-ton ship, *Atlantic*, was built in Port Royal in 1773. The *Heart of Oak*'s size was perfect for Charleston, however, in more ways than being able to get across the bar. While larger ships could carry more cargo, it took longer to find enough cargo to fill their holds. This meant more time at anchor and at the wharf. Smaller ships, vessels the size of the *Heart of Oak*, filled quicker, resulting in shorter turnaround times. Ship registers show that during this period, the average size of Charleston-based ships was 151 tons.

The *Gazette*'s account of the *Heart of Oak*'s launching on April 23 noted, "The best judges all agree, that she is one of the most compleat vessels ever set up in America, equal to any built on the river Thames, and will last longer." This boast may have been a not-so-subtle advertisement for Carolina shipbuilding, as local shipwrights sought both northern and English markets for their products. Two years later the *Gazette* for September 28, 1765, while discussing local shipbuilding, boasted that "as soon as the superiority of our Live-Oak timbers and Yellow Pine plank, to the timber and plank of Northern colonies, becomes more generally known, 'tis not to be doubted, that this province may vie with any of them in that valuable branch of business."

Rose was a passenger on the *Heart of Oak* when it sailed for Cowes on June 22, 1763. He went to England to recruit shipwrights to come to Carolina. He returned in February 1764, his mission considered a failure.

When the *Heart of Oak* was registered, Rose listed himself as sole owner; one-fourth of the ship, however, was owned by his friend Laurens. In 1766 Laurens valued his one-quarter interest in the *Heart of Oak* at £4,000. By comparison he valued New Hope, his three-thousand-acre plantation on the south side of the Altamaha River in Georgia, at £3,150.

In February 1773, while anchored in the Thames River, the *Heart of Oak* was driven ashore by a storm. Apparently the ship received little damage as it sailed for Carolina in March, arriving in Charleston on May 1.

Rose launched the 160-ton ship *Liberty* in 1767. According to the April 27 issue of the *Gazette*, the *Liberty*, built for the Bristol trade, had a figurehead in the image of William Pitt "and was intended to be called the *Pitt,* 'till he was created Earl of Chatham; so great a veneration have the Americans for Pitt and Liberty." Apparently the owners felt that accepting the title of earl was something of a sellout. In 1773 the *Gazette* listed both the *Liberty* and the *Heart of Oak* as being "constantly employed in the Trade between this Port and Europe." It would be interesting to know what the Europeans, and especially the English, thought of the name *Liberty* in 1773.

More repair work consumed the yard following the launching of the *Liberty.* On July 11, 1767, the eighteen-gun HMS *Cygnet* sailed into Charleston Harbor after a Caribbean cruise. Because of rot and decay in its hull, it went to the Hobcaw Shipyard the following day for repair. Its repairs took almost two months.

Whether because of age, reaching financial security, or, as a Loyalist, disenchantment with Charleston politics—we'll probably never know— John Rose soon began thinking about getting out of the shipbuilding business. In 1769 he sold the shipyard to William Begbie and Daniel Manson. With his profits from shipbuilding and the proceeds of the sale of the shipyard, considered to be around thirty thousand pounds, Rose bought several lowcountry plantations and adopted the lifestyle of a gentleman planter. First he bought the 1,000-acre Plainfield Plantation on the Stono River. He then bought the 7,061-acre Southernmost Barony on the Coosawhatchie River and several adjoining plantations in Christ Church and St. Thomas parishes totaling 1,855 acres. He also owned two lots in downtown Charleston and a 350-acre island in the Coosawhatchie River.

During the British occupation of Charleston, Rose and twenty-four other Carolinians petitioned the British commandant to be armed as a loyal militia. When the Patriots regained control of the city, they confiscated his estates and banished him from the state for signing the petition. He moved to Jamaica and subsequently to England, where he lived until his death. It is in the nature of this civil war, for in large part that is what the Revolutionary War was, that one man, Rose, was loyal to one side while his friend Henry Laurens became a champion of the other. During the war Laurens became president of the state's first legislature and later a member of the Continental Congress, becoming its president when John Hancock stepped down.

The shipyard's new owners, Begbie and Manson, bought it along with "all the stages, punts, steamers, fixed pitch kettles, and all the tools and utensils for conducting a shipwrights business," according to the deed. They were soon busy at their craft, launching the ship *Magna Charta* in 1770.

The *South Carolina and American General Gazette* for November 27, 1770, notes that at the ship's launching, "There was a very numerous Company of Ladies and Gentlemen, who partook of a cold Entertainment, and afterwards had a Ball." I assume "cold Entertainment" meant some sort of buffet with cold dishes. A ship launching at this time was apparently an important social event. Ann Manigault, wife of Gabriel Manigault, reputed to be the colony's wealthiest citizen, mentions in her journal attending many of Charleston's leading social events, including balls, marriages, horse races, baptisms, and Hobcaw ship launchings.

The *Magna Charta* was noteworthy not only for being Begbie and Manson's first ship but also for the ornately carved woodwork ordered by the ship's owners. The following description of the figurehead and stern ornamentation appeared in the *South Carolina Gazette* for January 17, 1771. Unfortunately the left edge of the page is missing, as indicated by the brackets.

> [On] Sunday the new Ship called the Magna-Charta, Bur-
> [then ab]out 300 Tons, built by Messrs. Begbie and Manson, for
> [Capt]. Richard Maitland in the London Trade, and launched
> [on the] 23d of November last, at Hobcaw, came down from thence,
> [the] Hull being completely finished, and neatly decorated with
> [C]arved Work: and is allowed, by good Judges, to be as well
> [made] and likely a Ship as ever came off the Stocks in this
> [Provin]ce. The Head, is a Bust of Brittania upheld by two
> [??????]ans; one on the Right, armed for her Defence; the
> [one o]n the Left, offering her the Horn of Plenty, filled with
> [var]ious Productions of America. The Decorations on the
> [stern]e, in the Center, a Scroll representing Magna-Charta,
> [uphel]d by Liberty and Justice; on the Right, is Fame,
> [holding] a Label with the Word Unanimity, as recommending
> [??????] Americans; on the Left, Mercury, as a Messenger,
> [holding] another Label, with the Word Repealed; Under
> [Fame i]s Mars, with his Sword in one Hand and a burning
> [torch i]n the other; and under Mercury, Neptune with his
> [trident] in one, and a Dolphin in the other Hand.

The filled-in portions are best guesses, but it is evident that the *Magna Charta* was no ordinary cargo ship.

At the time of the *Magna Charta*'s launching, the shipwrights already had another ship on the stocks. This was the two-hundred-ton ship *Carolina Packet*, completed the following year. In 1773 the shipyard launched another two-hundred-ton ship, the *Briton*. These were only three of the vessels built or repaired while Begbie and Manson owned the yard.

In 1777, as the Revolutionary War was taking on a full head of steam, Begbie and Manson took on the refitting of the brig *Comet* for the South Carolina navy. They did this despite their Loyalist leanings; I guess, even under trying circumstances, business was business. However, a year later they sold their shipyard to Paul Pritchard, and the site became known as Pritchard's Shipyard. In 1782 the South Carolina General Assembly banished Begbie and Manson from the state and confiscated their estates for refusing to take oaths of allegiance.

Pritchard, a native of Ireland and a shipbuilder in the Charleston area as early as 1770, had been leasing Captain Cochran's shipyard on Shipyard Creek just above Charleston. A fervent patriot, Pritchard began getting work from the commissioners of the navy of South Carolina. The commissioners found the Shipyard Creek site unsuitable, however, since it was so near to Charleston. They noted in their records that "the sailors belonging to the Vessels do Frequently come to Town, get Drunk, and [quit] the Service." So in partnership with the Navy Board, Pritchard bought the Hobcaw site in 1778. The commissioners also liked the larger size of the Hobcaw Shipyard. Their records also state, "there is on the Premises at Hobcaw a great deal of Store room, very Substantial good Wharves and Other Conveniences Sufficient to Heave down Three Vessels at the same time."

One of Pritchard's first jobs for the state navy was the construction of a boat for the brigantine *Hornet*. The commissioners then sent him the brigantine *Notre Dame* to be repaired and made fit for service. The *Notre Dame*, formerly the one-hundred-ton schooner *Islington*, carried sixteen four- and six-pounders. During its career with the South Carolina navy, it was involved in more than half the merchant captures made during the war. They also sent a large barge to the shipyard to be altered into a galley, meaning a vessel that had the ability to be rowed as well as sailed.

The commissioners continued to send Pritchard a variety of jobs related to keeping the naval war effort afloat. During 1778 Pritchard built a two-masted brig for the navy. The new warship was the *Wasp*. Its first captain was William Fisk, who had been second lieutenant of the *Notre Dame*.

In August 1779 the commissioners sent the prison schooner *Pack Horse* to Hobcaw to have its bottom cleaned. They also directed Pritchard to make twenty-five pairs of oars for "Boats & Schooners."

One of the most unusual requests Pritchard received was in September 1779 concerning the French fleet that was operating off the coast. The commissioners sent him a letter noting that "in the late Gale of wind Count DeEstang's ship had her Rudder hurt and is in want of Timber to make a New One also Timber to make three of four Rudders for Ships of the Line." In their letter they specified the types and sizes of timber needed by the French. This included:

One piece of oak 42 ft. 8 in. long, 2 ft. 1½ in. square
Two pieces of oak 35 ft. long, 13 in. square
Two pieces of oak 37 ft. long, 9⅓ in. square
One piece of oak 30 ft. long, 10⅔ in. square
One piece of oak 15 ft. long, 15 in. square for an anchor stock
One unspecified piece 52 ft. long, 2 ft. 2 in. in diameter for a bowsprit
One unspecified piece 59 ft. long, 20 in. in diameter for a bowsprit
One unspecified piece 80 ft. long, 17 in. in diameter for a yard
One piece of pine 77 ft. long, 20 inches in diameter for a jib boom
One piece of pine 37 ft. 4 in. long, 1 ft. 7½ in. square
One piece of pine 32 ft. long, 1 ft. 4 in. square

More cleaning and general repair work on the state's galleys and brigantines occupied the shipyard for the next several months. The brigantine *Notre Dame*, Capt. William Hall, and the galley *Lee*, Captain Boitard, were sent to Hobcaw in November. The galley *Marque de Bretagne*, Captain Corversier, was sent there in December. The galleys *Marque de Bretagne* and *Lee* had been converted from barges and each carried two eighteen-pounders. In addition, by January 1780, efforts at the yard were in high gear when the commissioners sent the ships *Bricole*, Capt. David Lockwood, and *Truite*, Capt. James Pyne, which the commissioners ordered be "put in good repair for immediate Service." The *Bricole* had been built as a large, two-decked armed transport in the 1750s. The *Truite* was built as a transport in Le Havre in 1776.

Shortly after departing Hobcaw Shipyard, presumably in good repair and ready for immediate service, they were turned over to the Continental navy. On December 26, 1779, a British fleet of some ninety vessels under the command of Admiral Marriott Arbuthnot left New York City with an invasion force of 8,500 British soldiers under the command of Sir Henry Clinton. The fleet's destination was Charleston. Early in 1780, prior to the arrival of the British fleet, Commodore Abraham Whipple of the Continental navy arrived in Charleston in command of the Continental frigates *Providence, Boston,* and *Queen of France,* plus the sloop-of-war *Ranger*. With the British soon to arrive, Governor Rutledge placed the vessels of the South Carolina navy under Commodore Whipple's command also. Little good it did. The British fleet arrived off Charleston in February. After mounting what was little more than a delaying action, the American vessels retreated into Charleston Harbor. To prevent the passage of the British ships, eight American ships were sunk between the city and Shutes Folly. These included the *Bricole* and *Notre Dame*. The *Marques de Bretagne* and *Lee* were captured by the British and presumably taken into the Royal Navy. On May 12, 1780, Charleston surrendered.

In his will dated November 10, 1791, Paul Pritchard left the shipyard to his son William along with "all the Materials at the Ship Yard at Hobcaw for carrying on the Shipwrights Business, and also all the Timber and Plank in the Said Ship Yard and Vessels on the Stocks." Also included were the shipyard's twelve slaves, listed as ship carpenters and caulkers. Their names were Portius, Sam, Moosa, Tom, Harry, Junk, Caesar, Ben, Little David, Big David, Cyrus Passage, and Gray. William Pritchard died in 1831, and the site's use as a shipyard seems to have ceased.

The property passed to Robert Muirhead, who purchased it in November 1853 and used much of the land for asparagus cultivation. It passed through several other owners. R. M. McGillivray purchased the property in 1953. Subsequently the land became Hobcaw Point subdivision, with the exception of the 7.5-acre tract of the shipyard. In 1974 the shipyard site was nominated to the National Register of Historic Sites.

The shipyard site remained intact until 1991, when the Hernandez family purchased it with the intention of building a home. They recognized the significance of the property (in fact the colonial shipyard was one of the reasons they purchased it) and agreed to consult with the institute well in advance of any development.

In 1992 we conducted a second brief reconnaissance of the property. Two areas were of special interest at this time. First was a one-acre lot the Hernandez family was selling to help pay for the construction of their home. The second was the proposed site of this house. This was the one that interested us most. A portion of the planned home's footprint required the removal of an old oak tree. Normally this would not have involved archaeology; however, surrounding the tree were the remains of a brick structure. The reconnaissance turned up colonial artifacts, and we decided to return in the future to test the entire area of the footprint and conduct a complete excavation of the brick structure area. This began a year later, in August 1993.

Unfortunately we only had one week in which to complete our project, so we decided to gather enough artifactual information to date the brick structure and determine its use. Because of the presence of the large oak tree that had grown up inside the remains, the building quickly acquired the misnomer "tree house." We managed to excavate 30 percent of the interior of the structure, expose and map the building's main features, and record soil profiles inside and outside its walls. The building was roughly twenty-four feet square. No evidence for a wall enclosing the north side of the structure was found, nor were remains of a builder's trench located as were for the other three walls. We know that in the 1940s this portion of the property was used to store heavy machinery. Perhaps the north wall of the existing structure was removed to provide shelter for some of this machinery. The artifacts recovered from the building location indicate that the structure existed during the time of the shipyard.

This led us to speculate as to the building's purpose. A clue as to one possible use comes from a letter written by the Navy Board to Paul Pritchard in 1779. The letter states that the board had learned that "the Stores belonging to the Different Vessels, belonging to the State, now at Hobcaw, are liable to be lost, or Embezzled by the People, for want of the Different Officers, for each Vessel, to take proper Care of them. The Commissioners of the Navy Board therefore Request, that you will cause all the Stores to be Removed, out of the Different Vessels into some safe store, and that the Clerk of the Yard do take an Inventory of each Vessel's Stores, and have them Placed Separate in the Store." Was this building used as the "safe store"? Perhaps. The artifacts indicate that the building probably served many purposes over the years.

In all we recovered more than twenty-eight thousand artifacts. Present in prodigious numbers were pipe stems and pipe bowls dating from 1750 to 1800, ceramic and bottle shards from the eighteenth and nineteenth centuries, fasteners of wrought iron and brass, and gunflints. Other items recovered include glass beads, buckles, thimbles, buttons, a horse bit, a 1720 Dutch trade token, ax heads, an adze, a pair of dividers, and wine glass stems dating to 1750–60. Burned and butchered bones were also recovered, with pig, deer, bird, and fish represented in great quantity.

Over the next few months, the remainder of the proposed house's footprint was tested at four-meter intervals, producing uniform concentrations of artifacts but no clearly delineated activity areas. Following this, preparation of the ground and construction of the house were monitored at each stage, including excavation of the footings and utility trenches.

In 1999 Sarah J. Morby, a University of South Carolina Department of Anthropology graduate student, conducted a ground-penetrating radar survey of the site, with the aid of SCIAA's Chris Amer. The project was to serve as the basis for her master's thesis. She picked four areas of the property to survey. Two were in the area of the "tree house," one near the slipways, and one in the area of the original main house. Unfortunately her results were inconclusive. In February 2000 she and Chris also performed ten shovel test pits in the area of a visible surface feature (Feature 100) on the eastern side of the property. The testing revealed wooden planking covering brick flooring, presumably of some sort of building. The area was heavily saturated with creosote. In her thesis Morby speculates on the possible use of the structure.

> It is my conjecture that Feature 100 may have been the site of pitch manufacture. The wood on top of the brick flooring would have supplied a stable platform for the heavy iron pitch pot. Further evidence is provided in the creosote soaked wooden planks covering the brick floor. Creosote is a byproduct of tar manufacture. Feature 100 would have provided an ideal location for such manufacture; summer winds generally blow from the south west and would have carried the odor away from the plantation main house and the remainder of the shipyard. Then again some shipyards did not make, but instead purchased pitch for their ships— Feature 100 could have been where the pitch was stored until it was needed on the yard.

In either event, whether used for pitch manufacture or simply for pitch storage, the structure was certainly part of the original shipyard. It is unfortunate that there was no time to perform a complete excavation of the building. The test pits we dug were unable to establish the structure's exact dimensions.

We periodically visit the Hobcaw site. The most visible remnant of the shipyard is the avenue of oaks that at one time led from the main house down to the slipways. Paul Pritchard's daughter Catherine referred to this as "Flirtation Walk," where couples strolled hand in hand during gala ship launchings. Elsewhere on the property, partially exposed brick and structural components and artifact distributions offer tantalizing prospects of eventually understanding the layout and operation of this site, once colonial South Carolina's largest shipyard. Moreover we enjoy the continuing gracious hospitality of the Hernandez family and their six-thousand-square-foot home on Hobcaw Creek.

The most recent plat of the Hernandez property is dated 1998. It shows the property as it is today. It shows an 8.757-acre lot and lake. It shows "view easements," "ingress/egress easements," and "drainage easements" and something called the "S.C. Coastal Council Critical Line." It also shows the outline of the Hernandez home. There is no little drawing of the house with little curlicues of smoke rising from chimneys, just a thin line representing the footprint of the house.

I miss the little curlicues of smoke.

Dredging for the First Americans

Huge cypress trees rising from the waters of Smiths Lake Creek in Allendale County shaded us from the August sun as we prepared our scuba gear. On the opposite bank, an eight-foot alligator slithered into the water, surfacing no more than thirty feet from where we intended to enter the creek. The critter nonchalantly eyed our activities—supposing, of course, that alligators are ever nonchalant. We ignored the threat. He would move off as soon as we entered the water. At least he had every day so far. To our right the creek narrowed, and the waterscape took on the appearance of a swamp. Here the cypress trees crowded the water, making passage by boat nearly impossible. Spanish moss dripping from the branches added to the primordial setting. Wading in the shallows near a small patch of dry ground, a great blue heron searched for a meal. A cover of dwarf palmetto fronds growing along the edge of the water disguised his movements. The large water moccasin that greeted us on the first day had moved off to a more peaceful area. We furtively scanned the area nevertheless. All was quiet except for the calls of some nearby birds and the clank of our aluminum scuba tanks as we unloaded them from the rear of our Suburban. Smiths Lake Creek was a place of seething beauty and familiar danger. If I didn't know better, I would think the scene hadn't changed in thousands of years. On second thought, perhaps it hadn't.

It was the summer of 1995, and SCIAA archaeologist Albert Goodyear had brought SCIAA's Underwater Archaeology Division to Allendale to search the bottom of Smiths Lake Creek for evidence of early Native American occupation. To the dive team, it was just another project in the backwaters of South Carolina. Little did we know that this site held the potential of helping answer one of the most elusive archaeology mysteries in the Western Hemisphere: when did humans first arrive here?

When I was in high school, back in the 1960s, I learned that humans arrived in North America about twelve thousand years ago. Teachers taught this as scientific fact. All the experts agreed. There was irrefutable evidence, specifically two pieces of evidence. First, the oldest artifacts found in North America dated no older than twelve thousand years. Second, the land bridge between Asia and North America, through which the first Americans supposedly migrated, did not open up until twelve thousand years ago. This was the start of what many archaeologists call the Paleoindian period. Archaeologists believed these people lived in highly mobile small bands of hunter-gatherers, hunting megafauna (mastodon and mammoth), bison, and caribou. The most abundant artifacts remaining from these people are stone tools. The famous Clovis point, named after Clovis, New Mexico, where this type of spear point was discovered in context with mastodon bones, has become symbolic of these early Americans. Archaeologists often refer to their way of life as "the Clovis culture." Clovis points can be six or seven inches long but are usually shorter. Their fluted stems identify and define these points.

Today archaeologists are discovering that the 12,000 B.P. (before present) date for the first Americans may not be correct. Over the past few decades several archaeology sites in North and South America have provided evidence that humans culturally different than the Clovis people may have actually populated the Western Hemisphere far earlier. Three of the most prominent of these "pre-Clovis" sites are Monte Verde in Chile, Meadowcroft in western Pennsylvania, and Cactus Hill in Virginia.

At Monte Verde, Tom Dillehay of the University of Kentucky has recovered lithic artifacts that show that people inhabited the area by 14,500 B.P. Dillehay believes these people subsisted on a varied diet that included mussels, crawfish, potatoes, fruits and nuts, small game such as birds, and the occasional mastodon. They lived in low, tentlike structures lashed together with cord and covered with bark and mastodon hide. The stone tools found by Dillehay consist of sharp-edged flakes or faceted pebbles that show signs of use.

The Meadowcroft site in Pennsylvania consists of an overhang jutting from a rock face forty-three feet above the ground. Excavations under James Adovasio of Mercyhurst College revealed an unfluted point and small bladelike flakes in a layer radiocarbon dated to about 17,000 B.P.

Two separate archaeological teams have excavated the Cactus Hill site in Virginia, resulting in the most extensive and best-documented "pre-Clovis" artifact assemblage. This assemblage includes two unfluted triangular points, small blades, retouched flakes, and abrading stones found in a layer dated to about 19,000 B.P.

A fourth site has recently taken center stage. This site happens to be in South Carolina—the very site we were gearing up to dive on in August 1995. At that time, of course, we knew nothing of this.

Not far from the town of Allendale, the site—a large chert quarry—encompasses three separate sites. Chert is a relative in the flint family. Specifically it is a fine-grained, silica-rich, cryptocrystalline sedimentary rock. It ranges in color from white to black, but is most often gray, brown, light green, or red. The chert from Allendale is commonly a rich caramel color. What makes chert important, at least in making stone tools, is that, like flint and obsidian, it fractures in "cones" when struck with some force. Little did I know as a youngster that I was seeing just such a fracture when one of my BB gun projectiles hit our living room window. When chert is struck on its edge, partial cones—what archaeologists call "flakes"—are broken off, leaving sharp edges. As a result the early Native Americans of the Southeast found it an ideal material for making a wide variety of stone implements, including spear points, drills, scrapers, and knives. One of the best sources of this material is this small section of Allendale County on the Savannah River. These early Americans mined chert from this site as far back as . . . well, no one knows for sure.

Dr. Goodyear learned of the quarry site in 1981 when David Topper, an Allendale County employee, told him about an area rich in chert along the side of a hill above the Savannah River. Topper picked the right person to tell. Goodyear joined the institute staff in 1975 and received his Ph.D. from Arizona State University in 1976. Whether at a staff cookout (venison is his favorite) or in the field (on his annual outings to Allendale County), he brings a boyish enthusiasm to everything he does. This trait comes in handy when in the field. Goodyear's digs feature one aspect of fieldwork that other archaeologists envy—volunteers who pay to work on the project. Recruiting and managing volunteers, especially ones who pay more than four hundred dollars a week for the privilege of shoveling dirt, require skills not taught in graduate school. One writer who visited the Allendale site described Goodyear as an "overseer, public relations guru, visitor's guide, and cheerleader." He smiles at the description, finding it amusing, flattering, and slightly embarrassing.

Goodyear and SCIAA archaeologist Tommy Charles visited the chert quarry area several times between the summer of 1982 and the spring of 1984. The area was part of the property of the Sandoz (now Clariant) Chemical Corporation plant. In addition to the Topper site, they found two other chert sites with Paleoindian components. These sites were on Smiths Lake Creek and became known as the Charles site and the Big Pine Tree site.

Members of SCIAA's Underwater Archaeology Division, namely division head Alan Albright and Mark Newell, first visited the site in August 1984. The pair spent two days dredging the bottom of the creek off the Charles site. They dredged numerous lithic artifacts, including six Paleoindian spear points. They also recovered several chert cobbles, indicating the site was a source of the lithic material.

In early 1985 Goodyear and a team of volunteers from the Archaeological Society of South Carolina, the Augusta Archaeological Society, and the Coastal Georgia Archaeological Society out of Savannah conducted a ten-day testing project at the Topper site. The team excavated seven two-meter squares down to a depth of one hundred centimeters.

In the bottom twenty centimeters of their excavations, they discovered stone lithic tools indicating a Paleoindian occupation. These included weathered flakes and both uniface and biface tools.

From thirty centimeters down to the Paleoindian level at eighty centimeters, they found lithics from the Archaic period. Beginning at about 10,000 B.P., the Archaic period is defined by the development of larger groups working "home territories" from seasonal camps. These people hunted deer and other smaller mammals but relied equally on the gathering of wild plants, for example, squash and gourds. They developed a wider variety of stone tools, including adzes, gravers, end scrapers, bone awls, and knives. About this same time, atlatls came into use. These were sticks used to increase the throwing power of spears. Spear points progressed from the Clovis point to side- and corner-notched varieties and then to stemmed points. Bone awls, used to puncture holes in leather and other materials, came into use. About 5,000 B.P. the use of dugout canoes became widespread. The oldest canoes found so far in South Carolina date to about 4,000 B.P. Pottery making began in the Late Archaic period, around 4,500 B.P.

In the top thirty centimeters, they found artifacts from both the Mississippian and Woodland periods, including ceramics as well as lithic remains. Semipermanent settlements and the beginning of food crop cultivation mark the Woodland period (ca. 3,500 B.P. to ca. 1,000 B.P.). There was more reliance on fishing and trade networks. Pottery became more diverse in form and surface decoration. These surface decorations included punctated designs made by jabbing the surface with reeds, periwinkle shells, and sticks; incised designs with geometric patterns; and both cord-marked and fabric-impressed designs. The Woodland period also saw the construction of the first shell rings as well as the widespread use of the bow and arrow.

The Mississippian period (ca. 1,000 B.P. to ca. 500 B.P.) follows the Woodland period. Large permanent settlements based on agriculture, particularly the cultivation of corn, characterize this period. These settlements, featuring large ceremonial mounds, formed complex chiefdoms ruled by hierarchies defined by heredity. As large game became scarcer, projectile points became smaller. Complicated stamped pottery, often with elaborated rim decorations, dominated the pottery designs. This period ends with the arrival of the first Europeans in the early 1500s.

Perhaps the most impressive artifact recovered by Goodyear's team was an intact late Mississippian burial urn. In the bottom of the urn, the team discovered the skeleton of a small infant six to nine months of age.

The Underwater Division also returned to the site in 1985. Funded by USC's Carolina Venture Fund Committee, the project focused on Smiths Lake Creek near the Charles site and the Big Pine Tree site. The underwater archaeology team, headed by Alan Albright, spent ten days dredging the Charles site using an airlift and screen boat. The screen boat had started its career as a military assault craft. Obtained from government surplus, the boat was sixteen feet in length and made of fiberglass. Cut a two-by-five-foot hole in the bottom of the hull, surround the hole with watertight bulkheads, *et voila!*—a military assault craft becomes an airlift screen boat. A wooden sluice built from the boat's stern to a screen fitted over the new hole received the airlifted, artifact-rich bottom sediments. As one screen filled with bottom debris and artifacts, it could easily be removed for further sorting and quickly replaced with a fresh screen.

The team airlifted twenty-one holes in the bottom of Smiths Lake Creek at the Charles site. Each hole measured from three to nine feet across. At the end of the ten days, artifact material recovered from the creek filled a total of forty gallon-sized plastic bags. The team then moved seven hundred feet up the creek to the Big Pine Tree site. During two days at this site, the team airlifted five holes and filled thirty-five gallon-sized plastic bags. The team also spent one day airlifting off the Allendale Chert Quarry's original site, the Topper site, which faces the Savannah River.

Most of the recovered artifacts consisted of bifacial blanks and preforms, which are preliminary stages in the manufacture of projectile points, and most of these dated from 6,000 to 5,000 B.P. However, a large number of flake tools, attributed to the Paleoindian period (12,000–10,000 B.P.) and the Early Archaic period (10,000–8,000 B.P.), came up the airlift as well. At the time Goodyear called the artifacts recovered the largest collection of Early Man chipped-stone technology the institute has in its possession.

While the presence of Paleoindian artifacts elevated the significance of the Allendale sites, at this point nothing Goodyear found on land or as the result of the dredging indicated the site might have a pre-Clovis component. Late in 1985, nevertheless, the three Allendale sites, designated the Allendale Chert Quarries Archaeological District, were accepted to the National Register of Historic Places.

Goodyear returned to the Topper site in 1986 with a team of volunteers and graduate students and funding for twenty-nine days of excavation. As many as fifty volunteers donated their time and efforts to the project. They managed to excavate a three-by-six-meter block down to 100 centimeters, adding to the artifact assemblage recovered the previous year. They also dug two trenches at the Charles site using a backhoe, discovering two crudely flaked Paleoindian bifaces at the 110- to 120-centimeter level.

SCIAA's dive team didn't return to Allendale until August 1995. On this trip to the chert quarries, the team consisted of Chris Amer, Lynn Harris, Joe Beatty, and me. Our goal was to accomplish a more systematic dredging of Smiths Lake Creek at the Big Pine Tree site than had been accomplished in 1985.

For accommodations while we were dredging, Goodyear suggested we camp on the Sandoz property along with his volunteers. He seemed taken aback when we declined, saying we would rather stay in Allendale. This meant motel rooms, an additional drain on his budget, but he agreed. After all he was staying in town as well. Chartered in 1873, Allendale is a typical small southern town. The motel in which Goodyear put us up was a typical small-southern-town motel. It was on the edge of town and on the edge of decline. Joe and I shared a room. On first inspection everything seemed in order. There was hot water in the shower, the air conditioner worked, and there was a color television. We soon learned that a partially plugged drain meant either a speedy shower or a flooded bathroom floor, the air conditioner worked sporadically, and the TV received only two channels.

The motel was also a favorite spot for truckers. This might be why a loud knock on our door woke us one night about 2:00 A.M. Our first sleepy thinking was that there was some sort of emergency. Perhaps the motel was on fire, or someone wanted to rob us. Or both. I went for the door. Joe went for a weapon. This turned out to be the first thing he could get his hands on—a Gideon Bible from the nightstand. I wondered if Joe intended to throw the book at the intruder or preach a sermon. Either could be an effective deterrent.

I opened the door to find a gaudily dressed woman who, it appeared, had been drinking. Heavily. Her profession was obvious.

"Wanna party?" she slurred. It was clear that playing pin the tail on the donkey was not what she had in mind.

"No, thank you," I said, trying to be polite. "Try next door," I added, closing the door.

Joe started to laugh. "Why did you tell her to try next door?" he asked, replacing his weapon back into the nightstand drawer.

"I don't know. I just wanted to get rid of her." I thought directing her elsewhere might hasten her departure. "Why?"

"Dr. Goodyear is next door," he explained, still laughing.

I didn't know. Honest.

This particular motel no longer exists—the victim of progress, specifically chain motels with cable TV, shower drains and air conditioners that work, and, happily/sadly (you pick), other forms of recreation than the one that knocked on our door at 2:00 A.M.

The bottom of Smiths Lake Creek is typical of many slow-moving creeks in South Carolina. The top layer consists of leaves, twigs, and mud. This is the newest material. Normally as we dig down the material gets older. This is a basic principle of archaeology. Layers of dirt or sediment are deposited over time. Therefore the deepest layers (and artifacts) are the oldest. As we dredged down into the bottom of Smith's Lake Creek, though, we found that this is not always the case.

We began dredging in roughly delineated squares. The first thing that occurred as we removed the top layer of leaves, twigs, and mud was that visibility immediately went to zero. With no water flow through the creek, the stirred-up sediments had nowhere to go. Once we removed the top layer, we came to a layer of sand and mud, and almost at once we began finding chert material. At first it sounded like broken glass going up the dredge head, but checking the screen at the other end of the dredge hose showed an abundance of chert flakes and many projectile point pieces.

Finding chert material so soon surprised us. We expected several more layers of historic sediments before reaching the prehistoric levels. But our surprise turned to astonishment when, after going through about a foot of this chert layer, we came to a layer of mud and decomposed

His bubbles roiling the muddy waters of Smiths Lake Creek in Allendale County, a diver dredges the bottom of the creek for evidence of early man as SCIAA staff and volunteers sort the dredged material. SCIAA photograph by Al Goodyear

leaves that contained pieces of cut timbers, Coca-Cola bottles, fishing lures, Budweiser cans, and all sorts of relatively modern trash. This was exactly backward—or more precisely, upside down—from what we expected. Goodyear provided the answer to the puzzle. At one time there had been some sort of wooden structure, perhaps a fishing shack, on the bank of the creek above where we were dredging. Reaching a decrepit state, the shack had toppled into the creek. Subsequently periodic flooding caused the bank of the creek to slide into the creek as well, covering the remains of the shack. Since the chert material had been in the dirt under the shack, moreover, it ended up on top of the remains of the shack.

Farther down the creek, closer to where it enters the Savannah River, Goodyear's team of volunteers slowly shoveled sand and dirt into screens for sifting as they skimmed down through the layers of time.

Once or twice a day, they would come across a few flakes or maybe a broken point. In comparison we were raking in the artifacts. When Goodyear's volunteers learned of our productivity, they slowly, one or two at a time, moseyed over to our screen boat to take part in, or at least watch, the action. This left too few for the land dig and forced Goodyear to add "volunteer herder" to his skill repertoire.

Joe Beatty and I shared most of the dredging duties. This suited me just fine. I admit that dredging is my favorite bottom activity. Even with no visibility, you are constantly active while dredging. The time goes quickly, and the results are tangible. So the long hours each of us spent underwater were more fun than work.

In 1996 Goodyear began the annual four-week, paying-volunteer journeys to Allendale that continue today. The emphasis here is on "paying-volunteer." After advertising in national and regional publications, Goodyear recruited twenty-nine volunteers, charging them $250 a week. Forty-two volunteers signed up for the 1997 project.

The Underwater Archaeology Division returned to Allendale in 1997. On this occasion our dive team consisted of Chris Amer, Lynn Harris, Joe Beatty, Jim Spirek, and me. We also had help from Brinnan Carter, a graduate student from the University of Florida, and three volunteer divers, Doug Boehme, George Pledger, and Michael Phipps. Our goal was to map the bottom of Smiths Lake Creek at both the Charles site and the Big Pine Tree site. This was accomplished by running multiple transects across the creek at both sites. Taking water depths at measured intervals across these transects gave us a profile of the creek bottom. While mapping the creek bottom, we discovered a large, natural outcrop of chert boulders. Analysis of these boulders revealed them to be of stone tool quality. We also did more dredging at both sites, resulting in the recovery of several Paleoindian biface preforms and Archaic points.

In 1998, because of high water levels in Smiths Lake Creek that inundated the Charles and Big Pine Tree sites, Goodyear and his volunteers returned to the Topper site. Having read of the recent pre-Clovis discoveries at Monte Verde and Meadowcroft, he decided to dig below the 100-centimeter Clovis level. Prior to the pre-Clovis discoveries, archaeologists almost never went below the Clovis level, thinking it a waste of time since they believed no humans lived here before then. Much to his surprise, Goodyear discovered chert artifacts at depths of from 130 centimeters to 210 centimeters. He also found a clump of rocks, possibly arranged deliberately, at 180 centimeters. The chert artifacts consisted of two thin, narrow prismatic blades, a tip of an early-stage biface, a retouched flake tool, a possible graver used for engraving bone, antler, or ivory, and two large cores, which are stones from which flakes have been struck.

Goodyear also took many charcoal samples and various levels for radiocarbon dating. In the meantime he had sediment samples in the sub-Clovis level taken for optically stimulated luminescence (OSL) dating. The OSL dating resulted in dates of from 18,000 to 20,000 B.P., clearly earlier than the Paleoindian period. Subsequently the radiocarbon dates came back. Astonishingly the results revealed dates of about—are you ready for this?—50,000 B.P.!

As you can imagine, this has caused a commotion within the archaeological community. Some doubters question the validity of the radiocarbon results. Others question whether the pre-Clovis artifacts were actually artifacts. Instead, the critics say, the items are "geofacts" shaped by natural processes. Time will tell.

The media were quick to pick up on the pre-Clovis results as well, creating a commotion of another sort. Almost all state and regional daily newspapers, including the *Atlanta Journal-Constitution,* ran the story. In June 2004 the *New York Times* featured the Topper site in its science section. Articles on the Topper site and the pre-Clovis artifacts also ran in several national magazines, including *American Archaeology, Discovery, U.S. News and World Report, Newsweek,* and *Time.* The site was also featured on PBS's *Scientific American Frontiers,* hosted by Alan Alda, and on a SCETV documentary titled *They Were Here: Ice Age Humans in South Carolina.*

In addition to the exciting developments of the past few years at the Topper site that now keep him busier than ever, Goodyear is currently working on plans to have SCIAA's Maritime Archaeology Division return to Allendale. Perhaps we can help him get a clearer picture of when humans first arrived here. Wouldn't that be something!

The Upside-Down Wreck

Divers, anglers, boaters, canoers, kayakers, and persons who just like to explore their local rivers, bays, and creeks stumble onto all sorts of maritime relics. These "explorers" are having eureka moments over dugout canoes, barges, ferry vessels, old rice field gates, and, now and then, the odd shipwreck. Often (although not often enough) they contact us to report their finds. Following up on these reports is one our most enjoyable and rewarding duties. We get to meet fantastic South Carolinians who are interested in the history of their state. We get to evaluate and record another piece of our maritime past. We get to escape from our offices, at least temporarily. Moreover we get to go diving, which is why we were on the Pee Dee River near Cheraw in 1990—to see the submerged remains of a vessel reported to us by a local sport diver.

It was a warm June day, and the river levels were down—perfect diving conditions. Our target was a small wooden vessel resting on the bottom of the Pee Dee just downriver from Laney Landing, Cheraw's public boat landing. The SCIAA archaeologists surfaced from their first dive on the wreck, let their regulators drop out of their mouths, and immediately began talking.

"Remarkable wreck," said one.

"Never saw anything like it," said another.

"Certainly is unique," agreed the third. When archaeologists get excited they tend toward simple declarative sentences.

Miller Ingram, the local sport diver, followed their conversation with interest. He must have wondered what type of wreck he had found. In what way could it be remarkable? Did someone actually say "unique"?

Miller S. Ingram Jr. is a prominent attorney in Cheraw, the county seat for Chesterfield County and a rustic, yet vibrant, town in the South Carolina sandhills. He has a penchant for the rich history of the area. He is also an avid scuba diver with several advanced certifications. For

Miller the three go hand in hand. His law practice allows him the time (and funds) to dive in the waters of the nearby Pee Dee River. And in these waters much of the history of the region can be traced.

Cheraw, some 165 river miles above Georgetown, sits at the historic head of steamboat navigation for the Pee Dee River, one of the most extensive river systems in South Carolina. Shelves of shale extend across the river just above Cheraw, making passage difficult, if not impossible, for all but the smallest vessels. As a result Cheraw became the center of trade for the area. Riverboats of all sorts, from pole boats to barges to steamboats, have been bringing goods to and from the area since the middle of the 1700s. At Laney Landing one can still see the remains of the tramway that brought these goods up the hill from the landing to be loaded into wagons and carts.

Miller became a certified scuba diver in 1986. He followed up his basic training with advanced courses with the intent of diving in the Pee Dee River. In May 1987 he applied for and received a South Carolina hobby diver license, allowing him to collect artifacts and fossils from state waters, and before long was reporting finds from the bottom of the Pee Dee River.

His first discoveries consisted of ceramics and bottles, but he soon began finding numerous Civil War military artifacts, including several artillery projectiles. This is understandable, considering what happened on March 6, 1865. Three days earlier Confederate forces under Lt. Gen. William J. Hardee fought a running battle with Union forces under Maj. Gen. William T. Sherman as the Confederates crossed the Pee Dee River at Cheraw. Sherman's army of 60,000 men, 4,500 vehicles, and 30,000 horses, having just devastated Columbia, was headed to Fayetteville, North Carolina. Hardee's Confederate army of 11,000 had abandoned Charleston and was marching to join Confederate forces gathering in North Carolina to stop Sherman. Hardee arrived in Cheraw ahead of Sherman and set up defenses to slow Sherman's advance. Seeing the hopelessness of his position, Hardee made plans to withdraw. With the Union forces hot on their heels, the Confederates managed to flee across the river, burning the bridge behind them. The shooting continued as the Confederate forces fired on the Union forces, who were trying unsuccessfully to extinguish the flames. A lively cross-river exchange of rifle and artillery fire continued throughout the afternoon, ending at sundown.

Because of their hasty retreat, the Confederates abandoned a large cache of artillery, shells, gunpowder, and ammunition. This included twenty-five field artillery pieces, sixteen complete limbers, sixteen complete caissons, five thousand artillery rounds, twenty thousand rounds of small arms ammunition, and more than twenty tons of gunpowder.

The Union forces quickly built pontoon bridges across the Pee Dee in several places and began to move across the river and into North Carolina. They took with them three captured Blakely guns as souvenirs. They discarded most of the Confederate gunpowder and artillery shells in a ravine, however, resulting in a pile of explosives several feet deep. This ravine happened to be near the path used by the soldiers to get from town to the pontoon bridge at Cheraw. Late in the morning of March 6, Union soldiers passing by the ravine accidentally ignited the gunpowder. The blast flattened buildings, shattered trees, stupefied animals, and threw artillery shells high into the air, where they exploded or landed in the surrounding landscape and nearby river. It also killed one officer and three men.

Miller Ingram also began exploring the wreck of a steamship that had the misfortune of sinking just downstream from Laney Landing, collecting a variety of artifacts from the site. These artifacts included several ceramic shards, kaolin clay pipe bowls, five coins, eight padlocks, and forty-three buttons. In 1990 he decided to expand his exploration to the area downriver from the vessel's remains. After all the steamship had apparently exploded, and parts of the wreck (and artifacts) could be scattered over some distance. Working his way downriver, he discovered the remains of a wooden sailing vessel partially buried in sand.

Ingram reported his discovery to SCIAA's Underwater Archaeology Division staff. We decided to conduct a reconnaissance and brief survey of both the steamship and Miller's new wreck. We arrived at Laney Landing in June 1990 with our dive boat, all our dive gear, and what archaeological gear we thought we would need, including probes, tape measures, and slates to write on underwater. We were the picture of professionalism. Our team consisted of archaeologists Chris Amer, Lynn Harris, and David Beard, along with divers Joe Beatty and me. Miller Ingram came with us. We have a policy of never diving on a wreck site without notifying the wreck's finder and inviting him or her along. The extra help comes in handy.

After listening to the archaeologists' tantalizing conversation about the wreck, Joe decided to don his scuba gear and take a look for himself. He returned to the surface within minutes. We were still discussing this "unique wreck."

"Construction is unusual."

"Not at all typical."

"I concur."

Joe broke into the discussion. "Hey, guys," he said to get our attention. "The wreck is upside down."

The archaeologists gaped. Miller laughed. Joe shrugged. After assuring everyone he was not kidding, a minor commotion ensued. Chris, Lynn, and David hurriedly donned their dive gear and returned to the water, skeptical of Joe's quick assessment. While river sand covered most of the vessel's remains, it soon became obvious that the wreck was indeed upside down. This was highly unusual. Most wrecks we see sit upright. Some are on their sides. This was the first one that was upside down. Despite our curiosity about the wreck's position, though, it was obvious that extensive excavation was needed to get a full picture of the vessel's dimensions and construction aspects. Since time was short, we turned our attention to the remains of the steamer.

The first steamboat to haul passengers and cargo to Cheraw on a regular basis was the *Pee Dee,* which began operating between Georgetown and Cheraw in December 1819, making the 330-river-mile round trip voyage in four days. By 1823 two steamboats were making runs from Cheraw to Georgetown and Charleston. Moreover another steamer, the *Maid of Orleans,* was already on the stocks. In that year Cheraw had a population of seven hundred and consisted of about 250 dwellings, an academy, a library, four public houses, and one church. Produce taken to Georgetown and Charleston consisted mainly of cotton but also included large quantities of tobacco, beeswax, tallow, flaxseed, flour, and corn. In the local newspaper, the *Cheraw Intelligencer,* merchants advertised the steamboats' return cargoes for sale. "Just received" items included dry goods, hardware, medicines, salt, iron stock, sugar, molasses, coffee, and an assortment of international goods, specifically French brandy, Jamaican rum, Dutch gin, Irish whiskey, and Madeira wine.

For the river steamboats, navigating the Pee Dee River was risky business. Shallow water, narrow banks, and endless twists and turns waited to snare the intrepid riverboats. In addition steamboat technology was still in its infancy, and boiler explosions accounted for many a mishap.

In January 1825 the steamboat *Columbia* was on its way downriver, pulling two towboats laden with eight hundred bales of cotton, when one of the boats hit a snag about sixty-four river miles above Georgetown. The boat filled with water in less than four minutes, damaging about one hundred bales of cotton.

On March 29, 1843, the steamers *Utility* and *Osceola* left Georgetown for Cheraw. Near Uhany (Yahany) Ferry (a little more than twenty-seven river miles above Georgetown), the *Utility* was a short distance ahead of the *Osceola* when the *Utility's* boiler exploded. Severely damaged, it quickly sank. Owing to the quick work of the two vessels' crews, however, most of its cargo was transferred to the *Osceola*. Only a few hogsheads of sugar and about fifty sacks of salt were lost. Several of the crew received minor injuries.

The *Osceola* itself had been the victim of several mishaps. In March 1841 it ran ashore at Wright's Bluff while descending the river. The incident was blamed on violent currents caused by the heaviest rains anyone had seen in twenty-five years. The grounding stove in two of its planks but caused no other damage. The *Osceola* was subsequently gotten off and taken to Georgetown for repairs. A little over a year later, in May 1842, the vessel snagged a submerged obstruction near Society Hill. After discharging its cargo without any loss, the *Osceola* was freed.

On November 19, 1853, after taking on wood near Port's Ferry (about sixty-five river miles above Georgetown), the steamer *Robert Martin* was just getting under way for Cheraw when its boilers exploded, flinging fragments of machinery, cargo, ship parts, and crew members in every direction. According to contemporary newspaper accounts, the ship's anchors, chains, and iron capstan landed on the nearby riverbank. The explosion killed ten of the twenty-seven persons on board, including the second engineer, the cook, and one of the firemen, all of whom were never found, presumably blown to bits. Built in 1849 in Charleston, the *Robert Martin*, a wooden, side-wheel steamship, was 129 feet 6 inches long, with a beam of 29 feet 4 inches and a draft of 7 feet 2 inches.

All that remains of the unidentified steamboat on the bottom of the Pee Dee River near Cheraw is an eighteen-foot-by-ten-foot section of the hull, a portion of the deck, a large wooden gear on a wooden shaft, parts of several barrels, and a scatter of miscellaneous artifacts. The hull section appears to be from the bow area of the vessel. We found remnants of the red lead paint that must have covered the hull in the seams of the planking. The small portion of deck found on the site had planking that measured eight inches wide and a half inch thick. The large wooden gear and shaft would have connected the paddlewheel. It was reinforced with longitudinal strips of metal running between two metal bands. None of the steam machinery was located, but the wreck's accessible location in proximity to Cheraw means it was probably salvaged shortly after the sinking. With time short we mapped in the various remains, packed up our gear, and headed back to our offices.

After our brief visit to the upside-down wreck, however, our interest in the small wooden vessel was piqued. The remains of a ship-built riverine craft in an upland South Carolina context had never been studied. What type of craft did the early settlers find most advantageous in such an environment? How did it differ in design and construction from craft used in other contexts? Would different types of wood be used in its construction? We suspected that a vessel specially built for the local river conditions would be of shallow draft, beamy, and lightly built. It would have to have a shallow draft to navigate the shoals of a river whose depth at times is measured in inches. It would have to be wide, not only to carry heavy cargoes, but also to spread the load out over a larger area. In addition we speculated that it might be lightly built. Without the need to stand up to heavy ocean swell, its frames and timbers could be less heavily constructed than those for an oceangoing vessel. We decided that a full excavation and recording of the wreck was in order.

But first the most important aspect of archaeological research—funding—had to be obtained. Meanwhile the Archaeological Society of South Carolina (ASSC) awarded Miller its 1990 Distinguished Archaeologist of the Year Award. The award is given to avocational archaeologists who have done outstanding work assisting the professional archaeology community. Miller received the ASSC award not only for his diligence in reporting the steamboat and upside-down vessel and helping us in our preliminary visit to both sites, but also for his educational efforts in giving talks about the history of the Pee Dee region to schools, historical societies, and dive clubs. Dr. Bruce Rippeteau, then director of SCIAA and the state archaeologist of South Carolina, presented the award at the ASSC awards banquet.

For funding to conduct further work on the upside-down vessel, Dr. Suzanne C. Linder, whose doctoral dissertation was on the Yadkin / Pee Dee River system, was approached to write a grant proposal. She agreed and subsequently submitted the proposal to the South Carolina Humanities Council on behalf of the Historic Cheraw Foundation. The funding was approved in July 1993.

We returned to the site in the fall of 1993. Our team consisted of SCIAA staff members Chris Amer, Mark Newell, Joe Beatty, and me. Assisting us was William Barr, a University of South Carolina anthropology department graduate assistant; Britt Nickels, a volunteer diver from Augusta, Georgia; Dr. Frank Barnes of the University of North Carolina at Charlotte; and Miller Ingram. Just as important to our efforts was Miller's wife, Gale, who graciously fed the tired, hungry, and often waterlogged crew after a day in the swift currents of the Pee Dee River.

Cheraw attorney Miller Ingram, standing left, and William Barr watch Chris Amer gather gear prior to a dive on the "upside-down wreck." SCIAA photograph

Our plan was to measure and draw the exposed portions of the wreck before using our water induction dredge to expose the portion covered by a small mountain of sand. Since the vessel was upside down, the construction aspects that would be most revealing, those of the interior structure of the vessel, were hidden from us. There was also the chance that any cargo the craft was carrying might be trapped underneath. The possibility that an intact cargo lay beneath the hull of a vessel is as enticing to an archaeologist as a cookie jar is to a six-year-old. Not only could the cargo be helpful in dating the wreck, but also, by comparing the cargo with recorded shipping manifests, it might be possible to learn the exact identity of the vessel. We decided to cut a hole in the vessel's bottom to gain access to the interior once the exterior was recorded.

Immediately we ran into a slight problem. Upriver from Cheraw is a hydroelectric dam that has the unpleasant habit of dumping huge amounts of water at unannounced intervals. A manageable half-knot current could speed up to a whopping six knots in a matter of minutes, raising the level of the river several feet at the same time—sort of like a mini tsunami. Trying to work underwater in a six-knot current is like trying to inflate an air mattress in a windstorm.

Nevertheless we managed to record the exposed portion of the wreck. We then began dredging the sand-covered portion of the vessel and recording its timbers. After several days of dredging, we had moved several tons of sand and gravel off the remains of the small wooden vessel. To our surprise we discovered that our dredging had created a new sandbar downstream of the wreck, reaching all the way to the surface in a semicircular shape at the end of our dredge outflow hose. We hoped no local boater would discover this new hazard to navigation, at least not at high speed.

To get to the possible "goodies" inside the hull, we cut a hole about eighteen inches square in the hull and inner planking. We then dredged inside the hull down about one meter until we hit hard marl. What we found was disappointing. Actually it was what we did not find that was disappointing. Inside the hull we found no cargo, no ballast, and no artifacts that could be linked to the boat. Either the hull was empty when it overturned and sank, or it overturned upstream and spilled its contents as it drifted to its resting spot. We also found no evidence that the boat was decked, although a vessel this size (a little more than fifty feet long) would probably be at least partially decked. Also we were unable to determine the vessel's rig. Our limited access to the interior precluded the ability to count mast steps to determine whether it was sloop or schooner rigged. We did take measurements of the framing members of the boat, along with some wood samples. We then replaced the plank sections we had cut out and covered the area with sand and gravel to protect it.

A close examination of the outside of the hull did reveal some information about the vessel. For one thing, the boat was relatively new when it sank. The bottom of the hull showed little wear, with none of the abrasion marks one would find on a boat after years of scraping over the rocks and sandbars of the upper Pee Dee River. There was also no indication of any hull repairs. We dated the boat's construction to the first part of the nineteenth century. This is indicated by the presence of wrought-iron nails in the hull. Cut nails (nails that were sliced from sheet iron by a machine) were first produced in 1790; however, wrought nails were commonly used well into the nineteenth century.

While we were examining the small riverine vessel, we had one of those days that make archaeological projects memorable. While anchored over the site, we were taking a lunch break after a morning of diving.

With our wet suits cushioning our butts on whatever piece of equipment substituted for a seat, we ate out of our coolers and talked about the upcoming diving. Our conversation stopped as a distant buzzing drew our attention downriver. A few hundred yards downriver from the wreck, the Pee Dee turns to the east and disappears between the high, tree-covered riverbanks. The buzzing sounded like a large swarm of angry bees, and it was coming our way. Approaching unseen, the noise became frighteningly loud as it reverberated off the riverbanks. It sounded like an airplane engine, but it was too close to the water. Must be an airboat, someone said.

Suddenly a small, single-engine aircraft zoomed around the corner and into view. The plane was flying so low its wheels were dragging in the brown river water, kicking up rooster tails like a wide-legged water skier. We stared in disbelief, frozen like deer in headlights, as it came straight for us. Less than fifty yards before crashing into us, the pilot gunned the engine and soared upward, missing us by a scant few feet. It was probably more like seventy-five feet, but that seemed scant to us. Once we calmed down, and checked to see if we needed to wash out our wet suits, we wondered why the pilot would fly up the river in such a manner. Perhaps he did not realize how close to the water he was. Perhaps he had a bet with a passenger in the plane. Perhaps the plane was full of illegal drugs, and the pilot was flying low up the river to avoid detection. The speculation that followed became even more illogical.

The upside-down wreck indeed turned out to be made for its environment, at least as far as compared to the other riverine vessels we have studied in South Carolina. Perhaps the best comparison is with the Mepkin Abbey Vessel, so named because it was discovered near the Mepkin Abbey in the Cooper River—a definitive lowcountry environment. Both vessels were about the same length—50 feet 10 inches for the upside-down boat versus 49 feet for the Mepkin vessel. Both were of the same period, the early nineteenth century. Both were riverine cargo vessels—the Mepkin wreck was carrying a cargo that included a load of cypress shingles. This is where the similarities end. As we suspected the upside-down vessel was built for the upcountry river environment. It was shallow drafted, indicated by its flat keel (6 inches compared to 10 inches for the Mepkin wreck), and beamy (15 feet 1 inch wide compared to the Mepkin wreck's 11 feet). Even more revealing is how lightly built it is. Its frames are $3\frac{3}{8}$ inches by $3\frac{3}{8}$ inches and spaced $23\frac{3}{8}$ inches apart. They were made from soft southern yellow pine. The Mepkin Abbey Vessel's hull is supported by 6-by-5-inch frames that are spaced, on average, 12 inches apart. Not only larger and closer together, they are also made of stronger live oak. Both vessels have outer planking made of pine. The planks are ³⁄₄ inch thick on the Pee Dee River vessel, however, compared to 1¹⁄₄ inches thick on average for the Cooper River vessel. Moreover on the Mepkin wreck the keelson is through bolted to the keel at every frame. On the upside-down vessel, the keelson was treenailed to the frames but not through to the keel.

Interestingly the upside-down vessel was made of only one type of wood—southern yellow pine. The Mepkin Abbey Vessel is made of oak and pine as is typical of vessels found in a lowcountry environment. The use of pine alone could indicate a vessel not only used in an upcountry environment but one constructed in the upcountry as well. As we find and record additional upcountry vessels, we will reveal more answers about these riverine craft. In archaeology, as in other sciences, knowledge is cumulative. We do know that shipbuilding was a thriving industry in the early history of the upper Pee Dee. Linder, in her doctoral dissertation, documents early shipbuilding in the Cheraw area.

Stephen Parker operated a boatyard as well as a tavern, a ferry, and a mill on Marks Creek, just above Cheraw, as early as 1776. In 1801 Achilles Knight, another boat wright, bought land on Marks Creek adjacent to the Parker property. This proved convenient as he was married to Parker's daughter Elizabeth. Knight died in 1809. His estate papers list many tools used in boatbuilding, including mallets, caulking irons, a pair of compasses, a gouge, wood planes, augers, adzes, a square, and a broadax. When Parker died in 1821, he gave another son-in-law, Cannon Weaver, the use of his boatyard for fifteen years. Weaver, however, moved in 1828 to Mississippi, where he became a wagon maker. What types of vessels were constructed at these yards? No one knows for sure, but the upside-down wreck may have been one of them.

We debated what to name the wreck for the records. The Upside-Down Wreck was the obvious name; but archaeological sites have been named for some amusing aspect or obscure reference far too often. During a 1979 project on Wadboo Creek, off the west branch of the Cooper River, a small wooden wreck was discovered. Apparently finding nothing distinguishable about the vessel to use as a name, someone must have looked up into the trees that hover over the creek. This site is recorded in the South Carolina Statewide Archaeological Site Inventory as the Eagle Nest Wreck. In another instance SCIAA staff member

Facing: Plan, backbone elevation, and section views of the excavated portion of the upside-down wreck, officially known as the Ingram Vessel. SCIAA illustration by Christopher Amer

KEEL SCARPH DETAIL

SECTION AT FRAME 14

RIVER BOTTOM

SECTION AT FRAME 10

SECTION AT FRAME 7

BACKBONE ELEVATION

KEEL

KEELSON

SECTION AT FRAME 5

FREE

FREE

PLANS

PLAN

TREE

ROCK MESA (10 METERS FROM KEEL)

CHANNEL

GUNWALE

ROCK

PLAN

PLANK

05

03   04   05   06   07   08   09   10   11   12   13   14   15

METERS
0   1   2

SOUTH CAROLINA INSTITUTE OF
ARCHAEOLOGY AND ANTHROPOLOGY

INGRAM VESSEL (38CT204)

SCALE 1:20   NOVEMBER 11, 1993
CHRISTOPHER F. AMER

Ralph Wilbanks, while cruising the New River in 1979, stopped for his noon meal on Daufuskie Island. There he discovered old pilings and a road leading off into the woods. Nearby he found prehistoric and historic pottery. This site is now officially designated the Lunch Break Site.

We decided not to name the wreck the Upside-Down Wreck. Instead we decided to honor its finder. The remains of this interesting upland riverine vessel are listed in the site inventory files as the Ingram Vessel. This seems appropriate. After all, as Miller reminded us, his birthday *is* June 13—the feast day of St. Anthony of Padua (the patron saint of lost objects).

Salvage License #32

State archaeologists cringe at the thought of dealing with salvage divers. They would rather eat glass. Archaeologists see these treasure hunters as human termites, devouring archaeological sites through their greed— a kind of blight on the scientific landscape of archaeological research. Archaeologists perceive the artifacts taken by salvage divers as a loss to our cultural heritage. Salvors, of course, see artifacts as objects devoid of scientific information but full of profit potential. After all, they argue, what scientific value can there be in, for instance, South Carolina Dispensary bottles lying haphazardly near a shipwreck or in a crate of dinnerware found in the wreckage of a blockade runner? Archaeologists, naturally, see thing differently. To them every artifact, every ship timber, every loose bottle lying near a shipwreck is part of the story, and its loss is tragic. They would be perfectly happy to see treasure hunters shot, hanged, or at least crucified. These options are, of course, out of the question, so archaeologists have a tendency to want nothing to do with treasure hunters.

Since the South Carolina Underwater Antiquities Act provides for the salvage of shipwrecks in state waters, however, institute archaeologists who administer the law have little choice. As good public servants, they have to work with those salvors who come up with salvage plans that fit all the legal requirements. They may not like it, but they at least have to "make nice." Yet no matter how friendly and cordial the relationship between the archaeologist and salvor begins, it often degenerates into squabbling, bickering, and occasionally legal action. Mistrust and misunderstandings frequently lead to animosity and accusations. Such is the case of salvage license #32.

In May 1985 Howard B. Tower Jr. of Jacksonville, an engineer with Southern Bell, applied to SCIAA for a search license (now called an intensive survey license) to look for shipwrecks off Bowman's Jetty on

Sullivan's Island. This is a precursor to receiving a salvage license (now a data recovery license). The idea is that before the institute issues a salvage license, the prospective salvor should precisely delineate the area he wants to salvage and conduct historic research on the area and shipwrecks he is looking for, giving everyone a better idea of what is down there before going further. It also gives the institute archaeologists an idea of how the salvor operates before allowing him to retrieve a large number of artifacts. In this case the applicant previously held a salvage license. Issued in 1980, that license allowed Tower to salvage the remains of the USS *Boston*, a 215-foot army transport ship that caught fire and sank in the Ashepoo River in 1864. Because of Tower's prior salvage record with the *Boston*, the state underwater archaeologist, Alan Albright, approved the application, and Tower's search for Civil War blockade runners near Bowman's Jetty began.

The U.S. Army Corps of Engineers built Bowman's Jetty in 1839 to control the erosion of Sullivan's Island near Fort Moultrie. Jutting four hundred feet into Charleston Harbor, the jetty was an immediate success. Within months more than one hundred feet of additional beach had accrued in front of the fort.

Some years later, in 1850, Lt. John Maffitt of the U.S. Navy discovered a new channel into the harbor while resurveying the Charleston bar and the entrances to Charleston Harbor. This winding channel ran close to Sullivan's Island, almost paralleling the beach. During the Civil War, "Maffitt's Channel" became popular with the blockade runners. With Union batteries on Morris Island and the blockading fleet guarding the regular channels, the blockade runners, either coming to or leaving from Charleston, found the near shore channel gave them the best chance of avoiding the Union artillery. This put them dangerously close to Bowman's Jetty, however. As a result several were lost on the protruding rocks.

Over a period of several months, Tower conducted his search in the area on the ocean side of Bowman's Jetty. He and his team located the remains of several shipwrecks believed to be the *Minho*, the *Stono*, the *Prince Albert*, the *Beatrice*, and the *Flamingo*. All these vessels were indeed blockade runners lost while trying to enter or leave Charleston Harbor.

Between 2 A.M. and 3 A.M. on the night of October 20, 1862, the Union blockading fleet spotted the blockade runner *Minho* attempting to enter Charleston Harbor. Built at Paisley, Scotland, in 1854, the *Minho* was a screw-driven steamer with a wood hull on an iron frame, 175.3 feet in length with a beam of 22 feet and draft of 13.5 feet. Purchased by Fraser, Trenholm and Company in 1862, it made five successful runs into Charleston before being sold to the Navigation Company in September of that year. In October, as the *Minho* was making its first run into Charleston for its new owners, it came under fire from the USS *Flambeau*. Faced with certain capture, the *Minho's* captain ordered it to full speed and ran it aground on Bowman's Jetty. It was sold at auction several days later for six thousand dollars, and most of its cargo was salvaged. This consisted of the expected types of war goods and necessary staples, including cases of Enfield rifles (plus their associated bullets and percussion caps), cavalry swords, and even uniform buttons. Desperately needed staples included medicines and drugs (morphine and opium among others), shoes (461 pairs), hardware (tools, latches, hinges, and pulleys, plus assorted pots, pans, and eating utensils), dry goods ("4¾ dozen Girl's drawers, assorted" and "1 case Children's White Diapers" were just two of the listings in this category), and groceries (from sugar to sardines, coffee to candles). The *Minho* was also carrying a surprising amount of luxury goods. In addition to the other items, the blockade runner was carrying quantities of Italian silk, wine glasses, decanters, tea trays, curtain rings, bread baskets, cigars, smoking pipes, playing cards, scented soap, and alcoholic beverages (including cognac, sherry, brandy, claret, gin, whiskey, port, ale, porter, and champagne). By today's thinking these goods would seem extravagances in time of war. To the war-ravaged Charlestonians, many of these items (especially the alcoholic beverages) may have seemed more like necessities.

The *Stono,* built as a propeller-driven river steamer, was purchased by the federal government on September 9, 1861, for the sum of fifty thousand dollars. It was 171 feet 6 inches in length, 31 feet 4 inches wide, and had a draft of 9 feet. The navy converted it to a gunboat, arming it with eight eight-inch Dahlgren guns and a thirty-pounder Parrott gun in its bow, and christened it the USS *Isaac Smith*. On January 30, 1863, it was captured by the Confederates as it patrolled the Stono River south of Charleston. It was brought to Charleston, converted to a blockade runner, and renamed the *Stono*. Its first attempt to run the blockade proved fatal. The *Charleston Mercury* for June 8, 1863, ran the following story:

> Marine Accident—The steamer *Stono,* outward bound, having
> on board a cargo of about six hundred bales of cotton, went to sea
> on Friday night. Soon after crossing the bar she was seen by the
> blockaders, who fired at her and gave chase, when she had to put
> about and made for the harbor to prevent her falling into the

clutches of the Yankees. On nearing the Sullivan's Island break-water, owing to a mistake on the part of the wheelsman, she was run ashore on the rocks, where she now is, with every prospect of her being totally wrecked. The bulk of her cargo has been taken out and brought to the city, some of it damaged. She is now being stripped, and everything taken from her that can be got at.

The USS *Wissahickon* was the Union ship that gave chase. It fired at the *Stono* from a distance of three-quarters of a mile with its twenty-four-pounder howitzer, its twenty-pounder Parrott, and its two-hundred-pounder Parrott gun. For the crew of the *Stono*, having shells from a two-hundred-pounder coming at them must have been terrifying. It's easy to understand how the wheelsman could have gotten flustered and ran the ship aground.

The third vessel in Tower's salvage sights was the propeller-driven *Prince Albert*. The 132-gross-ton blockade runner, built in Dumbarton, Scotland, in 1849, was 138.1 feet long by 16.7 feet wide with a draft of 7 feet. Its loss was a matter of luck—both bad and good. As it was running into Charleston Harbor during the night of August 9, 1864, good fortune came in the form of a negligent Union naval officer. Acting ensign Joseph Frost, captain of the tug *Dandelion*, had picket duty that night, but instead of following standing orders to patrol the harbor entrance, he ordered his crew to anchor the tug around 9 P.M. While he and his crew slept, the *Prince Albert* slipped through the blockade. Unfortunately it ran into the wreck of the *Minho* as it came by Fort Moultrie. At daylight the USS *Catskill* spotted the stranded *Prince Albert* and commenced firing with its rifled howitzer on the hapless blockade runner. The Union battery on Morris Island joined in, and the *Prince Albert* soon caught fire and sank. According to the official reports, the *Dandelion*'s captain was placed "under suspension" for failing to patrol the harbor entrance. I suspect that meant he was in deep naval doo-doo.

On December 11, 1985, Albright received a salvage license application from Tower for the recovery of artifacts from three of the wrecks. The wrecks, Tower stated, were the blockade runners *Minho*, *Stono*, and *Prince Albert*. According to Tower's application, these three wrecks were located in a 100-by-300-yard rectangle on the offshore side of Bowman's Jetty. This was later changed to a 100-by-500-yard area. Tower listed his associates as Larry Tipping, a personnel manager also from Jacksonville; Gerald Mahle, owner and manager of an auto repair business in Hampton, South Carolina; and Mike Zafoot, a salesman of water treatment systems from West Columbia. One week later, on December 18, the institute approved the application and issued salvage license #32.

The license stipulated that the licensee receive ownership of 50 percent of all artifacts recovered, and the state would keep 50 percent. Under the provisions of the license, Tower agreed to keep a daily log that "shall list and describe all submerged antiquities recovered; shall include sketches, photographs, or other descriptions of submerged antiquities located." The agreement also stipulated that the licensee would be "responsible for marking his site location and for protective measures to insure against encroachment on his location by others." These were standard requirements at the time and were part of all salvage licenses issued. Tower paid the institute $250 for the license, which was to expire in one year. Albright signed the license on behalf of the institute and the state. Little did he know that before it was all over there would be disputes over artifacts, accusations of theft, and a police investigation.

Tower's "proposed method of excavation," which was attached to his salvage license application, noted that the wrecks of three blockade runners "lie scattered and intertwined on a hard bottom of compacted sand/gravel south of Bowman's Jetty." Not surprising. The U.S. Army Corps of Engineers had the wrecks deliberately demolished in the 1870s. According to their records, the corps's work consisted of the removal of 125 linear feet from the outer end of the jetty, the lowering of several hundred more feet, and "the removal of sundry wrecks sunk in the harbor during the civil war." The removal of these wrecks was, in a word, brutal. Benjamin Maillefert, who held the contract for the work on the jetty, employed what the corps's officer in charge, Q. A. Gillmore, described as a "set of claws, run by steam power," mounted on a large scow to remove the jetty rock, rip apart the wrecks, and scatter their remains. At that time the term "cultural resource management" was in no one's dictionary. What remained of the site, in Howard Tower's words, was "a nautical junk pile of Civil War vessels, their tackle and cargo."

Tower's plans also called for positive identification of the shipwrecks in his salvage area. This proved difficult because of the limited visibility and strong currents near the wrecks. In his first progress report, submitted to the institute on July 16, 1986, Tower included a preliminary site map showing the locations and orientations of the three wrecks. At least as far as could be determined. The remains of the *Minho*, the report states, lie roughly north-south, intermingling with those of the *Stono,* which lies roughly east-west. There was little of the *Minho* left. He attributes this to the Army Corps of Engineers' work in the 1870s.

Conversely much of the *Stono* remained. Of these remains the report states that "the east end of the wreck is buried in a sand bank and pieces of wooden hull are visible 120 feet west of this point. Only that portion of the hull that once was well below the waterline remains. A forty foot section sheathed with brass is well defined and rises, at points, two feet off the bottom." There is also a 25-by-35-foot area of "boiler wreckage" rising about eight feet off the bottom. This is a considerable amount of remains, considering the abuse from demolition and environment. On future dives, the report concludes, they hoped to find the remains of the *Prince Albert,* which they had not seen since January. Tower also requested permission to raise the anchor they found in the wreckage. Albright refused this request.

With relatively little accomplished during the first year of working the recovery site, Tower requested and received a one-year renewal of salvage license #32. In March 1987 he again requested raising the anchor he and his group exposed early in 1986 and another one they had subsequently found. Dr. Bruce Rippeteau, SCIAA director and state archaeologist, handled the request this time. Noting that both looters and deterioration now threatened the exposed anchors, Rippeteau approved the request with one small stipulation. In a letter dated April 9, 1987, he told Tower he could raise the anchors and would be given title to them provided he "offer them only to a public or non-profit organization, who would agree to conserve and display, at their cost, both anchors, within South Carolina." A month later Rippeteau wrote to Tower suggesting he offer the anchors to Patriots Point Naval and Maritime Museum in Mount Pleasant.

The most significant aspect of the 1987 salvage activities, however, was the raising of the Enfield rifle cases, at least for those of us on the SCIAA staff who were involved. The rifles, packed twenty per case, were arranged trigger guards up in four alternating layers or tiers with wooden frames for support. Five bayonets rested atop each layer. In addition to being packed in grease, two types of containers protected the rifles. The inner was a kind of box made of folded, one-sixteenth-inch-thick lead sheathing. An outer wooden box, consisting of inch-thick tongue-and-groove boards, acted as a shipping container. Each case measured sixty inches by twenty inches by twenty inches and weighed about five hundred pounds. The first rifle case saw the light of day on June 10, 1987, after 125 years of lying submerged on the bottom of Charleston Harbor. Visibility that day was little more than one foot as Mark Newell and I reached the case of rifles that lay exposed on the sandy bottom in twenty feet of water. Even in the dark water and limited visibility, we could tell the box was highly deteriorated. The wooden outer case was totally gone, probably eaten by marine worms. Only the lead inner case remained, but it too was in poor shape, having been pulled apart either at the time of the vessel's sinking or subsequently during the work done by Benjamin Maillefert in the 1870s. Several of the rifle butts were visible but were severely corroded, with no wood being evident. We checked the lift lines attached to the crate and decided more were needed. To make it more secure we added three more lift lines that were attached to a fifty-five-gallon drum. Meanwhile SCIAA staff members Peggy Brooks and Joe Beatty checked things topside.

Once everything was set, more air was added to the drum, and the case of rifles rose easily to the surface. The rest of the recovery required the use of considerable muscle power. We dragged the case onto the beach and wrestled it onto our Trendelenburg board. Thankfully this is the only time we have used this emergency spinal injury transporter. We then grunted the five-hundred-pound case onto our eighteen-foot McKee for a short ride to Patriots Point, where we manhandled it, with the aid of Patriots Point staff, into a fiberglass tank aboard the NS (Nuclear Ship) *Savannah*. While we were doing this, Tower, who remained on the site, found two more cases of rifles. These rifles and the ones already raised were model 1853 three-band Enfields, also called long Enfields. Used by both Union and Confederate armies, the Enfield was the second most widely used rifle in the war. Civil War historians estimate that more than nine hundred thousand Enfields were imported to America between 1862 and 1865. Only the American-made Springfield rifle was more abundant. The 1853 long Enfield was fifty-five inches long, weighed 9.5 pounds, and had a thirty-nine-inch barrel attached to the stock with three metal bands, hence the name "three-band Enfield."

Tower also recovered a box containing 1,023 Enfield bullets. Ten days later, on June 20, he and his partners recovered another 1,609. They were located in clumps amid the vessel remains. In all Tower retrieved nearly 13,500 of these .577-caliber lead bullets, measuring just over an inch in length and weighing 1.1 ounces each. They are a variation of the famous "minié balls." The minié ball was not a ball but the first conical-shaped bullet. French army captains Claude-Étienne Minié and Henri-Gustave Delvigne designed the innovative bullet in the 1840s. Not only did it allow faster loading than a round ball, but it also was more accurate, had greater velocity and longer range, and left less gunpowder residue in the barrel. At the time the rumor was that at 1,200 yards the bullet could penetrate a victim and his knapsack and still kill anyone standing behind him. Rumors aside, tests in 1849 showed that at 15 yards the bullet could penetrate two pieces of poplar wood, each more than a half inch thick and separated by twenty inches. In addition to its conical shape, the soft lead minié ball had a hollow base filled with a small iron plug. When a rifle was fired, the exploding gases pushed the iron plug deeper into the bullet's hollow base, expanding the lead for a better seal against the rifle barrel. It also had three exterior grease-filled grooves, allowing a quicker and cleaner passage down the barrel. The bullets retrieved by Tower were devoid of the three grooves and had wood plugs in their hollow bottoms. Removing the plug revealed a letter L stamped on the inside.

In October one of the anchors and another case of Enfields were recovered by Tower and his group. The anchor was taken to Patriots Point, where it was submerged in the mud at the end of the museum's pier. As far as anyone knows, this is where it remains. The case of Enfields was taken to Columbia and placed in the institute's conservation facility. Keeping them submerged while being transported was out of the question, so we loaded the case into the back of our Suburban and covered it with wet blankets. I had the honor of delivering the case to Columbia. Being out of water enticed all sorts of marine creatures to evacuate the crate as I sped west on I-26. When I arrived in Columbia, the back of the Suburban resembled an exhibit at the South Carolina Aquarium. We disposed of all the creatures we could find, but I suspect we missed a few. There was the smell that emanated from the back of the Suburban for months as evidence.

December 1987 was a pivotal point in time for salvage license #32. The license would soon be up for renewal. This meant, for the first time, a public hearing on the license. At the same time, there would be the first division of artifacts between the salvors and the state. Moreover on November 1, Christopher Amer joined the institute as the new head of the Underwater Archaeology Division. This meant Amer would now be overseeing the license, inevitably changing the relationship between Tower and the institute. Amer brought a new focus to the Underwater Archaeology Division. This manifested itself in new archaeological standards not only for the division's projects but also for salvage projects as well, standards Tower would find constraining, if not superfluous.

The artifact division and public hearing were held on December 15, 1987. Even though the method of artifact division varied from what Tower was used to with Albright, the new procedures were agreed upon in advance, and the event went well. In addition to the two cases of

Enfield rifles, the two anchors, and the small mountain of minié balls, the salvors recovered several thousand brass percussion caps, six sword hilts, four rifle butt plates, one one-hundred-pounder Parrott shell, one brass sabot, one eight-inch cannonball, one two-hundred-pounder Parrott shell, one nine-inch solid shot, and one ten-inch solid shot. Miscellaneous items collected included an eight-inch-diameter green glass ship running light lens, a brass compass gimbal, and eighty-four brass spikes. The artifacts were divided fifty-fifty (or thereabouts).

The public hearing went less well. The purpose of the public hearing was to question the salvors about the work already completed and to review their plans should the license be renewed. Howard Tower attended, of course, along with Tipping, Mahle, and Zafoot. Chris Amer moderated. SCIAA conservator Curtiss Peterson; state archaeologist and SCIAA director Bruce Rippeteau; deputy state archaeologist Steve Smith, head of SCIAA's Services Division, of which the Underwater Antiquities Management Program was a part; SCIAA staffer Dina Hill; and Fritz Hamer of the South Carolina State Museum made up the rest of the participants.

As the hearing progressed, it soon became evident that there was a new sheriff in town. SCIAA's new staff members immediately brought procedures and activities allowed by Alan Albright into question. The first of these was the location of recovered artifacts. Tower admitted that many of the smaller artifacts were being taken to his home in Jacksonville for storage. Amer requested that these artifacts be returned to South Carolina. He then asked Tower if he was providing adequate security for the salvage area to prevent encroachment by others. It was a standard requirement of all salvage licenses that the licensee was responsible for security. Tower informed those present that he had worked out an arrangement with Fort Moultrie personnel to notify him of trespassers when he and his partners were not present. Tower added that SCIAA had never before shown any desire to prosecute violators of salvage license boundaries. Times are changing, Amer told him. Steve Smith told Tower that in the future any violation was to be reported to SCIAA for legal action.

Amer then questioned Tower about the sketches being submitted by the salvor, noting there was a lack of locational data concerning the artifacts being found by the divers. "From an archaeological point of view we need to determine which artifacts come from which wrecks," Amer said.

"This is a loose end that needs to be tied down," Curtiss Peterson said.

"The artifacts are tied to specific locations," Tower insisted.

"Not that we can find," Peterson answered.

"An example would be the [artillery] shells," Amer said.

"It is not important to know the provenience of the shells," Tower retorted. I am sure several of the archaeologists recoiled at hearing this. This is precisely the wrong thing to say to an archaeologist. Artifact provenience is one of the major tenets of archaeology. For a salvor to tell an archaeologist that the provenience of an artifact is not important is like a nurse telling a doctor that an X-ray of a broken limb is not important. Often more can be learned from an artifact's locational information than from the artifact itself.

Nevertheless Tower agreed to produce a comprehensive site map, showing the locations of all artifacts and ship remains, prior to the renewal of the license. He conditioned his agreement, however, by saying, "If I go to the trouble of producing the map, I would expect that the license would be issued."

"You would not consider this as winding up loose ends under the old license?" Peterson asked.

"I had an agreement with Mr. Albright that the map would be completed when the project is completed. The project is not completed," Tower said, apparently still not grasping that there was a new sheriff in town. In any event he got his new license, but there were conditions:

1. A site map was to be produced to illustrate the various vessel remains, the areas of excavations, the areas from which artifacts have been recovered under previous years' licenses, and the locations of additional artifacts. Moreover the map was to be submitted within ninety days, and no new recovery of artifacts would be permitted until the map was completed to the satisfaction of SCIAA staff.
2. Artifacts not yet divided with the state were to remain in South Carolina.
3. The institute was to be notified two weeks in advance of any visit to the site by Tower or his group.
4. Tower needed to add more specific information relative to artifact provenience and recording controls to his periodic reports. What this specific information was and how it was to be gathered then followed. In detail.
5. A screen must be fitted to the intake portion of the dredge hose. This may seem a small thing. It was intended to prevent artifacts from being sucked up the dredge and lost. However, this would slow down the dredge operations considerably, especially dealing with the layers of seashell.

6. Work was to be limited to the 100-by-500-yard delineated area. Chris Amer was concerned that the divers would supplement their artifact production with items from other nearby shipwrecks.
7. The unexposed portions of the shipwreck remains were to be left undisturbed.
8. Tower was required to state in any public statements that he was licensed by SCIAA to conduct his salvage activity. This stipulation was intended to prevent other salvage divers from thinking ship-wrecks were being salvaged without being licensed by the state.

On March 31, 1988, Tower submitted a progress report containing the required site map. He also reported that all recovered artifacts would be stored in Mike Zafoot's garage in West Columbia.

Keeping with stipulation number three, Tower notified Amer that he intended to begin his 1988 salvage season on April 8 and 9. He invited Amer to visit the site during this time. His purpose was for Amer to assess both the site and "our desire to perhaps use a modest prop wash in future activities." A prop wash, or "mailbox," is a device fitted over a propeller to direct the force of the water downward. The force of water removes the sand and mud covering a shipwreck much faster than dredging. It also blows away in situ artifacts that may be in and around the wreck. In maritime archaeology using a prop wash to excavate a shipwreck is like doing heart surgery with a hammer and chisel.

For scheduling reasons we were unable to visit the site at that time. During the two days, Tower's group recovered a lead sounding weight, two more sword handles, another thousand Enfield bullets, and about one hundred thousand additional percussion caps.

Chris Amer and SCIAA staff members Bruce Thompson, Joe Beatty, and Peggy Brooks finally visited the site on October 3. Amer and Thompson went down to inspect the cases of Enfields still lying near the wreck of the *Minho*. Thanks to a down line rigged by Tower, the two SCIAA staffers landed on top of the rifle cases. Visibility was less than six inches, though. All they could do was grope the cases. "It was virtu-ally impossible to see them [because] it was so dark and muddy in the water," Amer wrote in a memo to file about the visit, "but we could feel that the cases were fairly well intact." After investigating the rifle cases, Amer and Thompson felt their way to the stern area to get an idea of its extent. Amer wanted to get some basic measurements of the hull and framing but found "it would be ridiculous to have tried to have taken any measurements, because we wouldn't have been able to read the tapes." They then tried to find their way to the line that ran across to the remains of the *Stono*. Unable to locate the line, they came to the surface to discuss what to do next.

On a second dive, Chris and Joe went down to again try to find the line that would take them from the *Minho* over to the *Stono*. After fifteen minutes of groping around in the dark water, they gave up and returned to the surface. Following the dive Tower reiterated his desire to use a prop wash on the wreck site. Amer told him he would have to discuss this with other senior SCIAA staff members.

The 1988 season ended without further work on the site.

Things took a turn for the worse between Tower and the state during a May 16, 1989, public hearing on renewing the salvage license for another year. Tower took exception to comments by Patricia A. Cridlebaugh, an archaeologist with the State Historic Preservation Office at the South Carolina Department of Archives and History. The transcript of the hearing could not be found in SCIAA files; however, Dr. Cridlebaugh subsequently submitted her objections in writing. These objections centered on her belief that "there is no evidence that the applicant understands or had knowledge of basic archaeological techniques and the scientific goals of archaeological investigations." Picking up on a theme from previous hearings, she also noted that "based on the Tower group's responses to several questions raised at the hearing, I do not believe they comprehend or appreciate the purpose and importance of recording data through mapping, photography, field notes, and technical reports. It appears that 'archaeological context' is a meaningless concept to the applicant." She was also critical of the articles Tower had written for popular magazines about the project. "As a professional, I find it is especially discouraging to read articles which are void of technical data, repeatedly state the project was sanctioned by SCIAA, and then conclude with price list information."

Nevertheless the license was renewed—with additional stipulations. These "conditions appended to salvage license #32" consisted of seventeen points. Some of these conditions were the same as those added previously. Some were new. Tower was forbidden from using a prop wash device to remove the sand covering the artifacts. SCIAA's conservator was to approve the storage methods of all recovered artifacts, including the type of container. Moreover the size of the salvage area was reduced from a 100-by-500-yard rectangle to one that was 30 yards by 60 yards. This took the *Prince Albert* out of the approved salvage area. On the other hand, the institute lifted the requirement that a screen be installed at the intake end of the dredge hose.

Despite receiving his renewal, Tower phoned Amer on June 12, complaining about the treatment he was receiving from the institute. According to Amer's recollection of the phone call, Tower's complaints centered around the delay between submitting his application for renewal and the license being granted, the fact that the state would not consider his renewal application until SCIAA staff members had assessed the site, and the fact that SCIAA staff members attempted to assess the site without him being present. He also told Amer that he considered Cridlebaugh's comments at the public hearing slanderous and that he was not happy with the conditions attached to the renewal but that he would abide by them.

Tower concluded the conversation by asking Amer about the whereabouts of three rifle butt plates that were recovered with the case of Enfield rifles brought up in 1987. Amer reminded him that their status had not changed—they were still missing. Tower then told Amer that this was another example of institute employees pilfering artifacts. When Amer asked him to explain, he told Amer that he had an inside informer who was giving him names, dates, and the artifacts they were stealing. Tower declined to give specifics, telling Amer he just wanted to let him know.

Subsequently a meeting was set up with Howard Tower for July 21, 1989, at our Charleston office aboard the *Savannah* at Patriots Point. The purpose of the meeting, as far as the salvor knew, was to return the three Enfield butt plates to him. The butt plates resurfaced, so to speak, when the SCIAA conservation lab moved from the old Booker T. Washington Building to the Brown's Ferry conservation lab on campus. They had apparently been buried in the clutter of the old facility.

I doubt Tower was prepared for what awaited him as he entered our shipboard office. He greeted the SCIAA staff members present. This included Amer, Joe Beatty, Peggy Brooks, and me. What caught him off guard were two men in suits. It was obvious he did not know what to make of these men, especially when Amer introduced Tower to them. They were Investigator W. R. Snyder of the University of South Carolina Police Department and Agent Mark Murray of the State Law Enforcement Division (SLED). Amer returned the rifle butt plates to Tower. Then, as if on a prearranged signal, the SCIAA staff members all stood and walked out, leaving the office to Tower and the two law enforcement officers who were there to ask him what he knew about SCIAA staff stealing artifacts.

We did not mean to ambush Tower like that. Okay, maybe we did. Yet the allegations were disturbing. If indeed Tower was receiving information about thefts by institute personnel from an inside informer, the allegations implied that any one of us could be the culprit, or at the very least that we knew what was going on. If it turned out there was a thief, this would reflect badly not only on the institute but each one of us as well, whether we had known about it or not. Much of what we do, from soliciting donations and volunteers to working with other state and federal agencies, depends in large part on a good reputation with the public. We wanted the thief or thieves caught as soon as possible. If Tower had credible evidence of artifact pilfering, we wanted him to tell the investigators without the hindrance of having SCIAA staff, possibly including the thief or thieves, present to hear the testimony.

Three days later Investigator Snyder issued his report. It was short, less than two pages, and to the point. According to the report, the interview went straight to Tower's allegations of artifact pilfering. Tower told the investigators that he had no direct evidence of any criminal activity by SCIAA personnel. He did say that he witnessed incompetence and mismanagement by institute personnel. He also told the officers about "his problems with current Institute personnel and the difficulty he was having with his salvage permit."

Tower's statement that he had no direct evidence of any criminal activity by SCIAA personnel was perceived as his attempt to backtrack on his accusation. According to Amer's memos regarding his telephone conversations with Tower, however, Tower never said he did have direct evidence, just that an institute staff member was telling him about thievery—in other words, hearsay evidence. Apparently Tower did not want to tell the investigators the identity of the person who was feeding him this information or what he was being told. The report mentions neither. This is unfortunate. Even though hearsay, the information could have led to a real investigation and to the thief, if there was one, being revealed. The law enforcement officers ignored the charges of incompetence and mismanagement. Bad management at a state agency is not against the law (an oversight on the part of the South Carolina legislature, no doubt). The report concluded, "This investigation is closed as unfounded."

Since salvage license #32 was in effect until the middle of 1990, our relationship with Tower and his associates continued. As it turned out, Mother Nature affected Tower's salvage operations more than the conditions added to his license. In September 1989 Hurricane Hugo swept through Charleston, disturbing not only the landscape above water but below water as well. On November 4 Tower and his associates dived on the site to assess the affects of the hurricane. Before descending down to the wrecks, he noted that the sand dunes that once rose behind the beach, blocking the view of Fort Moultrie, were now gone and that the fort was plainly visible. On the bottom he found, despite the limited visibility that extended no more than fifteen inches in the beam of a strong light, that much of the area had been changed. The *Stono* was almost completely covered by two to three feet of sediment. All but an eight-foot section of the *Minho*'s stern was filled with sand, and the cases of Enfield rifles, previously exposed, were covered by five to six feet of sand.

As a result of his assessment, Tower requested that his salvage license be extended by four months since the boat landing he had been using on Sullivan's Island had been taken over by the navy and the Army Corps of Engineers and wouldn't be available to him for several months. He also requested that the state lift the ban on using a prop wash to clear the overburden of sand and mud (especially now that there was so much more of it). The reason for not letting him use a prop wash in the first place centered on the fact that any in situ artifacts literally would be blown away by the down force of water from the propeller. It was Tower's contention that the new overburden would not contain any in situ artifacts.

Meanwhile the salvage activities ceased while Charleston and the lowcountry regained some normalcy.

After a visit to the site by SCIAA staff on April 17, 1990, Amer acquiesced to Tower's requests. He extended the license to November 1, 1990, and agreed to let Tower use a prop wash, provided it only be used to move the sediments deposited by Hugo and that SCIAA staff be on-site when it was used. Tower agreed, and the date of September 28 was arranged for a trial of the prop wash. Tower showed up with a new dive boat, a twenty-four-foot Stamus with twin 120-horsepower engines and a twenty-inch-diameter prop wash attached to one engine. He also had a new trio of associates. These were Donald C. Young of Winter Park, Florida, John E. Provinsky of Jacksonville, and Leonard Wheeley of Fort Pierce, Florida.

And, in this corner of the ring, wearing white wet suits, is . . . the state. Sorry, couldn't help the comparison. SCIAA staffers on hand to observe were Mark Newell, head of the institute's Underwater Antiquities Management Program (UAMP); David Beard, UAMP archaeologist; Joe Beatty from the Underwater Archaeology Division; and me, then a member of UAMP.

Beatty, Beard, and Tower toured the site before Tower tried the prop wash. They found excellent visibility, in the three- to four-foot range, allowing them to get a good picture of the area. The port side of *Minho*'s stern section protruded three feet up through the sand. Sand buried the rest of the wreck. The salvors were interested in reexposing the cases of Enfield rifles, which Tower estimated were now under about six feet of sand. They first ran the prop wash for ten minutes. This removed about two feet of sand. The prop wash was then run for twenty minutes. These times had been agreed upon by Beard and Tower after some discussion. Following the twenty-minute run, Beard and Beatty inspected the results. They found that the prop wash had removed another five feet of sand in a twelve-foot diameter. A portion of *Minho*'s starboard side was now exposed, consisting of several iron frames and a section of wooden ceiling planking. Beard concluded that several feet of new sand still covered the site. He then agreed to a thirty-minute prop wash run. By now the wind was picking up, and there was a slight chop, bringing the activities to the brink of discomfort. Nevertheless the prop wash performed a thirty-minute blow. This time Beard and I went down to inspect. We found that the rocking of the boat in the rising seas while the prop wash was being used had actually filled in the hole, negating much of the work already performed. Tower decided to wait on-site to see if the weather moderated. We, however, decided to leave, confident that the deteriorating weather would not permit further work.

We were wrong. Tower continued to use the prop wash after we left. He called Chris Amer in October 2 to apprise him of the results. Tower revealed that they had been able to uncover seven cases of Enfields. To Amer this was a violation of their agreement, since Tower was not to uncover anything that had not already been uncovered. David Beard agreed. In a memo to Amer on October 3, Beard asserted that Tower's overuse of the prop wash "undoubtedly caused substantial adverse impact to previously undisturbed cultural deposits on the site." Painting with a broader brush, Beard noted, "It is obvious that left to their own devices, commercial salvors will violate any agreement signed and do an immense amount of damage to shipwreck sites in the name of expedience."

Amer wrote to Tower on October 12, accusing him of operating the prop wash "during a period which was not monitored by the monitoring archaeologist," meaning after we left that afternoon. Amer also noted that Tower "went beyond the condition that allowed you ONLY to remove sterile, Hugo-related, overburden." As evidence for this accusation he cited that fact that before Hugo only two cases of Enfields had been exposed, whereas now there were seven.

Less than a week later, Tower fired back a response to Amer's accusations. "Your comments concerning my use of the propwash are disconcerting," he began. He claimed that when we left that afternoon as much as four feet of "Hugo sand" still covered the wreck. "I asked [Beard] for and received his permission to continue using this tool [the prop wash] for the duration of the day." He also disputed removing sterile overburden. In what can only be another example of miscommunication, Tower stated that when he ceased using the prop wash only three cases of Enfield were exposed and that these cases had been first exposed in 1988 by himself and Larry Tipping.

Newell, Beard, Beatty, and I returned to the site on October 25. Our intent was to examine the work done by Tower and the prop wash after we left on September 28. There was a stout wind out of the northwest that day, however, and small craft advisories had been posted. We abandoned any attempts at trying to dive the site. Nevertheless Tower and his divers visited the site the next day, October 26. In a letter to Amer dated October 29, he said that the Enfield rifle cases were now covered with three to four feet of new sand and that the interior of the *Minho,* exposed by the prop wash, was now filled in.

Tower and his salvage group ceased operations on November 1, 1990, a little more than a month less than five years since salvage license #32 had been issued in December 1985. Tower submitted his final report to the institute on February 14, 1991. There is no small amount of irony in the fact that the date happens to be Valentine's Day.

Neither Howard Tower nor any of his partners have ever again applied for a salvage license in South Carolina. Perhaps these men have taken up other pursuits. Perhaps they are no longer interested in salvaging shipwrecks in South Carolina waters. Perhaps no other wreck site caught their interest.

On the other hand, perhaps they no longer want to deal with SCIAA's new crop of underwater archaeologists and all the new rules and procedures and seventeen-point "conditions" being imposed on their salvage activities. Perhaps they did not want to repeat salvage license #32.

Perhaps they would rather eat glass.

The Wreck of the
SS *William Lawrence*

As I lowered the milk crate full of artifacts over the side of our vessel and watched it sink beneath the waves, I thought how strange it was to be returning artifacts to a wreck site. It is most often the other way around. Usually we retrieve artifacts from a site. These are then cleaned, cataloged, and analyzed in the hopes they can tell us something about the shipwreck from which they came. We knew all about this wreck, however. It was the steamship *William Lawrence,* which in 1899 ran aground and sank in an area off Hilton Head Island known as the Great North Breakers.

Now, some ninety-one years later, we were returning artifacts, bottles mostly, that a group of divers had salvaged from the wreck two years earlier. In those two years, we had been in federal court to prove that the wreck was in state waters and that the court had wrongly given the divers custody of the *Lawrence* and its artifacts.

It all started in 1988 when two groups began vying for salvage rights to the remains of the *William Lawrence.* Believing the wreck to be outside state jurisdiction, the two groups, Sea Dweller Diving Company of Delaware and J & W Investments of South Carolina, went to federal court over the wreck. On April 5, after hearing testimony from both parties, U.S. District Court judge Falcon B. Hawkins issued an injunction naming J & W Investments as the custodian of the wreck. Under the injunction Sea Dweller was enjoined from conducting any further salvage operations on the wreck and was required to turn over all items already recovered from the wreck to J & W Investments. The judge also ordered that J & W Investments display a copy of his order at the salvage site at all times during their salvage operation and "shall show a copy of said Order to any third parties entering upon the salvage site, and such third parties shall thereafter refrain from interfering with [J & W Investment's] on-going salvage operations." Apparently J & W Investments considered "any third parties" to include anglers or anyone else who happened along and not just other divers.

We first heard about this on April 6, 1988, when Joe Beatty of SCIAA's Underwater Archaeology Division began receiving phone calls from anglers who said they were being chased away from the site by a group of divers who were salvaging the *William Lawrence,* claiming they had an exclusive permit to work the site. These anglers were irate that the state would allow salvage divers to keep them from a prime fishing spot. We assured them that we had issued no such permit. Nevertheless their complaints got our attention.

Then on April 11 we received a call from Charlie Zemp, a law enforcement officer with the South Carolina Wildlife and Marine Resource Department (now the Department of Natural Resources). He said that a shrimp trawler called the *Captain Robert* was anchored over the *Lawrence* site, it had hoses going down over its side, and its crew was running off anyone who came near, telling them that they had both a federal and state license. The *Captain Robert* had been hired by J & W Investments to serve as its salvage vessel on a daily hire rate. We decided to investigate.

Several days later Chris Amer and Mark Newell, both with SCIAA's Underwater Archaeology Division, visited the site with wildlife officers. They found the *Captain Robert* still anchored over the site. The captain of the trawler claimed the wreck was outside state waters and therefore none of the state's business. They showed the state officials the federal court order giving them the right to salvage the vessel. Since we believed the *Lawrence* to be within state waters, the state initiated court action to prove that claim.

In August 1988 Judge Hawkins granted permission to the state of South Carolina to intervene so that it could assert its claim over the wreck. The dispute arose over exactly where state jurisdiction ended. Answering this question turned out to be a matter of determining exactly where state jurisdiction started. Established law said state waters are defined as from the mean low waterline to three statute miles offshore. Charles Harrington of the National Oceanic and Atmospheric Administration (NOAA) testified at the hearing that the three miles start at the most seaward isolated landmass that is within three miles of the mainland. Harrington testified that NOAA considered the most seaward isolated landmass to be a sandbar about two miles offshore of Bay Point that is exposed at low tide. The *Lawrence* was less then three miles off the sandbar, so the state argued that this put it squarely within state waters.

On December 20, 1989, Judge Hawkins ruled that while the *Lawrence* was more than three miles from the mainland of South Carolina, it was indeed within three miles of the exposed sandbar and thus within state waters and state jurisdiction. Hawkins dismissed J & W's claim, saying he had a "lack of subject matter jurisdiction."

So there we were, in September 1990, returning the artifacts the salvagers had recovered from the *Lawrence* back to the *Lawrence*. We were anchored over the wreck with a down line directly into the vessel's hull. We would fill the milk crate with artifacts and clip it to the down line, lowering it slowly to divers waiting on the bottom to distribute the artifacts. We quickly discovered that the salvagers had ripped open part of the ship's hull to get at the cargo and that the remains of the cargo were being pulled out of the wreck by the strong currents of the Great North Breakers.

The Great North Breakers stretch for more than two miles along the east side of Port Royal Channel like a lazy sea serpent waiting with tentacles of sand to snare vessels that wander too close. The screw steamship *William Lawrence* was one of its most notable victims. Contemporary news accounts in the *Savannah Morning News* tell the story of the ship's loss. It is a story that can only come from a mariner's worst nightmares.

By 8 A.M. on Saturday, February 11, 1899, Capt. A. L. Willis knew he was in serious trouble and had ordered his ship to slow. The *William Lawrence*, owned by the Merchants and Miners Transportation Company, was heading to Savannah with a cargo of general merchandise, having left Baltimore three days earlier. An icy winter gale was whipping the seas into angry mountains, and a thick fog reduced visibility to less than thirty feet. Captain Willis later called it the "the worst weather he had experienced in twenty years on the coast." Making his situation even worse, the ship's compass was malfunctioning, and the latest soundings revealed they were in shallow water. Ten minutes later the *William Lawrence* struck.

The *William Lawrence* found itself on the Great North Breakers. Even in nice weather, the Great North Breakers are inhospitable. The crew members tried everything they could think of to get their ship off the vast sand flats. They even threw a considerable portion of the cargo overboard in an effort to lighten the ship. Their efforts were to no avail. By the next morning, it became evident that the ship was breaking up, and Captain Willis made the decision to abandon ship.

The twenty-eight crew members scrambled into the ship's four lifeboats. Although the boats tried to remain together as they made their way toward shore, the howling winds, mountainous seas, swift currents, and limited visibility caused by falling sleet and snow soon separated the boats. One of the boats, containing six of the crew, made the Parris Island Naval Station around 4:30 P.M. Sunday.

Another of the boats, with seven of the crew, made buoy number three at the mouth of Port Royal Harbor. Exhausted, they tied up to the buoy and awaited rescue. After two hours of punishment by the weather, they cut loose and made for shore. But the currents pushed them out to sea and back toward the wreck. The boat soon ran aground, and the crew abandoned it, making their way through the surf to land, presumably on Bay Point Island. Despair set in, and several members of the crew even talked of suicide. However, one of the crew, described as a tall, rawboned Irishman, kept the crew members' spirits up by telling stories and jokes. The Irishman, named John Montgomery, also kept a lookout. After two days of misery, he spotted a pilot boat looking for survivors and signaled to it. According to the newspaper account, Montgomery was the only one of the seven who looked as if he had not suffered any particular hardship. The other six were hospitalized.

The two other boats, one containing Captain Willis, were at sea for more than twelve hours before finally making land on Capers Island, which is barely more than a small sand spit. Coming through the surf, both boats were stove in. Here they spent two harrowing days and nights, as the island provided no shelter. They managed to build a fire using driftwood and the wooden seats from the lifeboats. On Tuesday the weather moderated, and the men patched the boat with the least damage. They left Capers Island in the boat and made their way to the military camp on Hunting Island, a distance of eight or nine miles. From there they were taken to Savannah.

The prolonged exposure to the elements resulted in six of the crew members being hospitalized once they reached Savannah. Chief Engineer Edward Roach, who suffered from frostbite on both his legs and hands, died on February 21, and Second Officer Robert A. Beale was "taken to Baltimore for treatment, his sufferings having affected his mind. Mr. Beale is well advanced in years," the news account explained. The other four crew members recovered over time.

The *William Lawrence* was an iron-hulled, screw-driven steamship, with two sailing masts as auxiliary power. A pilothouse and cabins, punctuated by a tall black smokestack with a large red band painted near the top, were situated between the masts. Its top speed was listed as twelve knots. The Merchants and Miners Transportation Company commissioned the Atlantic Ironworks at East Boston, Massachusetts, to build the 1,049-ton steamship in 1869. This was a time when the use of iron for shipbuilding was first becoming widespread. It was 207.8 feet long and 25.1 feet wide, and the depth of its hold was 20 feet. Thirty years old by the time of its demise, it had made 1,040 voyages, mostly along the Atlantic coast.

A wide variety of items constituted the ship's cargo, which was valued at the time at thirty thousand dollars. Unfortunately none of the cargo was insured. It included a large quantity of furniture, much of which was said to have washed ashore and to have found its way into the best homes in Beaufort. Other cargo included various clothing items such as leather shoes and men's socks, cases of patent medicines, bottled pickles and preserves, children's toys and dolls, and even toilet paper. Some of the artifacts showed remarkable preservation, including the socks and toilet paper. We know of one diver who claims he actually wears socks he recovered from the *Lawrence*. We did not ask about the toilet paper. The bottled pickles and preserves looked in good condition, but finding someone to try them has proven difficult.

An ample quantity of Dr. DeWitt's Liver, Blood & Kidney Cure was cargo aboard the steamship. Dr. DeWitt's came in square-sided, amber-colored glass bottles with embossed lettering. Several of these, still corked and containing the "cure," were recovered from the wreck. We had the contents of one of the bottles analyzed. Considering the amount of alcohol it contained, Dr. DeWitt's would have to be considered an excellent "cure" for sobriety, if nothing else. In 1899 patent medicines were still widely sold as remedies for a large assortment of ailments. The Pure Food and Drug Act of 1906 essentially ended the patent medicine business. This law banned the use of misleading claims, such as the word *cure* on bottles. It also stipulated that these "medicines" had to have labels that revealed the presence and amounts of certain harmful ingredients. These ingredients included alcohol, morphine, opium, cocaine, heroin, alpha or beta eucaine, chloroform, cannabis indica, chloral hydrate, or acetanilide. The law also stipulated that patent medicines be examined and tested by the Bureau of Chemistry at the U.S. Department of Agriculture. These stipulations were something patent medicine makers found bad for their business.

A large part of the cargo was a shipment of South Carolina Dispensary bottles bound for the dispensary at North Augusta. There they would be filled with whiskey and sold by the state monopoly. The dispensary system and its associated bottles are unique to South Carolina. The system was the brainchild of Governor Benjamin "Pitchfork Ben" Tillman. Caught between the temperance and antitemperance forces in the early

1890s, Tillman came up with the idea of a state monopoly on the sale of liquor. The South Carolina Dispensary system, which lasted from 1893 until 1907, proved not only to be a political compromise but also an excellent tool for promoting graft and patronage.

Until 1902 out-of-state bottle manufacturers supplied all dispensary bottles. The cargo on the *Lawrence* consisted of quart cylindrical bottles and pint Jo-Jo flasks made by E. Packham Jr. and Company of Baltimore, Maryland. The Jo-Jo flask was the most common form of dispensary bottle. It is oval with rounded shoulders and base, a pedestal bottom, and flat front and back. The bottle occurs in pint and half pint sizes only. In addition to E. Packman Jr., four other northern companies supplied the bottles: the C. L. Flaccus Glass Company of Pittsburgh, the Olean Glass Company of Olean, New York, the Williamston Flint Glass Company of Williamston, New York, and the Illinois Glass Company of Alton, Illinois. To bring this business home and to make bottles less expensive, the Carolina Glass Company was formed in Columbia. In 1902 they began making dispensary bottles for the state. As it turned out, their bottles were just as expensive, and they became involved in the corruption that permeated much of the dispensary system.

Dispensary bottles came in four sizes (half pint, pint, quart, and gallon) and thirteen different shapes (six cylindrical and seven flask shapes). Unless paper labeled, the bottles came with two basic embossing designs, the palmetto tree and the monogram designs. The palmetto tree emblem is similar to, but not an exact replica of, the palmetto tree on the state seal. The monogram is the entwined letters *SCD*. These two designs came in myriad variations. There were seventeen versions of the palmetto tree and thirteen versions of the monogram on the half-pint Jo-Jo flask alone. The *Lawrence* bottles were all of the palmetto tree design. The palmetto tree design was discontinued about 1900 when temperance groups complained about the state symbol being on bottles that contained liquor. The *SCD* monogram continued until the end of the dispensary system in 1907.

In November 1990 we returned to the wreck. Our goal was to ameliorate the damage done by the salvage divers from the *Captain Robert*. To get to the cargo more easily, they had created a ten-by-twenty-five-foot hole in the bow section of the hull. We wanted to protect not only the remaining cargo but also the hull from further damage. Our plan was to cover the wreck with geofabric. We had used it with great success in the Santee Canal and had a good quantity of it left over. This alone made it perfect for covering the hull of the *Lawrence*. After placing the geofabric over the damaged area, we covered this with sandbags.

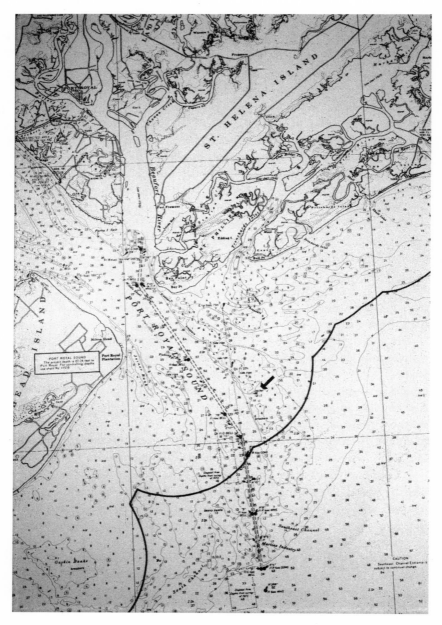

A portion of navigational chart showing location of the *Lawrence* site (arrow) and extent of state waters (arched line). From NOAA Navigation Chart #11513

We planned to dredge sand over the fabric and sandbags to hold down the fabric and protect the wreck further, but a cold front moved in, creating high seas and making dredging operations impossible. The fabric and sandbags should work just fine, we decided as our dive boat rocked in six-foot seas.

The site of the SS *William Lawrence*'s remains is the one wreck site in South Carolina waters that most closely resembles the public perception of what a shipwreck site should look like. The *Lawrence* sits upright in the sand in about thirty feet of water. Its hull, except for the stern area, is mostly intact. At low tide the boiler is visible just below the surface. The bow area of the ship shows the best preservation and rises off the bottom some twelve feet in height. The forward companionway, galley ventilator, windlass, and anchor are all recognizable. The stern section consists of scattered components, including the propeller and rudder skeg, which appear to be still attached to a section of the hull.

In 1995 the institute nominated the *William Lawrence* site for inclusion in the National Register of Historic Places.

The wreck site of the steamship *William Lawrence* is a favorite destination for both sport divers and saltwater anglers. An abundance of marine life calls the wreck home. Soft corals and sponges cover the iron hull. Angelfish and butterfly fish swim in and out of the hull structure. Overhead black sea bass, rock sea bass, and sheephead cruise the area. Not only is the site excellent for the angler; it also provides an excellent venue for the scuba diver interested in underwater photography. Moreover now that the wreck has been protected from salvagers, divers can even find the odd bottle or two.

Hobby Divers

Licensed hobby diver Doug Boehme's artifact reports for the third quarter of 1994 were startling, even amazing. During those three months, he reported finding fifty-three whole projectile points (arrowheads and spear points), twenty-three broken points, thirty-one scrapers, two bannerstones, two drill points, two prismatic blades, and three prehistoric pottery shards, all from one dive spot in the west branch of the Cooper River. Over the next year, Doug found even more prehistoric Native American artifacts, including several bannerstone pieces, two hammer stones, several baked clay objects, a grooved ax, and a couple dozen more points—all in this same spot.

Doug is a postal worker who lives with his wife and daughter in Summerville. He became a licensed hobby diver in June 1992 and attended our field training course (FTC) a year later, in June 1993. With his license and the knowledge gained at our FTC, he and his dive partners began exploring the rivers of the South Carolina lowcountry.

In the Cooper River, Doug had found a gold mine of stone and pottery artifacts covering all periods of Native American prehistory—too many to be there through the usual haphazard scatter of artifacts along river bottoms. Did these relics of the past indicate a nearby Native American site? A village, perhaps, or a hunting camp?

Doug's artifact reports are required under conditions of his South Carolina hobby diver license. That the information provided us by a sport diver could lead to the discovery of an unknown Native American site is precisely what the South Carolina hobby diver licensing system is all about. Briefly, license divers are allowed to keep the artifacts and fossils they pick up in South Carolina waters in exchange for reporting what they are finding, where they are finding it, and anything of interest they may have noticed in the vicinity. From this information the state learns of new underwater sites.

Just a few of the projectile points found by licensed hobby diver Doug Boehme in the Cooper River. Photograph courtesy Doug Boehme

Back in the early 1960s, as scuba diving was growing into an international leisure activity, South Carolina was one place where the new sport blossomed. This is because scuba divers are not only an adventurous bunch; they are also sentimental. In addition to exploring the underwater world, they like taking home souvenirs from the sites they visit. What better way to remember a great day of diving on a shipwreck than with some small keepsake as a reminder of the experience? Moreover South Carolina waters abound in keepsakes.

The early sport divers found the coastal waters littered with the remains of lost vessels, especially Civil War blockade runners. From these they were stuffing their goody bags with items from long-lost cargoes, items the sailors of these vessels risked and sometimes lost their lives attempting to bring into Charleston. These cargoes, for the most part, consisted of the three *m*'s: merchandise, munitions, and medicines. This included crates of dinnerware; mountains of small arms projectiles; armies of medicine bottles, wine bottles, lamp oil bottles, foodstuff bottles, and baby bottles; stoneware jugs of household commodities; and a variety of other objects the enthusiastic divers showed off with great pride, no doubt impressing their friends and boring their families. It was not long, however, before the divers were taking home slightly larger souvenirs, such as artillery shells and cannons.

At the same time, divers began braving the alligators and snakes of lowcountry rivers to pursue their new sport. Here they were finding fossilized animal remains of all sorts: whale inner ear bones, horse teeth, mastodon ribs, sloth claws, fish vertebra, mammoth molars, and shark's teeth—especially shark's teeth. These they were collecting by the bucketful. They were selling them to museums, placing them in display cases, putting them into glass lamps, and making them into mobiles. They were also finding significant cultural remains. They were gathering prehistoric artifacts, including ornately decorated Native American pottery, lethal stone axes, and finely made projectile points. They were finding historic artifacts as well, including creamware, pearlware, and porcelain dinnerware, clay tobacco pipes, pewter mugs, and stoneware jugs, plus coins of shiny silver and sparkling gold, not to mention bottles, buckles, and buttons of old. Again it was not long before divers were taking home more significant artifacts, such as whole cargoes from sunken plantation vessels.

Back then South Carolina had no laws governing the recovery of artifacts and fossils from state waters. Until three sport divers found a blockade runner with a particularly valuable cargo, the idea of regulating the collection of artifacts and fossils never dawned on anyone. When these divers approached the state with the idea of getting exclusive rights to the blockade runner's cargo, so they could of course become rich and famous, the state legislature had a rare brilliant idea. If these divers were going to get rich and famous, perhaps the state could at least get a little richer. So in 1968 the legislature enacted the first law governing the salvage of shipwrecks and the recovery of artifacts. It said that the state owned all the artifacts recovered under a state license and could grant ownership of all, a portion, or none the items to the finders. It also said: "A portion or all of such relics or artifacts may be sold or traded by the Institute [of Archaeology and Anthropology]." As could be expected, the law did not make the state, or anyone else, rich. However, it did do something that was, at that time, unique.

The law recognized that there was valuable information to be gathered from sport divers who were collecting fossils and artifacts on a noncommercial, recreational basis. Thus the "hobby diver" concept was born. Commercial salvagers or individuals seeking to recover and sell artifacts and fossils were excluded from this license. Persons or groups wishing to collect for profit had to apply for salvage licenses, which had much stricter rules and regulations. Under the law hobby divers were issued a hobby license for one year and were required to submit monthly written reports listing all objects recovered along with a description of the location from which each item was recovered. After submitting their reports, the divers had to make the items available to the institute for inspection. The institute, again, could grant the diver ownership of all, a portion, or none of the artifacts.

From the beginning this created a controversy among archaeologists that continues today. Archaeology pretends to be an unemotional science. Yet nothing will get an archaeologist's panties in a wad faster than the mention of amateur collectors. Many professional archaeologists believe it is criminal to allow nonarchaeologists to collect artifacts from state property, even if these are random finds not associated with an underwater archaeological site and despite the fact that we were gathering information about unknown submerged archaeological sites.

Divers did not like the program, either. With the possibility that the state could take their best finds, they were reluctant to report their artifact recoveries and either failed to submit reports or claimed not to have made any recoveries. Moreover when they did report the items they were finding, they often unknowingly misidentified their finds or supplied descriptions that were too vague to be of any use. In addition divers were hesitant to report the location of their finds, thinking that their report would become public information and that the next time they showed up at their favorite dive site there would be more divers than artifacts on the bottom.

Inevitably SCIAA underwater archaeologists realized the law needed changing. Even if they were not taking the divers' finds, just the fact that the state *could* do so was keeping the divers from providing the information archaeologists were looking for. Without honest and complete reporting from the sport divers, it was impossible to carry out the prime intention of the law—protecting South Carolina's rich submerged heritage.

As a result, in 1991 the law was revised. Saying it was revised is somewhat of a misnomer, actually. It was completely rewritten. We were determined to get it right. We held public hearings throughout the state, and many of the changes came as a response to diver's wishes. Instead of a one-year license and monthly reports, the diver now had the choice of either applying for a six-month license or a two-year license. Moreover monthly reports became quarterly reports. To make the hobby diver concept clearer and to distinguish it further from commercial salvage, the new law defined "hobby diving" as the recovery of artifacts and fossils that are exposed or resting on the bottom sediments and do not require excavation to recover. It also stipulated that "all powered mechanical dredging and lifting devices and buoyancy equipment, except a personal flotation device, of any sort are prohibited including, but not limited to, prop wash, air lift, water dredge, and pneumatically operated lift bags, under the [hobby] license."

To alleviate divers' concerns that his or her finds would be confiscated, all discussion of an artifact division with the divers was taken out of the new law. Instead the new law stated that "the institute shall review each list of objects and within sixty days from the receipt of the quarterly report release title to all specimens reported." To solve the problem of having artifact and fossil reports become public information, the new law specified that hobby diver reports "are not considered public record for purposes of the Freedom of Information Act."

When we receive a quarterly artifact report from a licensed hobby diver, several things happen. First, in the diver's database file, we note that the diver has submitted the form. If the diver has not done any collecting during the quarter, all he or she has to do is check the box labeled "No Recoveries Made During This Quarter." If the diver has collected artifacts, we record the locations and types of artifacts in the database. This provides information not only as to where divers are recovering artifacts, but also what they are collecting. We can thus monitor if divers are exploring near known shipwrecks and spot any possible artifacts from a shipwreck or ones that might denote a shipwreck or other submerged archaeological site. The major reason we reject reports is that the location or artifact information is not as precise or complete as we need. With the use of handheld GPS units to record locations and the Internet to research artifacts, this has become less of a problem in recent years. If the diver reports recovering something that piques our interest, such as Doug Boehme did in the third quarter of 1994, we contact the diver to follow up. We may ask for photos of the item or items, or we may ask to visit the diver so we can photograph the items ourselves. Occasionally we visit the site with the diver, such as we did with Doug.

Next we scrutinize the last question on the form: "Was there a shipwreck or structure in the vicinity of your finds?" When a diver answers yes, we check the reported location with the South Carolina Archaeological Site Inventory files. If the site already exists in the files, we file the artifact report form in the diver's file and continue to monitor the diver's reports. If nothing shows up in the site files, we contact the diver for more information. Based on this contact, we often decide that the site warrants a visit. When we decide to visit a reported site, we always contact the diver. We do this for two reasons. First, with the reporting diver along, it's much easier to find the site. Second, if it turns out to be a heretofore-unknown site, the reporting diver has some legal rights to the site. This comes into play if another individual or group should at some time in the future want to salvage the site. According to the

Antiquities Act, "If the finder of the wreck is other than the licensed salvor (commercial applicant), the finder must receive twenty-five percent of the licensed salvor's share." This is the proverbial carrot on a stick, meant to entice the hobby diver to report wrecks or other maritime sites.

While no statistical study has been done, saying that 75 percent of known maritime archaeological sites in South Carolina waters came from information provided by hobby divers would not be unreasonable. Maritime sites include shipwrecks, docks and wharves, ferry landings, rice gates, causeways, artifact scatters, mills, inundated forts, and shipyards. Shipwrecks account for about 40 percent of these maritime sites. A surprisingly large number of the shipwreck sites are untyped (about 20 percent), with the site files unhelpfully listing them as "wooden vessel" or simply "vessel remains." Of the typed shipwreck sites, sailing vessels make up about 60 percent and steamships make up about 20 percent. Barges and canoes each make up slightly fewer than 10 percent of the typed shipwrecks. Ferries account for about 1 percent. The remaining shipwrecks include early-twentieth-century fishing trawlers and cargo vessels. Without hobby divers seeing or, in the case of blackwater rivers, bumping into these sites and reporting them to us, we simply would not know about them and therefore we would be unable to protect them from the environment, from development, and from vandalism.

At the end of each calendar quarter, we also record who has not sent in an artifact report. We send e-mails to these divers reminding them that the reports are due. If a diver consistently fails to file timely reports, he or she risks having the hobby license revoked. More likely we will refuse to renew his or her license.

Over the past few years, the number of licensed hobby divers has averaged about two hundred. The majority (about 85 percent) are two-year licenses as opposed to the six-month licenses. Naturally most licensed hobby divers are South Carolina residents (about 65 percent); however, divers from all over the country come to South Carolina. Residents of twenty-eight states have had South Carolina hobby diver licenses, including divers from Maine, South Dakota, Texas, Arizona, and California.

When the law underwent the 1991 revision, one major change took the Hobby Diver Program in a completely new direction. In addition to simply issuing hobby licenses to divers and following up on their reports, the revised law stipulated that the program do something it had never before attempted. The new law directed the state to "establish and maintain an educational program for the training of interested members of the public in the identification, recordation, and registration of submerged archaeological historic property, and certify those who have successfully completed such training."

The thinking was that the benefits of an educational program would be twofold. First, the better the public understood the principles of underwater archaeology and the importance of preserving maritime sites, the less likely they would be to destroy these cultural resources. Second, the more divers knew about the artifacts they were finding, the better they would be able to report this information to us on their quarterly report forms. The diver who reported finding, for instance, an "old ceramic mug" would give us better information if he or she knew that the find was actually a late-seventeenth-century British stoneware mug. In addition the diver who reported finding an "old spear point with groove in bottom" would enjoy the find more and provide us valuable information if he or she knew it was a twelve-thousand-year-old Clovis point.

So the Hobby Diver Program became the Sport Diver Archaeological Management Program (SDAMP). Lynn Harris, a graduate of East Carolina University with a master's degree in maritime history, took the reins of the new and improved program that is part of the Maritime Research Division (then the Underwater Archaeology Division) at the institute. One of the first things she did was to create the underwater archaeology field training course. The aim of the course was to provide students with a comprehensive overview of the field of underwater archaeology with an emphasis on the underwater sites encountered in South Carolina waters. Lynn's goal was to train divers who could provide a pool of volunteers for SCIAA underwater projects. The course began with classroom instruction. Topics taught include discussions on the principles of underwater archaeology, the methods used in performing underwater surveys and site interpretation, and the basics of ship construction. In addition classroom lectures covered artifact identification and conservation as well as the laws governing artifact and fossil collection. The course consisted of more than classroom lectures, however. The students also learned artifact and shipwreck recording skills on the mock-up of a shipwreck in a pool session. Then, to practice what they have learned, the students performed their newly learned skills on an actual shipwreck.

Since its inception the SDAMP has graduated nearly two hundred participants from our FTCs. The first FTC took place in May 1990. We decided to conduct the first one specifically for scuba instructors and dive shop owners. The idea was to train these diving professionals so they could devise their own courses and pass along the principles of underwater archaeology to their students. After this our FTCs were open to all divers—including Doug Boehme.

Doug's artifact reports for his Cooper River site were exemplary. We like to think it was because of the training he received at our FTC. More than just reporting "points" and "stone tools," he was listing specific types. This is exactly the type of information archaeologists need to understand the time periods of his site and the origins of the prehistoric stone artifacts. The oldest point he found was a ten-to-twelve-thousand-year-old Clovis point. These are the oldest points found in North America (so far). The scrapers he found were stone tools used for cutting and skinning. Bannerstones are thought to have been weights used to counterbalance atlatls, which were wooden devices used in spear throwing. Doug's finds ranged in age from 12,000 B.P. to about 3,000 B.P. Doug's reports led Lynn Harris to visit the site with him in December 1995. This visit resulted in the site being added to the South Carolina Inventory of Archaeological Sites as site 38BK1766. It has yet to be determined whether Doug's site indicates a corresponding land site, but the odds are good.

Doug's Cooper River site is not the first site he has added to our site files. Prior to finding the Native American artifacts in the west branch of the Cooper River, he and his dive partner, Robert Bush of Goose Creek, discovered the remains of a wooden shipwreck while diving in Quinby Creek off the east branch of the Cooper River. According to Doug's report:

> Shipwreck is in approximately 10 ft. of water lying upright with the port side against the bank on the outside (north) bend of the creek. Length is 59 ft. from bow to visible end of keel. Width is 12 ft. from end of framing timber to opposite end of framing timber. Keelson is present from stern to approximately 25 ft. down the keel. Framing timbers are attached to the keel and keelson with two large iron bolts. Keelson is not notched to accept framing timbers. Bow has an iron strap bolted around it. Several treenails observed on framing timbers. Keel width is 12 in. Keelson width is 8 in. Framing timbers are 12 in. on center. Ship oriented 340 degrees to bow. Timbers charred on port side; heavily near bow. Outer planking present. Some floor planking present near stern. No mast steps observed. No stern post present.

Bush submitted the site file form for the site, which is now 38BK1672 and known as the B & B Wreck. The information provided by Boehme and Bush not only is exactly the type of information we like to receive from licensed hobby divers, it also caught the interest of Harry Pecorelli III, an underwater archaeologist from Folly Beach. His interest turned into a thesis topic for his master's degree in maritime history from East Carolina University. Pecorelli, who was a member of the Clive Cussler team that found the Confederate submarine *H. L. Hunley*, recorded the B & B Wreck in some detail. He found that the wreck was most likely plantation built, with its structural timbers made from oak and planking made from pine. According to Pecorelli,

> Vessel dimensions and construction leave little doubt that 38BK1672 is anything but a sloop or schooner, most likely the latter. The proximity to numerous plantations and a hull design maximizing cargo-carrying capacity while maintaining shallow draft suggests that 38BK1672 was used to haul cargo. The presence of wear damage, including repairs, Teredo worm holes, wear from shifting cargo, and 38BK1672's location in Quinby Creek suggest abandonment following a lengthy career.

Pecorelli's findings add significant information to the study of plantation-built vessels found in South Carolina and the Southeast. And this all came about from information provided by two licensed hobby divers exploring lowcountry waters. This is exactly what SDAMP is about.

In addition we have conducted numerous advanced projects with sport divers. These projects include a survey of a section of the Cooper River between Mepkin Abbey and the Strawberry railroad trestle and the recording of barges in the Waccamaw River.

The Waccamaw River Project was the brainchild of sport diver Hampton Shuping of Conway. Hamp is also the finder of the Brown's Ferry Vessel (see "Brown's Ferry Vessel Arrives In Georgetown"). In 1990 he and Don Stewart reported finding four sunken barges in close proximity while diving in the Waccamaw River near Laurel Hill Plantation. After a preliminary reconnaissance by institute staff, Shuping suggested the barge site would make an excellent cooperative project between archaeologists and sport divers. We agreed. For SDAMP this would be not only an opportunity to teach divers concepts in underwater archaeology, but also a means of learning more about the construction techniques used by the barges' builders. We also hoped to discover more about the life and perhaps loss of these river watercraft. The next year, in 1991, a group of sport divers assembled by Shuping, along with institute staff, began documenting the largest of the four barges. SCIAA staff provided advice and special equipment, such as a water dredge to remove the sand overburden on the barge. All artifacts recovered were taken to SCIAA for documentation and conservation. The four barges, while of differing sizes and construction aspects, dated to the early nineteenth century. There is no explanation for the close proximity of the four barges to each other. It may be simple coincidence.

We gave a preliminary look to all four barges; the divers only recorded the largest one in depth, however. In fact this barge turned out to be one of the largest barges ever recorded in South Carolina at fifty-five feet nine inches in length with a width of fifteen feet seven inches. An interesting feature was its chine log construction. The development of chine log barges came from the early settlers' method of splitting dugout canoes in half lengthwise and adding planks between the two halves. This greatly increased the cargo capacity of the craft. In time this method was used to make barges that were quite large with little remaining of their dugout origins. The chine logs were an efficient way to create a means of attaching the sides to the bottom of the craft. On the Waccamaw barge, planks or "strakes" were added atop the chine log to provide additional freeboard.

In addition to Shuping and Stewart, the volunteer divers included Steve Kelsay, Daryl Boyd, Butch Lishka, Patrick Harris, Debbie Lesser, Jan Mallindine, Donnie Edwards, Steven Lindsay, Wayne Martin, Miller Ingram, Wally Ketron, John Peace, and Richard Burdine. The sport divers paid their own expenses, including accommodations, travel, food, and air. The hard work of the divers provided valuable information about the constructions aspects of four very different examples of antebellum plantation barges.

Under the direction of sport diver Jimmy Moss of Abbeville, another FTC graduate, the Cooper River Project not only gathered valuable information about the artifact distribution patterns of this section of the river, but also recorded a new shipwreck near Pimlico Plantation. The project also allowed us to involve divers in an avocational project with the idea of teaching basic underwater archaeological principles.

With the information we learned from the Cooper River Project, Lynn Harris created the Cooper River Underwater Heritage Trail in 1998. The trail covers a three-mile stretch of the Cooper River between Strawberry and Mepkin Abbey. Funding for the trail came in the form of grants from the South Carolina Recreational Trails Fund Program, administered by the Department of Parks, Recreation, and Tourism, and from the Archaeological Research Trust, the fund-raising arm of the institute. We also received assistance from the Hightower Construction Company, the Berkeley County Public Works Department, and the

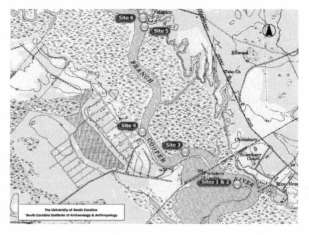

Locations of sites on the Cooper River Heritage Trail. Sites 1 and 2 are the Strawberry Ferry Landing and the Strawberry Wreck. Site 3 is the Pimlico Wreck. Site 4 is the Pimlico Barge. Site 5 is the Mepkin Wreck, and Site 6 is the Mepkin Plantation Dock. SCIAA graphic by Jim Spirek

Berkeley-Charleston-Dorchester Council of Governments. The Strawberry Wreck is one of six sites on the trail. Other sites include the Strawberry Ferry landing, the Pimlico Wreck, the Pimlico Barge, the Mepkin Abbey Wreck, and the Mepkin Plantation Dock.

Site number 1 on the trail, the Strawberry Wreck, is a wooden sailing vessel from the late eighteenth century. The presence of lead sheathing with a British "broad arrow" stamped in it suggests that it was a British vessel, perhaps one of the gunboats used by the British to move troops and loot plantations along Cooper River during the American Revolution. It may even be one of the British vessels captured and burned by Col. Wade Hampton and his men at Lewisfield Plantation in 1781. The vessel, which does show evidence of burning, is about forty-two feet in length and consists of a keel with stem post and sternpost, sixteen sets of frames, and some outer hull planking.

Site number 2 on the trail, the Strawberry Ferry landing, extends about twenty yards out from the riverbank. Rubble, the remains of the brick floor, and timbers are visible from the surface at low tide. Strawberry Ferry, established in 1705, is associated with the early settlement of Childsbury.

Further upriver, between the railroad bridge and Pimlico subdivision is the Pimlico Wreck (trail site number 3). Discovered by sport diver Jimmy Moss, this is the most enigmatic of the wreck sites on the trail. A large wreck, more than sixty-nine feet long and rising off the bottom more than three feet, it is periodically exposed, but more often than not it is completely covered by sand. Divers often call it "the disappearing wreck." Two mast steps indicate that the vessel was schooner rigged,

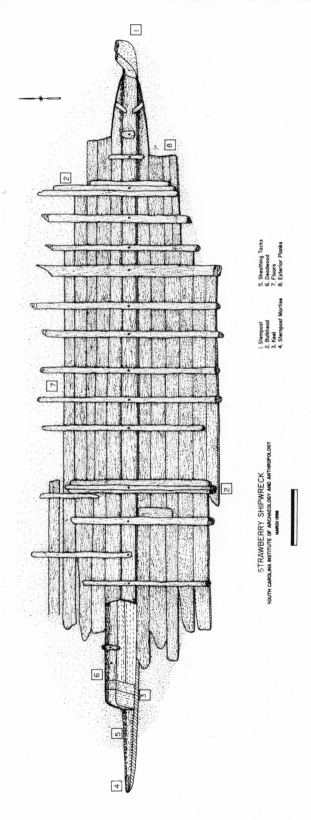

STRAWBERRY SHIPWRECK

SOUTH CAROLINA INSTITUTE OF ARCHAEOLOGY AND ANTHROPOLOGY

MARCH 1996

1. Stempost
2. Bulkhead
3. Keel
4. Sternpost Mortise

5. Sheathing Tacks
6. Deadwood
7. Floors
8. Exterior Planks

Plan view of the Strawberry Wreck in the Cooper River, believed to be a British Revolutionary War gunboat. The wreck is site number 1 on the Cooper River Underwater Heritage Trail. SCIAA illustration

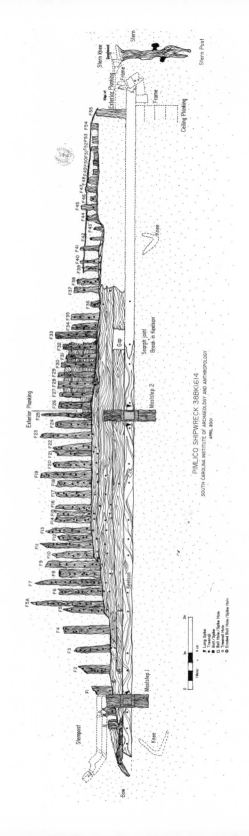

Plan view of the Pimlico Wreck, site number 3 on the Cooper River Underwater
Heritage Trail. SCIAA illustration by Sue Vezeau

and its length and large timbers suggest it was an oceangoing trader. What such a large vessel was doing so far upriver is one of its mysteries. It may have been upriver to take advantage of what the old-timers called "the freshes." This was the procedure of bringing a vessel far enough upriver to where the water is more fresh than salt. This kills many of the marine organisms present in salt water, organisms that attack the bottoms of wooden vessels. It also may have been upriver to seek shelter from a hurricane, a practice still used today by shrimp trawlers.

The Pimlico Barge, site number 4, sits in twenty feet of water just off the dock of one of the houses at Pimlico subdivision. Measuring more than thirty-nine feet long by fifteen feet wide, the barge has a large iron ring at each end. This suggests that it was probably one of a string of barges towed by a tugboat. A unique feature of the barge is the presence of chine logs forming the basis of its ends. Chine log barges are not unusual, but in all other instances we know about, the chine logs run along the sides. This barge has chine logs at the bow and stern. The reason for this is something research has yet to shed light upon.

Sites 5 and 6, the Mepkin Abbey Wreck and Mepkin Plantation Dock, are located near Mepkin Abbey. The abbey was once Mepkin Plantation, the home of Henry Laurens, a prominent colonial Charleston merchant and a leading patriot during the Revolution. The Mepkin Wreck is forty-nine feet long and consists of keel and keelson, twenty-three sets of frames, and a disarticulated stem post. In recent years its rudder, which had been removed for conservation, has been returned to the site. It is staked to the bottom near the stern. Part of the vessel's cargo, a load of shingles (house siding), lies off to one side of the wreck. The Mepkin Plantation Dock, now completely submerged, resembles the remains of the three-sided log cabin. It is typical of colonial plantation docks used to load products of the plantation for shipment to Charleston and to receive goods for the plantation as well as visitors. The dock extends more than twelve feet out into the river and rises off the bottom more than eight feet.

Permanent monuments mark each site, with lines running from the monuments to the sites. In the spring we place mooring buoys on the monuments to facilitate divers' exploration of these archaeological treasures. We retrieve the buoys in the fall for maintenance and cleaning over the winter. We often use the sites on the Cooper River Underwater Heritage Trail in the field training course. We are familiar with the sites and their surroundings, using the mooring buoys is convenient and saves time in an activity-filled day, and the students find the working on the historic wrecks rewarding.

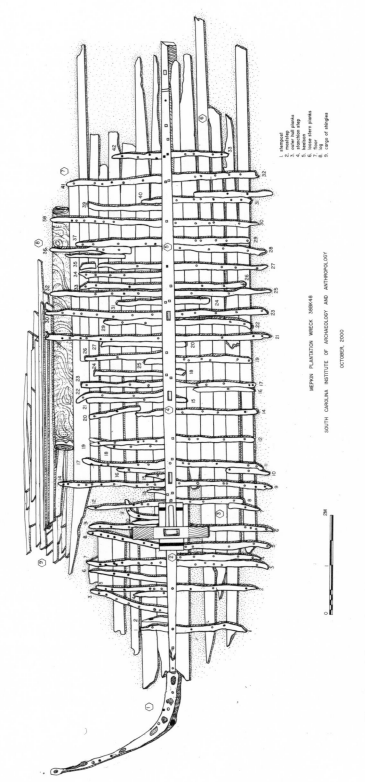

Plan view of the Mepkin Abbey Vessel, site number 5 on
the Cooper River Underwater Heritage Trail. SCIAA illustration

In 2006 the Sport Diver Archaeology Program took another new turn. By this time Lynn Harris had received her doctorate in history from the University of South Carolina and left the program to teach college-level courses in history and archaeology. She had developed the sport diver program since its inception. She had instituted the field training course, the Cooper River Underwater Heritage Trail, and the Ashley River Canoe Trail. She left to impart her experience to knowledge-hungry college students. In October 2006 Lora Holland took over the program. Lora has a bachelor's degree in history from Salem College in Winston-Salem, North Carolina, and a master's degree in anthropology from the University of West Florida in Pensacola. Her master's thesis, "Maritime Technology in Transition: Historical and Archaeological Investigations of the Schooner Barge *Geo. T. Lock*," centered on her research into an early-twentieth-century schooner converted to a barge. While at the University of West Florida, she also participated in a remote sensing survey of the Pensacola waterfront, an archaeological survey of the Old County Court House in downtown Pensacola, and a remote sensing survey of Cape Romano, Florida, for the Florida Bureau of Archaeological Research. Just prior to joining SCIAA, Lora worked with the *H. L. Hunley* project as a graphics intern. Her work there focused on the application of three-dimensional digital technology, including creating scans of the crew members' skeletal remains.

The first new direction she took the program in was to overhaul the field training course and change its focus. Instead of training divers to be volunteers on SCIAA projects, Lora revised the training to prepare divers as "first responders" of a kind. The participants would learn preliminary wreck site recording, basic vessel construction, the importance of artifacts in archaeology, and other cool archaeological stuff. The idea was that should they run into a site (sometimes literally) while they were out collecting artifacts under their hobby licenses, they would be able to gather enough information—basic measurements, locational information, and the like—to fill out a South Carolina Archaeological Site Inventory file for submission.

She also began a program for obtaining information from divers who were recovering artifacts from state waters before there was a hobby diver licensing program. Actually this came about at the impetus of diver Drew Ruddy. Drew was one of these divers who had been diving the South Carolina rivers, finding shipwrecks, and recovering artifacts before there was a law. He became a certified diver in 1967 and was one of the divers who originally found the Mepkin Plantation Wreck. He later became a U.S. Navy saturation diver. After the navy he worked as a commercial diver in Belgium, Scotland, and the United States. He currently works for CalDive, one of the largest commercial diving companies in the world. His job presently has him working in the Gulf of Mexico. He also holds a bachelor's degree in biology from Baptist College (now Charleston Southern University) and a master's degree in clinical counseling from the Citadel.

In 1997 Drew came to our offices at Fort Johnson with the idea of recording his activities at Willtown Bluff in the late 1960s. He and fellow divers Jim Batey, Steve Howard, Owen Batey, Lee Spence, Chris Beuter, Jim Stark, Eddie Phillips, Larry Roberts, Casey Herbert, Rick Rodgers, and Leon Robinson dived the Edisto River site then and had recovered scores of artifacts. Drew told us he wanted to report these finds to us as best as was possible after almost thirty years. After a Herculean effort in tracking down his old dive buddies, and with a little help from the SCIAA staff, Drew published a report on his diving at Willtown that would make any archaeologist proud.

For his new project, Drew had taken on the daunting task of locating the divers from the 1960s and 1970s and persuading them to open up their collections to be recorded and photographed while at the same time urging them to tell stories of their diving and recovery activities. Lora and Drew hope to produce an oral and pictorial history of early diving in South Carolina waters. The fact that Drew is one of these early divers makes this a project/task that perhaps only he could pull off—one that would be near impossible for a state (read *government*) archaeologist to accomplish.

So far Drew has photographed more than a dozen collections. His project has taken the Sport Diver Archaeology Management Program to heights only dreamed of when the Underwater Antiquities Act was revised in 1991. Under Lora's direction the sport diver program will surely attain even higher goals. I say this because she has the energy and drive it takes to do the job. I say this because she has the talent and perseverance to accomplish much with the program. I say this because, as my supervisor, she conducts my yearly employee evaluation.

Joe and the Alligator

We were on the Strawberry Wreck with a group of students in our underwater archaeology field training course when Joe Beatty had his first encounter with an alligator. The students had learned the proper methods of recording a shipwreck—measuring and drawing the frames, keel, keelson, planking, and fasteners—during classroom and pool training sessions and were now practicing these new skills "in the field." The Strawberry Wreck lies under about twenty feet of dark water in the west branch of the Cooper River. It is out of the main channel of the river, near the remains of the old Strawberry Ferry landing. Evidence found on the wreck suggests the wooden sailing vessel was a British gunboat of the Revolutionary War period. For the FTC students, this wreck was the real thing.

Lynn Harris and I were monitoring the student's activities from our twenty-eight-foot pontoon boat. Mostly this meant just watching the divers' bubbles. Joe Beatty had gone down with the students to act as guide. His task was to keep the students from wandering off the wreck and getting lost in the featureless river bottom around the vessel site, a surprisingly easy thing to do even though the diver might get no more than four or five feet away. Joe's dive partner was Furman Dabbs of Sumter, a volunteer helping us with the class. The students were on the remains of the hull, doing all that measuring and drawing, when Joe exploded to the surface and began waving his arms. Once he had our attention (monitoring students' bubbles can be distracting), he pointed down and shouted unintelligibly. Realizing he still had his regulator mouthpiece firmly between his teeth, he spit it out and shouted, "Big alligator." The strange looks on our faces must have surprised him. Before he removed his regulator, we thought he was shouting something about a figure skater.

I never saw Joe swim so fast. Back at the dive boat, he told us he was cruising around the wreck, making sure the students stayed put, when he spotted what he thought was a palm frond at the edge of his vision. In the Cooper River, the edge of vision is seldom more than a few feet. Wanting to get it out of the way, in case the students mistook it for a timber to measure, he grabbed the frond and discovered it was the tail of an alligator. He said he froze, still holding onto the creature's tail, not knowing whether he should gently let go of the tail and slowly move away or snatch his hand back and make a hasty getaway. Before he could react, the alligator turned toward him until they were face to face mask, eyeball to bulging eyeball. He was this close, Joe said, holding his hands no more than a foot apart. The gesture reminded me of an angler showing his friends how big the fish was that got away, only exaggerated in reverse. Joe had no idea how long the encounter lasted, but when he finally let go of the alligator's tail, he said it turned and swiftly swam away, flicking its knobby tail at him as it disappeared into the murk. Joe said the creature looked mean and nasty and had a grin like a used-car salesman. He finished his story by saying it was the biggest alligator he had ever seen.

We quickly convened a conference to discuss recalling the divers in light of the figure skater, er, big alligator being in the area. We knew that alligators are not aggressive (most of the time). We knew they generally leave divers alone (unless they perceive some threat to their young). We also knew that Joe is not prone to exaggeration (most of the time), and we knew that divers generally leave underwater creatures alone (unless they perceive some threat to their young). Ultimately since the incident happened some distance from the wreck and the alligator showed no real hostile intent toward Joe, we decided to continue with the training. Nevertheless we scanned the area around the boat for the alligator, knowing it had to come up for air eventually. Sure enough a minute later the great beast surfaced. It slowly swam toward shore, no doubt exhausted by its close encounter with Joe, hauled itself onto the riverbank and into the warm rays of the sun. Joe's alligator, the biggest one he ever saw, turned out to be all of four feet long. It looked bigger underwater, Joe explained.

Diving and working in South Carolina waters brings us in contact with a variety of wildlife, alligators being just one. As we survey offshore, we often see rays—some six feet or more across—leaping totally out of the water, only to crash awkwardly back into the sea. We see squadrons of pelicans dive-bombing schools of fish, seldom coming up without hapless victims. Inquisitive porpoises nose their way alongside

Attracted to the bubbles, an alligator cruising off Pimlico subdivision on the Cooper River closes in on Lora Holland, left, and Chris Amer as they head for shore after surfacing from their visit to a wreck site. SCIAA photograph by James Spirek

our boat, matching our course and speed, curious about our activities. Seagulls, squawking at our efforts, follow behind our survey boat, swooping low for closer looks at the magnetometer skimming along in our wake. Sea turtles come to the surface to breathe, at first glance looking like bald-headed human swimmers too far from shore, before slipping back beneath the waves. As we cruise the lowcountry rivers, anhingas perching on old dock pilings stretch their wings to dry in the sun. Osprey and bald eagles swoop down to snatch fish too close to the surface, returning to their nests in the tall trees along the riverbanks. Great blue herons stalk the marsh edges, stabbing their beaks into the shallow water to catch a wiggling meal.

One fall while surveying for the wreck of the French corsair *Le Prince* off Hilton Head Island, we saw one of the most remarkable displays of animal behavior we have ever witnessed. Winging their way south in a long ribbon stretching up and down the coast as far as we could see were millions of monarch butterflies. During September and October, virtually the entire population of East Coast monarchs migrates to wintering grounds in Mexico and Florida. I read somewhere that, assisted by prevailing wind currents, they use solar orientation, perception of polarized light, and the earth's magnetic field to guide their flight. At day's end they come ashore to rest on coastal foliage. Now and then one of the migrating monarchs would land on our survey vessel—on the sun top or the gunwale. The orange and black hitchhiker would fold and open its wings several times, as if stretching tired muscles, before resuming its epic voyage. Sometimes they would just get under our sun top and fly along at the boat's speed, apparently taking a respite from the sun's rays.

Yet when we give talks to the public, especially at elementary schools, our audiences inevitably ask about just two critters—alligators and sharks. In truth the two creatures that we have the most trouble with are snakes and jellyfish. (Actually the term *jellyfish* is as improper as calling sea stars by their more common name *starfish,* since neither are truly fish. Jellyfish are more properly called *jellies.*)

In 1990, to revive its once-thriving waterfront, the city of Conway proposed developing the area for public use by constructing a boardwalk along 3,500 feet of the Waccamaw River. For about half that distance the plan called for constructing the boardwalk on pilings 10 to 16 feet out over the water. The city contacted SCIAA's Underwater Archaeology Division in January 1991 to conduct a survey of the river bottom in the area of the proposed boardwalk. The purpose of the survey was to determine if the construction of the boardwalk would adversely affect any submerged archaeological features.

During our survey Chris Amer and I recorded a small wooden skiff that had rested for untold years on the bottom of the Waccamaw. Without a light we would have been in total darkness. Chris handled the tape, and I took the light. Chris had a white slate taped to his arm on which he would record each measurement in pencil. My job was to train the light from the measurement on the tape to the slate, trying to anticipate where Chris would be looking.

The skiff was a small, flat-bottomed, square-ended boat resembling a johnboat in shape. Only about five feet of the boat's length was exposed, and without having the time to excavate the entire hull, we were unable to get the boat's actual length. Our projections indicated a length of about ten feet. The widest part of the exposed hull was just under three feet. A single plank about ten inches wide at the widest point formed each side of the hull. Planks laid athwartship formed the bottom. These planks varied in width from eight to twelve inches. Iron staples attached the bottom planks to the sides. The boat was lightly constructed, as it had no gunwales or interior framework, making it relatively easy to build with only a few tools needed to complete its construction. No features were found that shed light on how the vessel was propelled. Most likely it was rowed or poled, but it could have been sailed or even motored, which of course covers about every type of possible propulsion.

At one point Chris took longer than usual recording notes on the slate. I kept the light on the slate for a moment longer than usual, curious as to what he had just written. Just before I moved the light back to where Chris was taking the next measurement, a water moccasin struck the slate and was gone. Chris and I looked at each other. I then swept the light around, looking for our attacker. Apparently satisfied that it had done its best to scare us witless (not far from the truth), the snake was nowhere to been seen. We shrugged and continued our work. Luckily the snake was unable to penetrate the slate and into Chris's arm.

This was not the only time I saw a snake strike underwater. We were in Kingstree surveying the bottom of the Black River where the South Carolina Highway Department planned to build a new Highway 52 bridge. As I crossed the bottom of the river looking for possible submerged cultural resources (a Viking ship, for instance), I was sweeping my Ikelite Superlight back and forth in the gloom when a moccasin struck my dive light. The force of the strike went through the light and up my arm, apparently causing some temporary nerve damage. What else would account for my inability to stop my arm from shaking as I tried to hold my dive light steady for the rest of the dive?

In 1996, while we conducted the initial excavations on the *H. L. Hunley*, jellies plagued our activities. Actually two types of jellies. One was the ubiquitous jellyball or cannonball jelly. A barrage of cannonball jellies bombarded us as we performed our tasks on the sandy bottom. Our dredges sucked them up, rudely shooting them out the effluent hose some distance away. It was as close to experiencing warp speed as any jelly could hope for. For the most part, they would just drift over, about, and under us. With their round shapes, some up to ten inches in diameter, and their milky bodies, it was like being downwind of a giant bubble machine in a gentle breeze. We were grateful these jellies were nonvenomous. The other type of jelly we encountered was venomous. Not being a marine biologist, I can only guess at this second type, but I believe they were common sea nettles. These jellies range from New England to Brazil in the western Atlantic and are the most common form of jelly found in South Carolina waters. Did I mention that these puppies are venomous? Though it was summer and the water pleasantly warm, we nevertheless wore full wet suits, hoods, and gloves. This provided protection for everywhere on our bodies except around our mouths. At the end of our dives, the jellies' stings would leave our lips swollen like a collagen job gone bad. To avoid this one of the divers, Harry Pecorelli, got in the habit of pulling women's pantyhose over his head like a prophylactic before donning his hood. With a cutout for his eyes and just a small hole for his regulator to fit in his mouth, his lips had some protection. While Harry had to put up endless teasing, the pantyhose nevertheless seemed to work.

Whether Joe's encounter with the alligator on the Strawberry Wreck sparked some sort of mental connection between man and beast or whether he has some latent affinity with alligators from birth would only be speculation. Either way the incident on the Strawberry Wreck was not the end of Joe's relationship with alligators.

During the 2003 FTC, we learned Joe Beatty in fact could talk to alligators. Moreover they would listen. We were tied up to the Mepkin Wreck buoy, getting students ready for their dive on this wooden plantation vessel, when we spotted an alligator swimming away from all our commotion. Joe cupped his hands over his mouth and made a noise that sounded something like "schmock, schmock." He repeated this several times, saying he learned the technique watching a *National Geographic* special. Suddenly the alligator turned and headed straight toward our boat. Joe's glee at having this effect on the alligator quickly turned to alarm. While we were accustomed to diving with alligators nearby, we had a boatload of students, many of whom we supposed were not going to be happy at being asked to dive so near the creature. Not knowing what else to do, Joe put up his arm, palm flat out toward the alligator, and shouted, "Stop." If Joe were auditioning for a job as traffic cop, he surely would have been hired, for the alligator suddenly stopped. Joe then bellowed, "Go away," and, with a flick of his wrist, dismissed the intruder. No sooner had he done this than the alligator turned and swam off, disappearing into the marsh.

We were stunned. The students were impressed. I wondered if Joe had learned *that* from a *National Geographic* special.

Brown's Ferry Vessel
Arrives in Georgetown

As they had for hundreds of years, the citizens of Georgetown awaited the appearance of a vessel. Since its founding in 1729, this port city has looked seaward for arriving ships. Only this one was not coming by sea, but by truck.

It was June 1992, and crowds worthy of a circus parade lined the sidewalks in front of the Georgetown Rice Museum, eagerly anticipating the arrival of a new exhibit for the museum's Kaminski Building. The exhibit would be the largest artifact on display in the museum, one that had consumed more than nine years of preparation—the remains of the Brown's Ferry Vessel.

News media abounded. Reporters interviewed local officials and got reactions from waiting townsfolk. Television crews and news photographers recorded shots of the crowd, of the Kaminski Building, and of Georgetown itself. The city's inhabitants tolerated the journalistic interruptions as every few seconds their eyes switched between Front Street and Screven Street, not knowing from which direction the nautical artifact would arrive.

Lynn Harris and I had driven up from Charleston that morning. Since SCIAA's Underwater Archaeology Division had been so heavily involved in the recovery and conservation of the vessel, we easily obtained permission from our bosses to attend the vessel's arrival and placement in the Kaminski Building. It seemed like a good way to get out of the office for a day. Actually we were just two of the SCIAA staff on hand. Dr. Bruce Rippeteau, state archaeologist and SCIAA director; Dr. Jonathan Leader, deputy state archaeologist and SCIAA conservator; and Christopher Amer, head of SCIAA's Underwater Archaeology Division, were among the institute staff there also. Since Lynn and I had no official duties, we joined the crowd on the streets.

The Brown's Ferry Vessel is not a ferry vessel at all but a sail-powered river and coastal cargo carrier from the early 1700s. It got its name by sinking in the Black River near the site of the old Brown's Ferry landing. Found by a sport diver while diving in the Black River in 1975, it carried a cargo consisting mostly of bricks. What makes the vessel historically significant, however, is not where it was found or what it was carrying. What makes the Brown's Ferry Vessel important to the maritime history of South Carolina is its design.

In 1979 Professor J. Richard Steffy of the Institute of Nautical Archeology at Texas A&M University called the Brown's Ferry Vessel "the most important single nautical discovery in the United States to date." He gives the following explanation for his claim:

> In the first place, it establishes primary evidence for American shipbuilding nearly fifty years earlier than previous discoveries. More important, this was a merchant hull, built without the anxiety, bureaucracy, and inefficiency often associated with vessels of war. As such, it defines everyday technology in a competitive atmosphere. Additionally, this was a local type—important to any maritime scholar—representing a period and area in which far too little maritime information has been forthcoming.

This "local type" of merchant hull has indeed been forthcoming in adding to the maritime information pertaining to shipbuilding in colonial America. The hull type of the Brown's Ferry Vessel provides a link in the evolution of ship construction. Dr. Fred Hocker of Texas A&M studied the vessel remains as part of his graduate studies and wrote in 1985 that the vessel's hull "represents the most sophisticated development in flat bottomed design and construction found in a commercial context. While its shape is probably not of European origin, its construction is clearly part of a tradition with roots or parallels in . . . the riverine craft of much of Europe." Hocker noted that the vessel "may also represent the merging of the European philosophy of boatbuilding with the traditions of the Indians of colonial South Carolina."

These are some lofty claims for a small wooden cargo vessel found abandoned and deteriorating on the bottom of the Black River. Even before Steffy and Hocker had a chance to study the craft and issue their statements, however, SCIAA's Alan Albright realized he might have something important when he first learned of the vessel immediately after its discovery.

This happened when scuba instructor Hampton Shuping Jr. of Conway had a class of new divers at Brown's Ferry in the winter of 1975.

While poking around the area, he and his students came across the remains of the wooden vessel no more than twenty-five feet from the end of the defunct ferry landing. It was lying partially on its side in twenty to twenty-five feet of water. Only a small portion of the wreck was showing. Sand covered much of the bow area. Thousands of bricks covered the rest of the vessel. In addition deposited on top of the sand and brick was more than two hundred years of debris and trash.

Shuping called Albright, notifying him of the find. Intrigued by what he heard, Albright asked Shuping to revisit the site and recover a few artifacts associated with the wreck for study by the institute. Shuping gladly agreed. The artifacts he recovered and brought to the institute were startling. The pieces of dark green glass English wine bottles, iron spikes, and clear glass bottles indicated a date for the wreck of about 1740. This would make the vessel the oldest ship-built cargo craft found in South Carolina to date.

Following a brief examination of the site by institute personnel, Albright made plans to raise the vessel in December 1976. This would give him nearly a year to arrange for the necessary equipment and come up with the all-important funding. Word of the find got out, however, and divers began visiting the site, removing small pieces of the wreck and other artifacts as souvenirs. This led Albright to move up his timetable.

Excavation of the vessel began in July 1976, led by Alan Albright. Assisting him was Dr. Newell O. Wright, an institute underwater archaeologist, along with SCIAA dive master Ralph L. Wilbanks and a corps of volunteers. The first two weeks were devoted to clearing the wreck site of debris—including trees, rocks, the remains of two automobiles, and the remnants of a horse-drawn buggy—and setting up a grid over the wreck. The team spent the next three weeks of the six-week project removing the brick and remaining artifacts from the hull. The divers used metal and wire baskets that held sixteen to twenty-four bricks each. Loading the brick disturbed the bottom sediments, and even with the tidal flow, visibility was zero for much of those three weeks. Albright estimated that the cargo comprised about two thousand bricks. The actual number reached a whopping ten thousand bricks, weighing an estimated twenty-five tons. The vessel's additional cargo consisted of four millstones, two dozen bottles, and three iron pots (one of which probably belonged to the cook). The artifacts recovered include personal items such as a slipware cup, a straight razor, and several gourd smoking pipes. Other items recovered include two oars and several wooden poles.

Perhaps the most interesting artifact found on the site was an improved Davis quadrant. Until the end of the sixteenth century, navigators took sun sightings with devices called cross-staffs. Unfortunately for the sailors relying on them, the cross-staff had problems. In addition to being hard to use properly, the user had to face directly into the sun. About 1594 British sea captain John Davis concocted a device that alleviated both problems—the back-staff. Not only easier to use, and therefore more accurate, it could be used with one's back to the sun. Subsequently Davis improved the design of his back-staff. In the seventeenth century, the "improved Davis quadrant" became standard navigational equipment on all English, and most foreign, ships.

With the bricks and other artifacts removed, Albright's crew then examined and labeled each frame, plank, and timber of the vessel. Loose pieces were also examined, labeled, and removed to the surface.

Now came the difficult and most exciting part of the project—raising the remains of the hull to the surface and loading it onto a truck. This was accomplished with a large metal frame constructed by the engineers and welders of the International Paper Company of Georgetown. Forty feet long, ten feet wide, and constructed with three-inch I-beams, the frame had twenty attachment points on each side. The idea was to suspend the frame over the wreck and run straps from attachment points on one side of the frame under the wreck to the attachment points on the other side of the frame. Before this could happen, however, slots had to be tunneled under the wreck for the wide nylon straps. The divers first tried pumping water through fire hose to cut through the sediment. This was only partially successful. The divers then used twelve-foot-long pipe, slightly bent to follow the curve of the vessel's bottom. By pumping air through the pipe, the divers easily pushed the pipes and straps under the wreck. With this done, it was time to schedule a crane to come to the site, lower the frame over the wreck, and begin raising the wreck.

The big day came on August 28, 1976. Reporters, a crowd of onlookers, a flatbed truck, and a crane arrived on-site. The spectators waited patiently (okay, reporters are seldom patient) while the crane smoothly lowered the frame down over the wreck and divers methodically hooked up the straps. The wreck was then lifted a foot off the bottom, allowing divers to readjust the straps for the final lift. Gently raised to the surface and placed on the truck, the Brown's Ferry Vessel was taken to Fort Jackson, near Columbia, for the first stage of its conservation. For the next sixteen months the vessel remained at Fort Jackson, being constantly soaked using a freshwater sprinkler system. In December 1977 the Brown's Ferry Vessel was taken to a spring-fed farm pond, where it remained until November 1983, when it was placed in the institute's

newly constructed, waterlogged-wood conservation facility on the University of South Carolina's Columbia campus.

While the vessel was at Fort Jackson, Albright invited Professor Steffy to come and assess the vessel's construction aspects. Steffy spent three days examining the remains. He then headed back to the Institute of Nautical Archaeology, where his measurements produced line drawings showing the vessel's overall shape. What Steffy found was a flat-bottomed craft designed to carry maximum cargo in both river and coastal environments. Its overall length was 50 feet 5 inches, and it had a maximum breadth of 14 feet. The vessel's oak frames, spaced approximately 24 inches on center, measured 4 inches by 5 inches on average. One-inch-thick pine formed the outer hull planking. While varying in width, the planking averaged 9½ inches wide. The keelson consisted of a single piece of cypress 36 feet $6\frac{1}{2}$ inches long and 4 inches thick. Amidships it was 12 inches wide, tapering to 10 inches wide at the bow and 8 inches wide at the stern. It contained steps for two masts. Steffy noted, "The keelson also served as a chopping block, presumably for the cook. Hundreds of random ax or hatchet marks marred its top surface between the two mast steps. Small charred areas, as if made by ash from the galley stove, were scattered among the chop marks." He estimated that the vessel's depth of hold was approximately 3 feet and that the hold had a maximum cargo capacity of thirty tons.

Interestingly the vessel lacked a keel. Instead three large planks of yellow pine formed the hull's bottom structure. Only the center plank, measuring 18 inches wide, extended the length of the vessel. The two side planks were edge-joined using $\frac{3}{4}$-inch treenails. These "bottom planks" varied in thickness from $2\frac{3}{4}$ inches to 4 inches, with the greater thickness being more predominant amidships and the lesser thicknesses near the bow. This flat-bottomed construction probably served two purposes. First, it allowed for a shallow draft, a necessity in navigating low-country rivers. Second, it allowed for easy beaching, an advantage when loading cargo in locations lacking proper docks and piers. As evidence of this, Steffy noted that the bottom planks "appeared worn near the bow, as if from beaching."

Flat-bottomed construction is the oldest boatbuilding technique, going back to ancient Egypt. However, once the more "modern" round-bottom design came into being, making long oceangoing voyages possible, flat-bottomed boats were relegated to rivers and sheltered waters. The reason for this is simple. While good for shallow waters and heavy cargoes, flat-bottomed boats are notoriously bad sailing hulls. Their lack of a keel provides little lateral resistance to counteract leeway, allowing the wind to push them more sideways than forward. Another problem is the inherent weakness of the flat-bottomed hull structure. "Even reinforced," notes Dr. Hocker in his report on the Brown's Ferry Vessel, "the flat-bottomed hull can rarely take the pounding of an extended open water passage."

This does not mean that flat-bottomed boats, including the Brown's Ferry Vessel, did not cruise in open ocean, or at least along the coast. According to Professor Steffy, "Teredo (worm) damage indicated the vessel must have wandered beyond the confines of the Black River." The presence of the improved Davis quadrant for navigating out of sight of land points to this as well.

Despite its drawbacks, flat-bottomed boat construction was used extensively by the European settlers of America, continuing to the end of the sailing era. French explorers and settlers in Canada and the North-east used a flat-bottomed, dorylike open boat—the bateau—that was between ten and forty feet long. Another example is the Chesapeake Bay ram. Designed to fit through the Chesapeake Canal, the ram had a flat bottom and vertical sides to expand cargo capacity. Both the Americans and British used flat-bottomed "gundalows" on Lake Champlain during the American Revolution. These warships were in the range of fifty feet long and usually single masted with large square sails. One of these gundalows, the *Philadelphia,* was raised from the bottom of the lake and is now at the Smithsonian Institute. It is 53 feet 4 inches long, 15 feet 6 inches wide, and has no keel, its bottom being completely flat.

Professor Steffy also made a model of the Brown's Ferry Vessel at 1:10 scale. Constructed out of pine to "museum quality" standards, the model even includes the ax marks on top of the keelson. While accurate with respect to what remains of the vessel, Steffy had to speculate on several aspects of the model. A major problem was determining its rig or sail arrangement. Although it is certain the vessel had two masts, its exact sail configuration remains unknown. The two masts allowed for any number of rigs. The vessel could have been square rigged, or square rigged on the upper masts and fore-and-aft rigged on the lower portion of the masts, or fore-and-aft rigged only. Steffy determined that the most likely rig for a vessel this size and purpose was a fore-and-aft rig, specifically a sprit rig. Sprit rigs differ from other fore-and-aft rigs in that a long gaff, attached to the mast near the deck, supports the top, aft end of the square sail. The bottom of the sail is loose footed, that is, not attached to a gaff. A small crew could easily handle a sprit rig that, according to Steffy's report, "would satisfy the requirements for sailing along the coast as well as among the fickle river winds."

Another area of speculation was the vessel's decking. While the vessel's remains showed evidence of decking in the bow, it was impossible to determine how much of the vessel was decked. Steffy decided to install decking in the bow and stern of the model, with walkways along the sides. "It seems unlikely that so shallow a hold would be completely decked over," Steffy concluded.

Meanwhile the vessel was undergoing conservation. Wood, subjected for long periods to wet environments, deteriorates. The bottom of the Black River is certainly a wet environment. First the starch and sugar in the wood's cells leach out. Then in time the cellulose in the cell walls disintegrates. This makes the cells porous, and they fill with water. If subsequently exposed to air, the water evaporates from the cells and they collapse. Conservation is required to prevent this. One of the most common methods for treating waterlogged wood involves displacing the water and reinforcing the cell walls with another substance. For the Brown's Ferry Vessel the substance used was a synthetic material called polyethylene glycol (PEG). The technique is simple. After placing a vessel in a large, stainless-steel tank, the tank is filled with a solution of water and PEG. The temperature of the mixture is then raised to about 140 degrees Fahrenheit. As the water evaporates, it is replaced with more PEG, until finally—after more than nine years for the Brown's Ferry Vessel—all the water is gone. The PEG is drained, and the vessel allowed to cool. As it comes to room temperature, the PEG hardens into a waxy substance, holding the shape of the wood's cells. The vessel is then ready for display. For the Brown's Ferry Vessel that meant a trip to Georgetown.

For Lynn and me, as well as for the crowd waiting outside the museum, the first clue that the Brown's Ferry Vessel had arrived in Georgetown came when the contingent of South Carolina Highway Patrol officers came into view. The troopers had escorted the boat's remains from Columbia, taking secondary roads to avoid the interstate. The trip had taken a cautious five hours.

Then the truck bearing the Brown's Ferry Vessel came into view. A feeling of anticipation vibrated through the crowd. A soft "ooh" escaped from the onlookers. Then I began to hear random comments.

"Is that all there is to it?" someone asked rhetorically. Granted the remains consisted of only keel, keelson, framing, and some planking, but that is more structure than many of the shipwrecks we find in South Carolina waters.

"Looks like a skeleton," I heard someone else say. I had the feeling the crowd was disappointed in what they saw.

It was difficult to fathom what I was hearing. What to me was a great achievement was a disappointment to others? A significant piece of our maritime history, one that already added to our knowledge of early American boatbuilding, was nothing more than a "skeleton"? Did they think that after more than two hundred years submerged in a South Carolina river the vessel would be intact? That its masts would still be stepped, its sails up, and all its woodwork in perfect condition? The typical remains of a wooden sailing vessel rarely consist of more than a keel, several sets of floor timbers and futtocks (frames), and, if we are lucky, the keelson and some outer and inner hull planking; and if they are still all articulated they look less like a ship and more like a . . . well, okay, a skeleton.

With the truck sidled up to the Kaminski Building, the riggers went to work. Days earlier the roof of the building had been removed to allow the shipwreck to be lowered into the third floor. The lift and placement went smoothly, taking about an hour. Almost immediately workers began replacing the ceiling rafters. A few days later the roof was back in place. Putting the wreck back together would take considerably longer. Dr. Leader estimated the reconstruction of the vessel would take several months. Local officials told news reporters the new exhibit should be open some time in 1993.

Reconstructing the Brown's Ferry Vessel actually took until 1998. One reason was that like most such projects, we were only able to spend a week or two a year in the reconstruction. Another reason was that much reconstruction was necessary. One hundred and fifty of the vessel's timbers had become disarticulated, that is, no longer attached to the hull, while it was lying on the bottom of Black River. Some of these lay near the wreck, others on the wreck itself. To make the reconstruction easier, the timbers had been marked with coded tags that indicated their placement back on the wreck. Unfortunately in the years since the tags were placed on the timbers, the codebook had disappeared, and no one knew how to decipher the tags. This meant that we had to take one timber at a time and, while walking around the wreck, try to fit it in one place and then another until its right place was found. It was akin to putting together a giant three-dimensional jigsaw puzzle. We then used stainless-steel rods to attach the timbers to the hull. We worked in teams, one team cutting the rods to the specific lengths necessary and then threading both ends. Meanwhile another team drilled the timbers to accommodate the rods and inserted them through the timber and hull. Washers and nuts then secured the assembled parts. In all we cut, threaded, inserted, and fastened more than three thousand stainless-steel rods.

Unexpectedly we ran into another problem. Halfway through the reconstruction, we learned that the vessel had one more voyage to make. While we were rebuilding the remains, the museum was renovating the Kaminski Building to accommodate the new exhibit. This renovation included the installation of an elevator. During construction, however, the architect took it upon himself to reorient the elevator, rotating it ninety degrees. This meant that instead of opening into a wide area parallel to the shipwreck, the elevator door now opened onto the stern of the vessel, where it would be impossible for someone in a wheelchair to exit onto the third floor and difficult for anyone else. Since the elevator was already in place, only one solution presented itself—move the vessel.

We determined that the whole exhibit had to be moved forward about six feet. But how were we going to do that? We estimated that the reconstructed vessel weighed about six tons. After much discussion we decided to jack up the vessel and attach heavy-duty castors to the ship-wreck's cradle. Then, with chains and a come-along attached to the third floor's main support, we inched the wreck forward. "Inched" could not be more accurate. From start to finish, it took us a whopping seven hours to move the wreck six feet.

The exhibit finally opened to the public in June 2000. Sitting atop the vessel is Steffy's 1:10 scale model, showing museum visitors what the vessel probably looked like. Displays include photos of the day the vessel was placed inside the museum and of its reconstruction. Many of the artifacts recovered from the wreck site are also on display, including the Davis quadrant.

The Brown's Ferry Vessel has found its proper home. This nautical artifact now adds an important chapter to the maritime history of the South Carolina lowcountry—even if it is only a skeleton.

Those Darn Dugouts

The reporter's question wasn't all that unusual. He asked if we knew anything about a prehistoric dugout canoe recently retrieved from the Cooper River by a scuba diver. For decades boaters, anglers, and divers have been discovering long-lost dugout log canoes in the marshes, mud-flats, and river bottoms of the South Carolina lowcountry. But no, we told him when he called the Charleston Underwater Archaeology Division field office in July 1997, we hadn't heard about this one. We did know, however, that the recovery of a prehistoric canoe from state waters without a license violated the South Carolina Underwater Antiquities Act of 1991. And we knew that no such license had been granted. We asked the reporter for the name of the person who had retrieved the canoe. At first he declined, citing confidentiality of sources. We asked the reporter if he knew that he was withholding information about a possible crime. We then heard the rustling of pages in a notebook. The diver's name is Joe Porcelli, the reporter revealed, and he lives in Mount Pleasant.

Lynn Harris, underwater archaeologist and head of the Charleston field office, called Mr. Porcelli. He admitted retrieving the dugout canoe from the Cooper River and said he had it submerged in a tank of water on his backyard patio. When told he needed a license from the state to retrieve such an artifact and that his actions constituted a violation of state law, he threatened to destroy the canoe and along with it the evidence of his "crime." We decided to pay Porcelli a visit.

The dugout canoe has to be the most popular type of watercraft in South Carolina history. For thousands of years before the coming of the Europeans, the Native Americans used them to travel along the coast and up and down the rivers and creeks. The early Europeans quickly adopted the vessel. The colonists used them for fishing and hunting, to get themselves and their goods to town, to take their families to church, or simply to visit their neighbors. This versatile form of transportation was made and used well into the twentieth century. We often see dugouts with square sterns and transom boards for mounting outboard engines.

Examples of this simple but effective watercraft are on display at many local museums. The South Carolina State Museum in Columbia, the Horry County Museum in Conway, the Berkeley County Museum in Moncks Corner, the McClellanville Museum, Middleton Place, Brookgreen Gardens, and the Charleston Museum are just a few. I have also seen them in the living rooms, backyards, garages, and flowerbeds of private homes throughout the lowcountry.

Over the years, SCIAA archaeologists have recorded and studied more than forty dugout canoes. These include both prehistoric canoes made by the early Native Americans and historic canoes made by the European settlers, colonists, and later inhabitants. Slightly more than half of those recorded are historic dugouts. Undoubtedly there are many more out there waiting to be discovered.

Distinguishing between prehistoric and historic canoes takes a basic understanding of how each was made. The Native Americans fashioned their dugouts from cypress, poplar, or pine. They hollowed out the log with fire, placing clay over the areas they did not want burned and fanning the flames where they wanted the burning accelerated. Occasionally they would extinguish the fire and scrape out the burned wood with a shell or stone tool. In the South Carolina lowcountry, they often used oyster shells. The European settlers almost exclusively used cypress trees and, of course, used metal tools—adzes, chisels, axes, and saws—to fashion their canoes. Before hollowing out the hull, they would drill holes in the bottom to the exact depth they wanted for the thickness of the hull. These are called gauge holes. Wooden plugs would then be driven into the holes. As the Europeans hollowed out the interior, they knew to stop when they reached the plugs. Somehow the Native Americans knew when to stop without the use of gauge holes. So the first thing we look for when we come across a dugout is tool marks and gauge holes denoting a historic canoe or burn marks indicating a prehistoric one.

As it happened, 1980 was a banner year for dugout canoes in South Carolina. Institute staff surveyed four canoes that year. These were the Kizer-Judy Canoe, the Ferguson Canoe, the Cut Dam Canoe, and the Chessey Creek Canoe. Three of the canoes were historic. Only one, the Cut Dam Canoe, was prehistoric. The builders of the three historic canoes used cypress to make their craft, while the maker of the Cut Dam Canoe utilized pine.

Discovered in the Edisto River near Branchville in September 1980, the Kizer-Judy Canoe was removed from the river by Furman Kizer, J. V. Judy, and eight others. Institute staff subsequently photographed and measured the canoe and assisted its finders in placing the dugout in a secure underwater storage area. Institute staff reported that the canoe was in excellent condition when they inspected it, despite the fact that loggers who attempted to remove it thirty years earlier broke off one end. In addition to adze marks, wooden plugs driven into gauge holes mark the canoe as historic. The remaining length of the canoe is 28 feet 7 inches. The canoe is 2 feet 5 inches wide at the widest point.

Also in September 1980, Ralph Ferguson discovered a canoe in the Edisto River near Cottageville. He and five others removed the canoe, took it to his home, and contacted the institute. It was visited by institute staff the next day. Tool marks, square nails, and a length of wrought-iron chain reveal it as historic. The staff members reported that the stern was rotted and a small portion was missing. There also was a hole in the bottom. Its flat bottom and shallow draft convinced the observers that the canoe was probably used in the local swamps. The canoe measures 15 feet 4 inches in length and 2 feet 5 inches in width.

The Cut Dam Canoe was discovered in Beach Creek in the Wateree Swamp. It was recovered by Bunk Cain, Jessie Singleton, and Tommy Mullis, all from Sumter, and taken to Cain's home. Institute staff who visited the canoe reported that only one end of it remained and that it was rotted and waterlogged. Despite its condition the canoe was determined to be prehistoric. What remained of the dugout was 8 feet 6 inches long and 2 feet wide. Institute staff and the canoe's finders subsequently placed the canoe in a pond near Cain's home.

An article that ran in the *Walterboro Press and Standard* in 1980 (coincidentally while I was the newspaper's managing editor) alerted institute staff to the recovery of a dugout canoe in Colleton County. Earl Marvin of Walterboro found the canoe in a swamp off Chessey Creek on property owned by Bink Sanders. Institute staff visited the canoe in October 1980 and found it to be in fair condition, considering a dragline digging a canal in the area removed it from its original resting place twenty years earlier and unceremoniously dumped it onto the dredge spoil pile. Part of one gunwale was missing, perhaps because of the dragline, and the interior of the canoe had filled with dirt and roots over the years. Tool marks and cut nails indicated the canoe was historic. The canoe was 12 feet 11 inches long and 1 foot 6 inches wide.

Institute staff members Alan Albright, Ralph Wilbanks, and Chris Craft returned to the Chessey Creek Canoe site in March 1982 with the intent of removing the canoe. The problem was that it was on the other side of the canal built twenty years earlier. To get over the canal, they brought along the institute's seventeen-foot johnboat. Their plan was to launch the johnboat, with seats removed, paddle across to the other side, drag the johnboat to the canoe, load the canoe into the johnboat, and then reverse the process. Everything went well until they got back to the other side. Getting the canoe into the johnboat, dragging it back into the water, and paddling both vessels across was one thing; getting them out of the canal and onto the trailer was another. To solve their problem, they tied a rope from a truck to the johnboat and dragged it out of the canal, stopping when they were under a large oak tree. They then rigged the canoe with ropes and slings and lifted it out of the johnboat using a strong limb of the oak tree and the truck. After wrestling the johnboat back onto the trailer, they lowered the canoe into it.

They drove straight to Charles Towne Landing, where the Chessey Creek Canoe was to be displayed. Once there a small front-end loader lifted the canoe out of the johnboat and onto a wooden cradle. A professional exterminator then applied an insecticide. Three months later institute staff returned. After cleaning the last of the roots and dirt out of the canoe, they applied a preservative consisting of Butvar B-98 (polyvinyl butyral) in ethyl alcohol. The crew brushed on four coats of the substance.

Dugout canoes, both historic and prehistoric, vary widely. To date the longest canoe reported to the state was found in the Wando River in 2005 by Walter Rixson of Awendaw. It measures 36 feet 9 inches long and 2 feet 4 inches wide. Only about four feet of the canoe is exposed at low tide. The rest is buried under marsh. Its length was determined by probing down through the overlaying mud with a metal probe. The shortest canoe measured 10 feet 10 inches in length. Found in the Edisto River, the canoe was made of cypress. Gauge holes make it historic. The canoe is 2 feet wide, making it six inches wider than the narrowest canoes yet found. Two canoes, the Chessey Creek Canoe and a prehistoric canoe found in the Ashepoo River, share this honor. Both measured 1 foot 6 inches wide. The widest canoe we have inspected is the Lawn Canoe, measuring a whopping 3 feet $4\frac{1}{2}$ inches wide.

The Lawn Canoe would also win the most interestingly placed canoe contest, if such a competition existed. Lynn Harris heard about the canoe in 2002 from a member of SCIAA's Archaeological Research Trust (ART) board of directors. The shifting sands of Myrtle Beach exposed the canoe some years earlier. To prevent its destruction by the elements, it was removed. It now resides on the banks of a small creek off the

Waccamaw River, specifically in the backyard of the Don Russell family of Pawleys Island. Lynn and I visited the canoe in March 2002. It rests near a corner of the lawn, seemingly afloat on a raised bed of ornamental grasses, pansies, and contrasting mulch. Gauge holes, a mast step, and tiller attachments indicate that the canoe is historic. Having a mast and being found on the beach suggest the canoe sailed in coastal waters as well as navigating lowcountry rivers. The canoe is 21 feet 3 inches long, not the longest canoe we have studied, but its record-setting width implies that it carried cargo.

Many historic canoes were used for personal transportation or fishing, but many more were built for hauling cargo. When John Lawson traveled through South Carolina in 1701, he saw dugout canoes carrying cargoes of lumber and as many as thirty barrels of goods. He noted that the canoes he observed were made of cypress. In 1731 the *South Carolina Gazette* reported that a large canoe had gone missing from White Point. It was carrying a cargo of 530 barrel staves. While the Lawn Canoe is the widest canoe we have recorded, there is evidence that even wider dugout canoes were common. Colonial South Carolina newspapers abound in notices of lost or found canoes. A notice in a 1741 *Gazette* describes a cypress canoe lost "from the Point of Pines on Edisto Island" as being 28 feet long and 4 feet 8 inches wide. In 1768 a notice in the *Gazette* describes two lost cypress canoes. Both were 16 feet long. One is described as being 3 feet 10 inches wide, and the other as 4 feet wide. Another notice describes a cypress canoe, found on "the North Bar," as being 24 feet long and 4 feet 6 inches wide.

Studying the physical aspects of both historic and prehistoric dugout canoes can give us interesting insights into how their owners used these versatile craft. But the fact remains that the study of dugout canoes is a study of the finished product. The dugouts we find and study are the result of hours and hours of work using long-forgotten construction techniques. Archaeologists never get to study the actual construction. They never get to look over the shoulder of a dugout maker and watch the vessel take shape, to observe the methods used in shaping the log into a usable watercraft. They never get to study the dugout canoe as a work in progress—well, almost never. In early 1977 institute archaeologists recovered a cypress dugout canoe from the Waccamaw River in Georgetown County. Discovered by Patrick O'Rear of Pawleys Island protruding from and partially buried in the riverbank, the canoe was routinely covered and uncovered by the tides. Mr. O'Rear, a member of the Archaeological Society of South Carolina, notified institute staff. Because its periodic exposure left the canoe vulnerable to possible damage,

Roots Canoe, still attached to stump of tree, shown after retrieval
from the Waccamaw River. SCIAA photograph

the institute staff decided to recover it. In February 1977 Underwater
Archaeology Division staff members Alan Albright, Dr. Newell Wright,
and Ralph Wilbanks arrived at the site with the intention of excavating
and removing the canoe. Funding for the project came from the South
Carolina Museum Commission and the institute. The institute team

figured it would take three days to accomplish the task. Boy, were they wrong.

An initial examination of the canoe revealed three things. First, clearly visible adze, ax, and saw marks confirmed that the canoe was historic. Second, it remained unfinished. Third, the uncompleted craft was still attached to its tree trunk, including the tree's base and roots, which were buried under the riverbank. As the archaeology team worked to uncover the canoe and free the tree base from the riverbank, days turned into weeks. Working with shovels and a water jet, they removed the mud covering the tree. This work could only be done at low tide, while the canoe and tree were exposed, limiting the team's workday to five hours at best. As they uncovered the tree's roots, they realized they would never be able to free all of them. They would have to cut them. The roots exposed at low tide were easily sawed. For the bottom roots, members of the team donned scuba gear and cut them underwater using a bow saw.

With most of the mud removed, the team began attaching fifty-five-gallon drums to the canoe and tree. The drums were filled with water and sunk alongside the canoe. The drums then were strapped to the canoe and tree with the cargo straps used to raise the Brown's Ferry Vessel the previous summer. At low tide, with the drums exposed, the water was drained and the drums were sealed. Fourteen drums were used in all, with an estimated total lift capacity of more than seven tons. On day fifteen of the project, an exceptionally high tide provided the opportunity to float the canoe and tree, and the team was able to pull it out into the river. Then it was a twelve-mile trip to Georgetown, pulling the canoe with the institute's twenty-foot McKee. Slowed by the drag of the tree, the trip took more than five hours. At Georgetown the canoe was tied up to a dock on the Sampit River. At first the team tried to lift the canoe out of the water using a boat lift, but after the lift began to twist with the weight, a crane was called in. Papco Construction Company, a subsidiary of the International Paper Company, supplied the crane, and the canoe was finally loaded onto a flatbed truck for the short ride to the Georgetown Rice Museum, where it was put on exhibit behind the museum. The institute team built a shed over the canoe and arranged for it to be watered at least once a day. They then returned to Columbia, seventeen days after the beginning of their three-day project.

If it had been finished and separated from the rest of the tree, the canoe would have been 14 feet 7½ inches long and 2 feet 9 inches wide, with a square stern and pointed bow. A large crack runs through both the bow and stern. Could this be the reason why the canoe was left unfinished? Did its maker misjudge the condition of the wood and, reaching a critical point in the canoe's construction, see his hard work go for nothing as the large crack suddenly appeared? We may never know. What can be presumed is that the canoe's maker figured the downed tree on the riverbank would save much effort. He wouldn't have to chop down a tree or transport the finished product to water. The remaining tree stump is 7 feet 10 inches long and 12 feet wide at the base. This would have provided a stable base from which to work on the dugout.

In 1983 the canoe and tree was moved to Columbia, where it was turned over to the South Carolina State Museum for display. The canoe and tree have become known as the Roots Canoe. The name could result from the tree's roots being a visible part of the canoe and tree. More likely, however, it comes from the seemingly endless roots the team had to saw through, both above and under water, to free the canoe from the riverbank.

So whatever happened with Joe Porcelli and the dugout canoe he retrieved from the Cooper River without a license? After her conversation with Mr. Porcelli, Lynn Harris called the institute and apprised them of the situation. It was decided that preservation of the canoe was the primary objective. If Porcelli was threatening to destroy it, then we would confiscate the ancient artifact. Dr. Jonathan Leader, then deputy state archaeologist and SCIAA conservator, and SCIAA staff underwater archaeologist Jim Spirek arrived at our office within hours. We wanted to act fast, before Porcelli had the chance to carry out his threat. We first went to the Mount Pleasant Police Department. While institute personnel have the right to confiscate illegally obtained artifacts under the law, we were uncertain about our rights to enter private property. We wanted backup.

We explained the situation to the officer who spoke with us. He agreed that we had the authority to visit Porcelli and retrieve the canoe. What would you like us to do? he asked. We were somewhat taken aback. We thought he would know the best way to go about this. The officer then went to get his sergeant. We again explained the situation. The sergeant asked what we wanted them to do. To say we were somewhat frustrated is understating the situation. Whatever it takes to accomplish the retrieval of the canoe with the least amount of trouble was our answer. The sergeant then went to get his lieutenant, and the whole explanation was repeated. The lieutenant decided to call in a South Carolina Department of Natural Resources (DNR) law enforcement officer. Perhaps he will know how to handle this, the lieutenant said. His ability to come to this conclusion is, no doubt, why he was a lieutenant.

A short time later, DNR officer Angus MacBride arrived. Once again we explained the situation. There was a dugout canoe retrieved illegally from the Cooper River, we told him, and we wanted to retrieve it before it could come to any harm. When we finished, Officer MacBride said without hesitation: "OK, here's what we're going to do. First. . . . "

We arrived at Porcelli's Mount Pleasant home late in the afternoon with a convoy consisting of a DNR law enforcement vehicle, two Mount Pleasant police vehicles, and our SCIAA Suburban. Porcelli was indignant, especially since the police presence at his home had raised a crowd of curious neighbors. We told him none of this would have been necessary if he had not threatened to destroy the artifact. Nevertheless he could not understand what all the fuss was about. We tried to explain. Prehistoric dugout canoes are delicate artifacts. Retrieving them without using extreme care could easily destroy the valuable artifact. Indeed several large chunks of the canoe had been broken off during Porcelli's recovery of the canoe. Not only that, but retrieval of the canoe without notifying the institute denied us, and therefore the people of South Carolina, the knowledge about early Native Americans that could be gotten through a thorough, professional study of the canoe in its original location. Our explanation fell on deaf ears. We finally got his attention when Officer MacBride cited him. He subsequently paid a fine of $125.

We had the canoe radiocarbon dated. It turns out that it was made 3,770, plus or minus 60, years, B.P. This makes the canoe one of the oldest found in South Carolina, indeed in the whole Southeast. We placed the canoe in a conservation tank at the institute's Charleston field office, located at the Fort Johnson Marine Resources Center on James Island, where it is now available for study.

The *Hunley*, the *Housatonic*, and the *Indian Chief*

They say the only true measure of an archaeological endeavor is how much it enriches the cultural record—in other words, how much we learn about our past and therefore ourselves. Based on that criterion, the *H. L. Hunley* project has been a smashing success. Numerous television documentaries and books, dozens of magazine articles, hundreds of newspaper and television news reports, and at least one movie have enlightened us on the story of the famous submersible, both past and present. The *Hunley* recovery project has deepened our knowledge of both the submarine technology developed during the Civil War and the motivations of the men involved. During my participation in the project, I learned about another form of human motivation, particularly where the Civil War is involved. This stems from the fact that the Civil War is often more than just "not forgotten" (as popular bumper stickers proclaim). It is revered. This goes for anything associated with it.

Summer 1994—The volunteer diver geared up for her dive in the coastal waters off Sullivan's Island. We were investigating magnetometer hits in the sandy bottom, any one of which could be the *H. L. Hunley*, recorded by best-selling author Clive Cussler and his National Underwater and Maritime Administration (NUMA) crew. After years of searching for the *Hunley*, Cussler had joined with the SCIAA's Underwater Archaeology Division for another attempt to locate the elusive submarine. The diver assembled her tank, regulator, and buoyancy compensator, then pulled a Confederate flag out of her gear bag and stuffed it inside the top of her wet suit before zipping it closed. As diving supervisor for the project, one of my jobs was to make sure the divers were properly equipped. As far as I knew, Confederate flags were not standard scuba gear.

I asked her what she intended to do with the flag. Her response was that she planned to rub the flag on the *Hunley*'s metal hull. We hadn't yet found the *Hunley*. This site was just one of many we would examine in our search. Nonetheless she had a Confederate flag ready. You couldn't fault her optimism. Should she find the *Hunley* on her dive and succeed in rubbing the flag on the submarine, I pictured her holding the now-blessed flag to her bosom much like a devout Catholic would the Shroud of Turin.

Summer 1999—One day during our excavation of the USS *Housatonic*, a diver returned to the surface with a surprise. Three years earlier, while performing our preliminary excavation of the *Hunley*, the flagpole holding our dive flag tangled with some line during a summer squall and was lost overboard. Little did we suspect the flagpole with flag still attached had migrated to the *Housatonic* site to be found by one of the divers. The flag was trash, marine growth covering much of the deteriorated and ripped fabric, but we were glad to get the stainless-steel pole back. I noticed one of the other volunteer divers watching me intently as I cut the remains of the flag off the pole. His eyes almost bugged out of his head when I stuffed the shredded flag into the plastic grocery store bag that hung from the cabin door handle pretending to be a trash bag.

He looked amazed and asked if I were throwing it away. I thought I just had. Nevertheless I answered yes. There was no point in keeping the tattered remains. The flag would never again be able to serve its purpose. It would never again warn others that we were conducting diving operations.

Noting that it was the very flag that flew over the first excavation of the *Hunley*, he grabbed it out of the plastic Piggly Wiggly bag, asking if he could have it. Apparently our laughter failed to deter the diver as he folded the flag and gently placed it in his dive bag.

"What are you going to do with it?" I asked him.

"I'm going to have it framed," he said seriously.

"Of course you are," I replied. I didn't know what else to say.

Shortly after our 1996 preliminary excavation of the *Hunley*, I went to my local Piggly Wiggly to get a gallon of milk. I was wearing a T-shirt emblazoned on the back with the words "Hunley Dive Team." Big mistake. No sooner had I entered the supermarket than I was accosted by a total stranger.

"Did you actually dive on the *Hunley*?" he asked. I smiled and answered yes.

"What was it like seeing it for the first time?" This is akin to a minor actor, say an extra in big-budget movie, being asked what it was like meeting Tom Hanks or Mel Gibson.

"It was really special," I said, almost meaning it. Actually it was very much like looking at an old boiler. After all the *Hunley* had been built from an iron boiler. So what else should it look like?

"Did you touch it?" he asked.

"Of course," I answered, still smiling. It would be nearly impossible to excavate a shipwreck without touching it. I start to say that, but then realize it's too late.

"Wow," he said, eyes glazing over. (It was about this time in the conversation when I began to regret wearing the T-shirt.) As my questioner's eyes refocused, he asked, "Just between you and me, who really found the *Hunley*? Did Clive Cussler really find it, or did Lee Spence?"

I'm often asked this question, which leads me to another cultural lesson I learned from the *Hunley* project—egos often take priority over science.

The controversy over who found the *Hunley* continues to this day. Cussler is officially credited with the discovery of the Civil War submarine. He is also credited with finding the German submarine *U-20*, which sank the *Lusitania*.

E. Lee Spence (he likes to be called "Dr. Spence") is a colorful character. He has found several shipwrecks, mostly blockade runners, off Charleston's coast. He claims he found the *Hunley* first. In fact he has made his claim so widely and so stridently that in 2001 Clive Cussler sued Spence for defamation. Spence countersued, claiming he lost between $100,000 and $309 million by not being officially recognized as the original finder. In May 2007 senior U.S. District Court judge Sol Blatt Jr. dismissed Spence's countersuit on the grounds that the statute of limitations on Spence's claim had expired. As Brian Hicks noted in his article in the *Charleston Post and Courier* about Judge Blatt's dismissal, "This fight has already lasted longer than the Civil War."

So who really found the *Hunley*? Should Cussler, the generally accepted discoverer, retain the title? Or should Spence be recognized as the true finder? The truth is it doesn't matter. Is the cultural enrichment gained by the discovery of the *Hunley* enhanced in any way by who made the discovery? Will the knowledge gained from the recovery and conservation of the submarine change in any way should Spence be ultimately credited with the discovery? Of course not.

The truth is there are some discoveries that transcend any one person or group. Can you name the person who found the Rosetta stone? Or the person who first excavated the tomb of Tutankhamen? How about the person who discovered the Dead Sea Scrolls? Not one of those questions will ever find its way into a game of Trivial Pursuit. The fame of those who found these astounding artifacts was short lived. Ultimately the identity of the finder becomes a mere footnote to the whole episode and one soon forgotten, while the discovery itself works its way into the vernacular of today's society. This is as it should be.

So why is Spence so hot on being acknowledged as the finder? His claim that he has lost millions of dollars by not receiving recognition as the true finder, presumably on movie and book rights, is pure supposition. So why has he spent endless hours publishing diatribes on the Internet trying to prove his case? Is it all ego? Does he hope to become the answer to a Trivial Pursuit question? Is that enough reason to become involved in a costly lawsuit with Cussler over *Hunley* bragging rights?

By the way the person credited with finding the Rosetta stone is army lieutenant Pierre-François Xavier Bouchard of Napoleon's French forces occupying Egypt in 1799. While clearing away debris in their fort just north of the town of Rosetta, he and his men came across perhaps one of the most significant artifacts ever found. In 1947 a Bedouin goatherd named Muhammad Adh-Dhib discovered the Dead Sea Scrolls while looking for a lost goat. And Howard Carter is the person who discovered Tutankhamen's tomb.

Obviously the tale of the *Hunley* involves the *Housatonic*. The historic encounter between the *Hunley* and the *Housatonic* on February 17, 1864, not only marked the first time a submersible vessel managed to sink a warship; it also marked the end of the two vessels in watery graves off Sullivan's Island. No retelling of the *Hunley* story fails to include the *Housatonic*. Yet another vessel's history weaves into that of the *Hunley*. Less known is the part played by the CSS *Indian Chief*, a lowly receiving ship anchored for much of the Civil War in Charleston Harbor.

During the Civil War, naval receiving ships functioned as barracks for transient sailors, as "boot camps" for training sailors, and as headquarters for a variety of other auxiliary functions. They were invariably older vessels, no longer useful as warships or no longer seaworthy. They spent their days in harbor, at anchor or tied up to piers. They served their cause in the only way that remained to them before being scrapped. Each of the major Southern ports had a receiving ship. The CSS *United States* served as receiving ship in Norfolk. The CSS *Arctic* was assigned to Wilmington. Savannah had the CSS *Sampson,* Mobile had the CSS *Dalman,* and New Orleans had the CSS *St. Philip.* In 1862 the CSS *Indian Chief* became Charleston's receiving ship.

Little about the *Indian Chief* is known. The where and when of its construction and its activities before coming to Charleston in 1862 have yet to be discovered. The only contemporary description of the vessel, albeit brief, comes in passing from a Confederate naval veteran who claimed he was assigned picket boat duty in Charleston during 1863. He notes that his headquarters was on the "full rig ship *Indian Chief.*" This would have meant a three-masted, square-rigged ship.

What little we know of its activities as a receiving ship comes from official records. On October 22, 1862, Lt. W. G. Dozier was relieved of command of the Confederate steamer *Huntress* and given command of the *Indian Chief,* relieving Lieutenant Ingraham. Dozier, a native South Carolinian, had been in the U.S. Navy prior to the war and served as lieutenant and acting master of the frigate *Richmond* of the Mediterranean squadron. His resignation from the navy was accepted the day following South Carolina's passage of the ordinance of secession. Offering his services to the state, he was appointed to the coast and harbor police before transferring to the Confederate States Navy.

On November 10, 1862, the Confederate navy paymaster approved a pay voucher of $12.50 to the Mount Pleasant Ferry Company for transporting fifty-two seamen and their baggage to the *Indian Chief.* Other references to the Charleston receiving ship during this time indicate similarly routine activities. In 1863, however, its role for the Confederacy expanded.

The official records of the Confederate States Navy indicate that one of the *Indian Chief*'s auxiliary duties was to serve as a workshop and assembly platform for the Confederate torpedo boats. On August 24, 1863, Flag Officer J. R. Tucker ordered Lieutenant Dozier to have "as many boats fitted with torpedoes [mines] as you can hoist up to the davits of the *Indian Chief* and have them ready for service." In addition to commanding the *Indian Chief,* Dozier seems to have been put in charge of the torpedo boat operations. The order from Tucker addresses Dozier as "commanding special expedition."

This involvement with the torpedo boats brought the *Hunley* into the picture. At this same time, the *Hunley* began practice runs underneath the *Indian Chief.* Witnesses aboard the *Indian Chief* watched the *Hunley,* towing a mock torpedo, dive as it approached the receiving ship, surfacing twenty minutes later on the other side of the ship. The crew of the *Hunley* practiced this maneuver repeatedly, sometimes several times a day.

Following the sinking and loss of the first *Hunley* crew at Fort Johnson on August 29, 1863, Confederate naval commanders gave command of the submersible to Lt. George E. Dixon, despite Horace Hunley's request to command the vessel. On October 15, with Dixon out of town, Hunley took command of the *Hunley* for a practice run under the

Indian Chief. The crewmen of the receiving ship watched the submarine approach their ship and dive beneath the waters of the Cooper River. Moving to the other side of their ship, they waited for the *Hunley* to resurface. After watching for some time, they realized the vessel was not going to surface. The submarine had gone to the bottom, entombing Hunley and the seven-man crew. Three days later divers found the submersible under the *Indian Chief,* which had to be moved from its anchorage so that recovery of the *Hunley* could be performed.

Shortly after raising and refitting the *Hunley,* Dixon was aboard the *Indian Chief* recruiting a new crew. He had no trouble finding more seamen to crew the lethal submersible. Apparently undaunted by the loss of the vessel's previous crews, volunteers eagerly stepped forward. Dixon now had his crew for the fateful attack on the USS *Housatonic* and the Union blockade.

After the historic meeting between the *Hunley* and *Housatonic,* things turned bleak for the blockaded city. On Thursday, August 18, 1864, the following item ran in the *Charleston Mercury:* "The crew of the C.S. *Indian Chief* beg respectfully to return their heartfelt thanks to the Rev. Mr. Yates—who is indeed the sailor's friend—for a liberal donation of clothing lately received, of which they stood greatly in need." Above this item the main headline for the day read "SIEGE MATTERS—FOUR HUNDRED AND SIXTH DAY." Underneath the headline the newspaper nonchalantly noted that, "from 6 p.m., on Tuesday, until the same hour yesterday [Wednesday] 121 shots were fired at Fort Sumter. Sullivan's Island fired 35 shots at Battery Gregg (on Morris Island), to which Battery Wagner (also on Morris Island) replied with 38 shots."

To keep the receiving ship from falling into Union hands, the Confederates burned the *Indian Chief* at its anchorage in Charleston Harbor shortly before evacuating the city on February 18, 1865.

Henry F. Rivers, an associate engineer with the U.S. Army Corps of Engineers, was in charge of dredging operations in Charleston from 1926 to 1948. He notes in his logbooks that in May 1929 he was overseeing the dredging of Town Creek by the dredge *Hallandale,* owned by the Arundel Corporation, when the dredge struck a large obstruction. He returned in July with the snagboat *Wateree* and, using clamshell bucket and dynamite, removed the remains of a vessel. Rivers had no doubt as to the identity of the wreck, recording in his logbook that

> it proved to be the Indian Chief, a three mast schooner of heavy design, used as a receiving ship by the Confederate Navy. Its ribs were 12" x 12" mahogany timbers, butting each other on the keel.

They were solid but as usual when sunken timbers are exposed they dry rot in a short time. The hull was sheathed with Muntz metal, marked Birmingham (I suppose England). Beautiful hand made brass spikes and long copper drift bolts held the hull together. The ship was 150' long.

It is interesting to note that engineer Rivers describes the *Indian Chief* as a "three mast schooner." How did he know the *Indian Chief* was schooner rigged? For that matter how did he know that the vessel remains discovered by the *Hallandale* were that of the *Indian Chief*? He fails to answer either question. He also fails to note what happened to the remains of the vessel. Considered worthless, they logically would have been dumped at the nearest out-of-the-way location—a nearby beach, perhaps.

Julian Weston of Mount Pleasant is like many South Carolinians. He likes to walk lowcountry beaches. One day early in 2002, while walking along the beach at Remley Point at an especially low tide, he came across spikes and metal bars sticking up out of the mud near the water's edge. Poking around in the sand and mud, he found wooden timbers. The spikes turned out to be brass spikes, and the metal bars turned out to be copper drift pins, both used to fasten ship timbers together. Realizing this might be the remains of a shipwreck, he called our office in Charleston. Lynn Harris and I met with Julian and his wife at their lovely old home in downtown Mount Pleasant, where Julian showed us some of the loose brass spikes he had retrieved from the site. He had wire brushed them and had the brass shining like gold. We couldn't wait to see the possible shipwreck he had found.

We drove over to Remley Point. The land adjacent to the beach had been cleared of underbrush. Stakes marked lots for upscale homes overlooking the Wando River. As we put on our boots and gathered our tapes and probes, we realized two things. First, we would need to proceed as quickly as possible, since the development would soon mean a lot more activity along the beach, including the construction of piers and docks that could impact the site. Second, we suspected it would take an archaeologist's entire lifetime earnings to afford just one of the waterfront lots.

A short walk over the marsh brought us to the site, where even from a distance we could see the spikes, metal bars, and deteriorated timbers on the beach. The exposed timbers consisted of a keelson, keel, outer hull planking, and frames. Brass spikes and copper drift bolts (the metal bars) were everywhere.

Mount Pleasant resident Julian Weston standing over remains of wreck at Remley Point. The remains indicate it could be the CSS *Indian Chief,* the Charleston receiving ship used for practice target by the H. L. Hunley. SCIAA photograph by Lynn Harris

Following this preliminary visit, we returned several times in August 2002 for a closer examination of the remains. In addition to Julian, Lynn, and me, we had Joe Beatty, Mike Ameika, Barbara Merchant, and her sons, James and Robert, to complete the team. Mike was a College of Charleston senior anthropology student interning with us. Barbara, from Covington, Georgia, is one of our field training course graduates.

Our first chore was to wash the mud and sand off the wreck. To do this we brought our johnboat and anchored it about fifty feet offshore of the site. We pumped water from the river through a fire hose, careful not to damage or move any of the timbers. This worked fine, and after several accidental slips of the hose that resulted in the crew becoming completely soaked, we soon had the remains uncovered. We found that the framing, although heavily constructed, was rotted and spongy, making measurements nearly impossible. We were able to get some preliminary measurements, however. What remained of the hull extended a little more than forty-four feet in length and was fifteen feet wide at the widest section. The keelson measured twelve inches by twelve inches. The framing members were placed close together, almost butting each other at the keel, but were too deteriorated to get useful measurements. The outer hull planking measured three-quarters of an inch thick and appeared to be covered with copper sheathing.

Subsequent to our work on Julian's wreck, Lynn Harris was researching shipwrecks in Charleston Harbor at the South Carolina Historical Society when she came across the logbooks of Henry F. Rivers. She read his description of the remains of the *Indian Chief.* "Heavy design," "timbers butting each other at the keel," "brass spikes and long copper drift bolts"—this sounded familiar. She realized the description matched much of what we knew about the Remley Point wreck. But what about the rest of the description, that is, the twelve-by-twelve-inch mahogany timbers and Muntz metal sheathing? The frames (ribs), apparently in poor condition even in 1929, proved too deteriorated to get satisfactory measurements. They could have originally measured twelve inches by twelve inches. We have not had the wood typed to see if the frames were mahogany. The consensus was that the wood was too spongy and worm eaten for type testing. So no luck there.

In 1832 George Frederick Muntz patented a new alloy for sheathing vessels. It consisted of 60 percent copper and 40 percent zinc. The addition of zinc slowed the deterioration of the sheathing, thus lowering the costs of keeping a ship protected from worms. It soon replaced copper as the most widely used method of sheathing wooden ships. We had the sheathing from the wreck analyzed, and sure enough it turned out to be Muntz metal. None of the sheathing we examined was marked "Birmingham," however, as noted by engineer Rivers.

Could Julian Weston's discovery at Remley Point be the CSS *Indian Chief*? Much of Rivers's description seems to fit the vessel remains we recorded. Although he neglected to specify what they did with the *Indian Chief* once they removed it, the beach at Remley Point would have been the logical place to dump the debris. It would be satisfying if we could definitively identify the Remley Point site as the CSS *Indian Chief.* It would provide closure to the story of this vessel that played a large part in the story of the *H. L. Hunley.* Archaeologists like closure. Our comparison of Henry Rivers's logbooks and the vessel remains do not provide conclusive proof that this is the *Indian Chief,* however. More information is needed. We can only hope that perhaps someday additional records will be discovered that provide the information required for verification. Nevertheless the logbooks of Rivers show how history and archaeology are as inseparable as the stories of some ships.

The Mysterious French Cargo Site

Every now and again maritime archaeologists come across an underwater site that defies explanation, one that leaves them scratching their heads in sheer bewilderment. One such site is in the west branch of the Cooper River.

In July 1995 sport divers Steve Nash of Holly Hill, South Carolina, and Phil Myers were searching for artifacts on the bottom of the river when they came across something that baffled them. Steve was a graduate of our underwater archaeology field training course, and he and Phil held current South Carolina hobby diver licenses. Steve realized his find might be important, so he called Lynn Harris, then head of the Sport Diver Archaeological Management Program. He told her that he and his dive buddy had found a mound of artifacts consisting of discrete groupings of various items, including wine bottle shards, pottery shards, brass and copper buttons, silver and brass buckles, and an abundance of musket balls and gunflints.

Lynn asked him about vessel remains associated with the artifacts. It was the standard question in such cases. His answer startled her: there were none. He said he could find no timbers or ship parts among the artifacts. He did find a block and some iron rings that could be ship hardware and a pile of "river rock" that could be ballast, but nothing else that indicated a vessel of any kind.

Intrigued by Steve's phone call, Lynn called the entire staff of the Charleston office of SCIAA's Underwater Archaeology Division into her office. That meant her and me. From what Steve told her, we believed the artifacts could constitute the cargo of some ill-fated sailing vessel. But Steve said no vessel remains were in the vicinity. Where did the pile of artifacts come from? Stumped, we had to see this site for ourselves.

A week later we met Steve and Phil at Cypress Gardens Landing on Durham Creek. A short ride down Durham Creek brought us to the west branch of the Cooper River, and an even shorter ride brought us to our target site. We hurriedly donned our scuba gear and entered the murky waters, colored a dark tea color by the tannin in the water.

Sure enough a mound of artifacts appeared out of the gloom when we reached the bottom. As Steve told us, a portion of the mound consisted of dark green glass bottle shards. The shards all appeared to be from bottles of a consistent shape, meaning they would be of a consistent date. We also saw the piles of green-glazed ceramics and musket balls. Poking around under the artifact heaps, we found the "river rock" Steve mentioned. It appeared to be flint cobble, indicating it definitely was a vessel's ballast. After our first dive, Lynn decided to make a map of the artifact mound on our second dive, while I would search up, across, and down the river for any indication of a vessel or at least some vessel parts.

The cargo, as we believed the pile of artifacts constituted, sits on a hard marl bottom in about twenty feet of water, fifty feet from the west shore. On the other side of the mound, the bottom gently slopes down to a depth of about forty feet before steeply rising to the eastern shore. Visibility was about as good as it normally gets in a lowcountry river, about five feet. I first swam downriver, zigzagging as I went to cover as much ground as possible. Judging distances underwater can be difficult, especially zigzagging along the nondescript, hard marl bottom, but I went at least fifty yards before turning and going across river. I went down into the channel and up the other side, coming to the other riverbank. I then slid back down into the deep part of the channel, thinking that any loose part may have found its way there. I zigzagged up the channel. When I was what I figured to be about fifty yards upriver from the site, I worked my way back. The entire bottom in the area was hard, dotted with areas of sand and gravel. I found no ship parts. No keel, no keelson, no frames, no planking. Nada, zip, zero.

From what Lynn and I saw during our dives, we had to agree with Steve and Phil, the site appeared to be a cargo neatly piled on the river bottom. The various types of artifacts that would constitute a cargo were clustered together with little mixing. For them to be deposited at the same time, however, the dates of the various artifact types would have to agree to some degree. This would strengthen the idea that they came from the same vessel.

The artifacts we observed included dozens, if not hundreds, of English dark green glass wine bottle shards. Dating these bottle parts, which are a common find in lowcountry waters, is easy thanks to a typology of such bottles compiled by Ivor Noël Hume. While director of archaeology at Colonial Williamsburg, Noël Hume excavated the site of a long-gone tavern, finding an abundance of these English wine bottles. There was a practice from the mid–seventeenth century until the mid–nineteenth century of placing glass seals on many of these containers. The seals were globs of molten glass added to the shoulder of the bottle and stamped with identifying marks. The marks could be initials representing a tavern owner or a gentleman of means who could have his own bottles custom made. Sometimes they indicate what the bottle contained. Years ago, while diving in the west branch of the Cooper River near the Pimlico community, we found the upper remains of a bottle with a glass seal clearly stamped "Claret." In the case of Noël Hume's Williamsburg tavern, the year of the bottles' manufacture was stamped into the glass globs. From studying these seals along with the evolution of the bottles' shapes, Noël Hume came up with his helpful typology. According to the typology, the Cooper River site bottles dated from 1760 to 1780. This gave us a base date range to compare with the other artifacts. If the dates of the other items were comparable, we had an even better case that the artifacts were deposited at the same time and therefore probably from the same vessel.

The two divers also discovered more than five hundred lead musket balls on the site. These were of four different sizes, the majority of which appeared to be the .54-caliber variety. Interestingly this is about the caliber used in American-made rifles before and during the American Revolution. The famous British Brown Bess muskets used a .75-caliber ball, while French muskets, widely imported into America during the Revolution, used a .69-caliber ball. The musket balls from the Cooper River site looked as if recently made. The mold seam lines were plainly visible around each ball. The divers also found several golf-ball-sized lead shot. These were probably canister shot. Since these items dated from the earliest dates of the Carolina colony until the mid–nineteenth century when rifles replaced muskets, they were interesting but did nothing to pin down the site's date.

One of most interesting group of artifacts was the hundreds of green-glazed pottery shards. These were all a form of coarse earthenware with a buff-colored paste body and transparent green lead glaze. These probably would have been packed in crates or barrels. Several barrel staves were found on the site. This was a new form of pottery on us, one we had not seen before. We took several pieces to Columbia and showed them to various members of the institute staff. The consensus was that they were French. The green glaze is called an "apple glaze." And the dates were right—middle to late eighteenth century.

Next we looked at the assortment of silver, pewter, and brass shoe and belt buckles found by the divers. Unfortunately metal buckles are not closely datable, as they are found on American sites dating from 1700 to 1800. One of the buckles appears to be a woman's shoe buckle whose style was common about 1750, however.

So far nothing refuted the 1760 to 1780 dates for the artifacts.

A portion of the cargo consisted of dozens of buttons, including bone, brass, and soft metal buttons. Like the shoe and belt buckles, buttons are difficult to date precisely, but the styles of buttons recovered were used primarily from 1726 to 1776. Forty-six of the buttons appear to be military uniform buttons of French origin.

The divers also found an abundance of gunflints. Two types of gunflints are found in South Carolina—English and French. English gunflints have square backs, while French gunflints have rounded backs. All the gunflints recovered by the divers had rounded backs. The fact that they were French is not surprising. The majority of gunflints found in colonial and Revolutionary archaeological sites are French. At that time French gunflints were considered superior to the English gunflints. Like the musket balls, gunflints were used until the mid–nineteenth century.

Other isolated artifacts found at the site were most likely personal items of the crew. The divers recovered several varieties of ceramics, the most datable of which was a piece of scratch-blue salt-glazed stoneware. Around 1750 English potteries began making a form of white salt-glazed stoneware decorated with incised lines forming simple floral designs. The incisions were filled with cobalt that when fired produced bright blue lines. These pieces most often took the form of bowls and pitchers. This came to be known as "scratch blue" and was popular until about 1775. The other ceramic pieces consisted of tin enameled earthenware. Several pieces of tobacco pipes were recovered. These were made with kaolin clay, the common material for smoking pipes until circa 1900. Dating pipes relies on the known evolution of the bowl size and shape. The specimens found are typical of smoking pipes used in America between 1730 and 1790. Also found were the brass top and bottom of a sword scabbard that appear to be of French origin.

The divers also found several coins on the site. These consisted of two Spanish silver half reals and a Spanish two-real silver Cobb coin. These Spanish coins were minted in Mexico and dated 1731, 1738, and 1744. There were also several British halfpennies. Unfortunately the dates on many of those were unreadable, but two had dates of 1749 and 1754.

Two silver half reals and a two-real silver Cobb coin, center, found at mysterious cargo site in Cooper River. These Spanish coins were minted in Mexico and dated 1731, 1738, and 1744. SCIAA photograph by Eddie Weathersbee

The 1754 halfpenny, being the latest coin, provides us with what archaeologists call a *terminus post quem*. This is Latin for "the site can't possibly be earlier than this because this artifact did not exist before that date," or something like that. Of course it could date much later. This dating technique works best with coins, but can also work less precisely with other types of artifacts.

So it seemed our site dated no earlier than 1754. Putting a similar end date, or a *terminus ante quem*, on a site is difficult. Artifacts can still be around long after their manufacture. Often, however, we can come up with a general end date for a site. One of the best types of artifacts used to determine *terminus ante quem* is ceramics. Ceramic styles and types changed often, and we know the dates of these changes. For example white salt-glazed stoneware replaced delft as the most popular and common form of dinnerware about 1720. Therefore one can generalize that if we find an abundance of delft but no white salt-glazed stoneware (or any other later ceramic) on a site, it probably dates before 1720.

So what about our site? Bottle shards dating 1760 to 1780. Ceramic shards dating 1750 to 1800. Buckles from 1700 to 1800 with one datable to around 1750. Buttons from 1726 to 1776. A stoneware shard dating from 1750 to 1775. Smoking pipes from 1730 to 1790. And that British halfpenny of 1754. The dates seemed consistent to us. We judged the cargo was deposited sometime between 1754 and about 1780.

The real question is what happened to the vessel? I suppose it is possible that the timbers disappeared through deterioration. This seems highly doubtful. Surely there would be some pieces of the vessel left. There are other sites of the same period where the vessel's timbers remain in remarkably good condition. More likely the cargo, in barrels and crates, was jettisoned accidentally from a vessel. Perhaps the vessel had gone upriver as a hurricane closed on the Carolina coast and was overturned in the high winds, spilling its cargo. Without the weight of the cargo, the vessel could have righted itself and survived the storm. Unless historic accounts are found detailing the story of this cargo and its vessel, we shall never know for sure. Another question was what to name the site. It is difficult to call it a shipwreck site without a shipwreck. As a result of there being mostly cargo items and many of them being French—the green-glazed ceramics, military buttons, sword scabbard, and gunflints—we call it the French Cargo Site. Still it is strange not having at least a part of a shipwreck to work with. And we will probably never know how the mound of artifacts ended up where it is. Perhaps we should have named it the Mysterious French Cargo Site.

The Cooper River Anchor Farm

What *is* it about old ship anchors? What exactly is their appeal as decorative items? I can see why a seafood restaurant would want a few of these barnacle-encrusted relics outside the premises, perhaps on either side of the front door. Should a prospective customer miss the forty-foot fiberglass lobster/crab/fish (pick one) on the roof or the red-and-green channel buoys marking the entrance to the parking lot, the anchors are sure to quell any doubt that seafood is served inside.

Old anchors are just gawky hunks of iron, usually rusting. Yet I see these nautical artifacts embellishing the most unnautical places. I see them as centerpieces in front yards of homes. I see them gracing flower-beds in back yards. I see them as mailbox posts. I see them displayed in public parks and in front of National Guard armories. I once visited a home near Charleston just before Christmas and was greeted by a seven-foot anchor propped upright in the corner of the living room, decorated like a Christmas tree with lights and ornaments. I wouldn't be surprised to see one marking a grave site in some cemetery.

I also see them in scuba shops, often in window displays showing off the newest dive masks and regulators or draped with this year's line of wet suits. Or they are strategically placed around the store as apparent evidence of the staff's diving prowess—subliminal messages to customers that they too could collect a maritime treasure from the ocean bottom (if they do business only with that dive shop).

Unfortunately these lawn ornaments, mailbox poles, and dive shop displays, now removed from their underwater resting places, usually lack proper conservation and are left to do what they do naturally, that is, corrode away to nothing. Or they are painted, usually black or silver (although I once saw a turquoise one), in a futile attempt to prolong their inevitable deterioration.

The problem is that iron does not get along well with seawater. As soon as an iron object, such as an eighteenth- or nineteenth-century anchor, settles on the seafloor, it begins to corrode through chemical reactions far too complicated (for me) to explain here. This corrosion can be due to biological as well as chemical reactions, as bacteria in seawater can account for as much as 60 percent of the deterioration. At the same time, minerals, bits of sand, and organic material in the seawater begin concreting on the surface of the iron, forming a coral-like encrustation. Often those who retrieve anchors from a saltwater environment believe they are rescuing the anchor from this corrosion. They are in fact making things worse. Without proper conservation, air accelerates the formation of rust. And worse, the saltwater that has infiltrated the cracks and crevices in the iron evaporates. The salt particles that remain solidify and expand, enlarging the cracks and crevices, causing huge flakes of rust to fall away from the iron. Despite all this, however, restaurants, home gardeners, public parks, National Guard armories, and dive shops continue to acquire old iron anchors.

The fact of the matter is that old anchors are easy to acquire. Commercial shrimpers snag them with their nets and pull them up to prevent future snags. Anglers grapple them with their boat anchors and bring them home in lieu of that record catch. Dredge barges suck them up as they go about their job of deepening the shipping channels. Even sport divers retrieve these pieces of maritime history from South Carolina waters (provided they are customers of the right dive shop, of course). Over the years the institute's Maritime Research Division has itself acquired a few of these salvaged relics. Conservation of the anchors, or rather coming up with the money for conservation, being out of the question for our meager budget, we are left with the problem of what to do with them. The answer: the Cooper River Anchor Farm.

In the history of ships, the anchor holds a special place—the seafloor. The first recorded anchors were rocks with lines attached. These rock anchors were flat and triangular with a hole chiseled in one corner for the line. Because they relied on weight to hold the bottom, size mattered, and the larger the better. It wasn't long before anchor makers started drilling holes in the other two corners and ramming wooden poles through them so the poles stuck out on both sides equally. These poles would dig into the bottom (it was hoped), thereby providing better hold for the vessel. Nevertheless these crude devices left much to be desired. This could be why you never see a rock anchor as a cap insignia in any of the world's navies.

By 600 B.C. the Greeks were using anchors made of metal or metal and wood. These anchors had shapes we would recognize today. They had large flukes attached to long shanks and wooden or metal stocks just below the anchor rings. We know this because detailed depictions of these anchors adorn Greek coins from about 600 B.C. until about 400 B.C.

When Mussolini ordered Lake Nemi drained in 1927, several sunken Roman ships emerged. These vessels are believed to be part of Caligula's fleet of about A.D. 40. Along with the ships, two anchors were discovered. These were metal affairs. Their flukes are on arms protruding from the bottom of their shanks. They have stocks, set at right angles to the flukes. Amazingly their overall design, with only slight changes, has come down through the centuries and is little different from anchors used up to the eighteenth and nineteenth centuries.

Ships of the eighteenth and nineteenth centuries carried three different-sized anchors. The largest was the main or bower anchor. It was used when the most holding power was needed, such as in heavy seas or strong currents. When in light seas or light current, such as in a river, a medium-sized anchor called a stream anchor was used. The smallest anchor carried by a ship was the kedge anchor. A kedge anchor moved the ship without using the wind, such as when working up a river against the wind. Lowered into a boat, the kedge was rowed away from the ship in the direction the ship needed to go. After dropping the anchor at the extent of its cable, the ship's crew moved the ship by pulling in the anchor cable, moving the ship to the anchor. This was repeated as many times as necessary. Naval warships carried as many as eight anchors, including one or two kedge anchors, one stream anchor, and as many as five bowers.

The first anchor placed at the anchor farm came to us as the result of nefarious activity. It seems several divers found the anchor while on an artifact dive in the Cooper River. The anchor was too large to bring up using only their personal buoyancy compensators for lift. The fact that recovery was therefore not allowed without a state license apparently never entered their heads. What did enter their heads was the possibility of recovering the anchor using fifty-five-gallon drums. So they returned with the drums and lifted the anchor to the surface. They then towed it to the Pimlico community's private boat landing. There a resident of the community spotted their activities. Perhaps the tow truck used to drag the anchor out of the water and up the boat ramp made him suspicious. In any event the Pimlico resident reported the activity to us.

Maybe it was guilt. Maybe it was being seen by the Pimlico resident. But before we could follow up on the report, one of the divers called us and reported recovering the anchor. We informed the caller that the recovery was illegal under the South Carolina Underwater Antiquities Act (allowing that he didn't already know) and that the anchor would have to be turned over to us. Now what were we going to do with it? The only answer we had was to put the anchor in water, and what better place than back into the Cooper River? We didn't want to put the anchor back were it was originally found. This might tempt the divers or others to retrieve it all over again. The best place to put it was somewhere where we could keep an eye on it. We decided the best place was near the Pimlico Barge. The barge is off the Pimlico community, not far from the Pimlico boat ramp. It is close to the riverbank, allowing a crane to lower the anchor directly to a safe resting place. We visit the barge periodically. There are houses along the banks with watchful eyes. It was a perfect solution, or as perfect as we could find (and afford).

We contacted Jimmy Hightower of Hightower Construction Company for use of one of his cranes. We had some experience with the construction company. When we placed concrete monuments on the Cooper River Heritage Trail, of which the Pimlico Barge was a part, Hightower had graciously donated the use of a crane and several of his employees to load the monuments onto our pontoon boat. He agreed to help us again. We then contacted the divers and set up a date for them to return the anchor. We all met at the Pimlico community. The anchor measured six feet in length and had a folding iron stock. Of course after years in the water, the folding stock no longer folded. Other than that it was in good condition, considering its time out of water did it little good. After our inspection of the anchor, Hightower positioned his crane in the vacant lot adjacent to the location of the Pimlico Barge. The crane lifted the anchor high in the air and lowered it into the water as near as possible to the barge. To make the anchor easy to find for divers visiting the barge (and us), we tied a line from the iron ring on the inshore end of the barge to the anchor.

The second anchor we planted at the anchor farm came from waters off Beaufort County. This was one of those brought up by shrimpers to keep it from snagging their nets. Apparently unable to find a seafood restaurant that wanted it, they donated it to the institute. It arrived at our offices at Fort Johnson Marine Resources Center, which is across the harbor from Charleston on James Island, in early 2000. The anchor measures 8 feet 3.6 inches in total length. The distance from one fluke tip to the other is 3 feet 11 inches. Its size indicates that it was the bower anchor on a sailing ship of about 60 feet in length. Interestingly it has a wooden stock. Iron stocks began replacing wooden ones on smaller anchors starting about 1800, completely replacing them by 1850. This dates our anchor to from circa 1700 to circa 1850. The stock consists of two pieces of oak 7 feet 8.5 inches in length, held together with two rectangular iron hoops. The stock tapers from 7.8 inches where it wraps around the anchor's shank to 4.7 inches at its tips. This tapering allowed the stock pieces to be tightened as they aged by hammering the hoops in toward the anchor's shank. Once again we called on Hightower Construction Company to help us place it at the anchor farm. To get it there, we borrowed a flatbed truck from the South Carolina Department of Natural Resources at Fort Johnson. It took several of us to wrestle the approximately five-hundred-pound anchor into the truck bed. Thankfully when we arrived at Pimlico, Hightower's crane lifted the anchor off the truck for us and deposited it near the first anchor. We then connected the two with heavy polypropylene line.

After placing this second anchor at Pimlico, we began calling the site the "anchor farm." We considered calling it the "anchor collection," since a collection is defined as having more than one of something you don't need, and we sure didn't need two iron anchors. But "anchor farm" stuck. It sounded better. It seemed appropriate. And like any good farm crop, the anchors need tending. We have to monitor their condition. We have to keep them clear of weeds (and fishing line). And we have to make sure they don't walk off and into backyard flowerbeds.

We thought it would end there, with just two anchors. We were wrong. Our farm continued to grow.

The latest addition to the anchor farm came from beneath downtown Charleston. While digging footings on East Bay Street in June 2007, construction workers came across a large iron anchor buried ten feet down in the muddy soil. The workers called Emily Jateff, an archaeologist with Brockington and Associates, a private archaeology firm in Mount Pleasant, who in turn called our Charleston office. Lora Holland and I went to look at the anchor. Emily and James Hunter of the Hunley Conservation project met us there. We were surprised at how large the anchor was. The shank measured 12 feet 4 inches in length. The distance between fluke tips was 7 feet 8 inches. The flukes themselves measured 27 inches long and more than 22 inches across. We estimated it weighed about one ton and dated to the early nineteenth century. It would have had a wooden stock, yet no stock was in evidence. What astonished us was the anchor's condition. Except for one small area where it was apparently in contact with another metal item

A large admiralty anchor is lowered into the Cooper River to join other anchors on the Cooper River Anchor Farm. SCIAA photograph by James Spirek

and some corrosion had formed, the anchor appeared as if new. We speculated that the anchor, brand new at the time, might have fallen into the water, settling into the mud, and was lost while loading it onto its intended ship. As time went by, the area filled in, resulting in the anchor being found underground on the river side of East Bay Street. We also speculated that since the anchor was new, a stock had not yet been attached. We speculated that this might have been why no stock was located by the construction workers. Archaeologists pride themselves on their ability to speculate.

Again we decided to put the anchor at the anchor farm. Again we called on Hightower Construction for assistance. In August 2007 we all met at Pimlico for what has become our anchor placing ritual. Since this was such a large anchor, we were not able to place it as far out in the river as the first two. Instead we lowered it onto the submerged ledge that sits between the bank and the drop-off to the river bottom. To make it easier to find, supposing we would have trouble locating a twelve-foot-long, two-thousand-pound anchor, we tied a line from it to the piling of a nearby dock.

Perhaps the Cooper River Anchor Farm isn't the best place for these relics of seafaring history. It would be more appropriate, of course, for them to be conserved and displayed in maritime museums. Nothing fosters a museum's nautical ambience like an anchor reclining nonchalantly amid the wooden figureheads and glass-encased ship models. If the anchor is from a known ship, moreover, then it gets a place all to itself, with a sign saying that the anchor is from the HMS *Whatever*.

Long ago I heard a tale of a young female archaeologist who claimed that whenever she saw an anchor in a maritime museum she immediately envisioned the vessel, usually under full sail. She said she could smell the sea, feel the sway of the hull, and hear the creaking of the rigging. Apparently it was a big turn-on for her. And should she chance to press her body up against the anchor, she would—

What? It's only a story.

Without a doubt maritime museums would be far better places for our anchors. There the public (as well as a certain female archaeologist) could fully enjoy them. Sadly they remain at the Cooper River Anchor Farm. At least they are not decorating front lawns, enticing scuba divers, holding up mailboxes, or adorning seafood restaurants. And they are not painted black, silver, or (thank heavens) turquoise.

Mowing the Lawn

Perhaps this would be a good place to discuss how maritime archaeologists find shipwrecks. The process starts with archival research. This means dreary hours in library stacks, historical society manuscript collections, public record offices, and newspaper archives and, today, online. Libraries contain a wealth of primary and secondary sources related to shipbuilding, shipping, shipowners, and shipwrecks. Manuscript collections at local historical societies may contain personal diaries and correspondence of seagoing families, shipping records of local merchants, and ship logbooks. At the various public records offices, one finds the deeds and plats regarding shipyards, ferry landings, and public wharfs as well as the tax records, land records, wills, and probate inventories of ship captains, shipowners, and shipbuilders. Newspaper archives give us contemporary accounts of ship launchings, ship voyages, and shipwrecks. Nowadays the Internet provides forums where archaeologists exchange information about current research pertaining to ships, shipwrecks, and maritime artifacts.

Surprisingly good sources of information about shipwrecks are "locals." Shrimpers know the precise locations of objects that snag their nets. Anglers have their favorite offshore fishing spot—that raised bottom where fish seem to gather. Objects that catch shrimp nets and raised bottoms fished by anglers are often vessel remains. Local "historians" and sport divers are other good sources of information.

Once the location of a shipwreck has been pinpointed as best as possible from written and verbal sources, the next step is finding it. In the old days, this was a hit-or-miss endeavor. Mostly miss. Depth finders have been used to find places where the bottom has relief. Grapple hooks and small anchors were dragged across the bottom, hoping to catch ship remains. If visibility allowed, divers could be towed behind a boat to survey the bottom. Of course this could be problematic if there were poisonous jellies in the water and the towing boat's propeller chewed them into small enough pieces to infiltrate wet suits. There is even a story of a researcher who lowered a tape recorder microphone to the bottom and used the changes in noise as the microphone skimmed over the bottom as clues. I kind of doubt this would work with any kind of effectiveness, but I have no doubt the story is true.

If these crude techniques were unsuccessful, divers could search for vessel remains. Using a variety of search techniques—circle searches, jackstay searches, swim line searches, grid searches—divers covered the area until they found the target, or not. Most often not.

Today searching for a shipwreck has gone high tech. Oh, we still do research in libraries, historical societies, public record offices, and newspaper archives. And it is still just as dreary. And we still talk to local sources, but actually finding a wreck now involves using remote sensing equipment—magnetometers, side-scan sonar units, and sub-bottom profilers. For the marine archaeologist, these instruments are the equivalent of the long-range sensors on Captain Kirk's starship *Enterprise*. They are as sophisticated as they are expensive.

Magnetometers detect variations in the strength of the earth's magnetic field caused by the presence of ferrous metals, that is, iron and steel. The advantage of the magnetometer is that it can detect objects buried below the bottom, provided, of course, that they are made of ferrous metal. The larger the object, the deeper it can be detected. We found the top of the *H. L. Hunley* under at least two feet of sand. We first came across the remains of the USS *Housatonic* a good six feet below the bottom. A magnetometer can locate shipwrecks such as these even though they may be much farther below the bottom. Magnetometers are towed behind a boat, keeping them far enough back not to pick up the ferrous metals of the boat itself.

While magnetometers are good for finding metal, it is almost impossible to determine what that metal constitutes. For this there is the side-scan sonar. Side-scan sonar takes a "picture" of the sunken object. By sending out sound pulses and analyzing the echoes, something like a black-and-white picture of the bottom under and to the sides of the survey boat is recorded. The sound pulses are transmitted from a towfish, but they can also be transmitted by hull-mounted devices. On early models the sonar picture was recorded on a paper plotter. Nowadays it's all on computer. Of course for the side scan to record ship remains, some of the vessel must be sticking up from the bottom.

What if there is no portion of the remains showing for the side-scan sonar to "photograph"? There is even an answer for that—sub-bottom

Author retrieving magnetometer towfish as Chris Amer coils the tow cable on board the SCIAA's twenty-five-foot research vessel. The missile-shaped object strapped to the boat's gunwale is the side-scan sonar fish. Photograph courtesy Jack W. Melton Jr.

profilers. These machines were designed to identify layers of sediment or rock under the seafloor. Like the side-scan sonar, the sub-bottom profiler transmits sound pulses, only a much different type. Some of these pulses bounce back off the bottom, but some penetrate down into the sediment and reflect off the different layers. Maritime archaeologists discovered that if the sub-bottom profiler could bounce sound pulses off sediment layers, it should be able to bounce them off buried ship remains.

We observed magnetometer and side-scan equipment in operation during the *Housatonic* project. One day during the project, we had local and state elected officials aboard. One of these was state senator Glen McConnell. After watching the National Park Service operate its magnetometer and side-scan sonar, Senator McConnell turned to us and asked if we had this equipment. We had to laugh. On our budget we would be lucky to afford a tape recorder and microphone to drag along the bottom. We told him no, although we would like to have such equipment and it would be invaluable in helping us manage the state's underwater archaeological sites. He turned to us and said something like, "You will." The following year there was a line item in the South Carolina state budget directing funds to the institute that made good on Senator McConnell's promise.

In 1998 SCIAA's Maritime Research Division purchased an integrated magnetometer, side-scan sonar, differential global positioning system (DGPS), and fathometer unit. Called the ADAP-III, it was custom designed by Sandia Research Facility in Albuquerque, New Mexico. The magnetometer is a Geometrics G-880 cesium marine magnetometer. The side-scan sonar is a Marine Sonic Technology Sea Scan PC. The fathometer is a Cetrek C-net COMBI fathometer. It reads out depths in feet and tenths. The magnetometer, sonar, and depth readings are all correlated with the DGPS. Ours is a Trimble Ag132 differential GPS (originally designed for farm tractors). A differential GPS works somewhat differently than a regular GPS. It records our position to submeter accuracy, specifically in tenths of meters.

When we survey, searching for *Le Prince* or Ayllón's Capitana, for instance, the side-scan unit gives us a continuous acoustic picture of the bottom, and the magnetometer is taking magnetic readings at the rate of up to ten times per second. (We usually change the magnetometer to a one-reading-per-second mode while surveying, saving the ten-per-second mode for pinpointing a known site.) At the same time, the DGPS is updating our position and the fathometer records our depths at the rate of four readings per second. The ADAP-III gives us accuracy a mad scientist would love. The whole array cost $109,000.

Conducting a remote sensing survey over a designated area is like mowing the lawn. I've heard that analogy more times than I can count. Newspaper and magazine articles use it when they talk about remote sensing. I have even seen it used in archaeology textbooks. It has become a cliché. It seems to me to be far too easy, describing how we go down one lane, back up the next, over and over and over, as "like mowing the lawn." You would think someone could come up with a better comparison. When I cut my grass, I don't have to swerve around crab pot buoys, avoid channel markers, steer clear of shrimp trawlers, or keep a wary eye on recreational boaters. Never have I run my Troy-Bilt model 546 lawnmower onto oyster beds, sand shoals, rock jetties, or mudflats. Mountainous waves, blistery winds, and swift currents have never buffeted my motorized grass-mulching machine. Other than that, yeah, it's pretty much like mowing the lawn—although some days it's more like mowing a rock garden during an earthquake.

To set up a survey block we run an "A–B line," point A being one corner of the block and point B being an adjacent corner. This line becomes the side of a survey block. With this information, and whether we want to go left or right of the line, how many lanes we want to run, and the spacing between lanes, the computer generates the survey block or "box." If the first lane is to the left of the A–B line, it becomes lane 1L. If it's to the right, then it's 1R, and so forth. On the dash in front of the boat driver is the "light bar." This has a horizontal row of thirty-six lights. The three middle lights are green. The rest are red. Above the three middle lights is a light that can turn either red or green. Below the row of lights is a digital readout. When the survey boat is in the block and on a lane line, the three green lights are lit, indicating that we are online. The light above will be green, signifying that we are in the block, and the lower level will read whatever lane we are on and the word *good*. When the boat wanders off-line, the three lights move off the green and into the red. The farther off-line, the farther they move. The bottom line will show the lane number, an arrow showing which way to steer to get back to the line, and how far away the line is in meters. "4L>7" means that to get back to lane 4L the helmsman— sorry, helmsperson—needs to move seven meters to starboard. As the boat moves back to the lane, the red lights move back toward the center. When the boat reaches the end of the lane, the top green light turns red, telling the helmsperson that it is time to turn the boat around and start down the next lane. With just the magnetometer out, we run between six and seven knots. With side scan we run a slower four knots. We typically run lanes that are about a nautical mile long, spaced twenty meters apart. We have found that in the type of waters we work, shallow coastal waters, this is the best combination. We once ran lanes that were three nautical miles long and found that to be about the maximum prudent length. Concentrating that long on the little green and red lights of the light bar as they move back and forth tends to be hypnotic, and we figured it would be too tempting for the crew to start giving the driver subliminal commands such as "cluck like a chicken" or "strip down to your underwear." While entertaining during long days of "mowing the lawn," it would do little to further the progress of the survey.

Ground truthing is nothing more than diving down to identify the anomaly. Perhaps this is oversimplifying it. It also includes doing circle searches with a hand-held magnetometer, using a variety of probes, and digging with a water-induction dredge. While there are a variety of search patterns divers use, we have found the circle search the quickest and most efficient. We start by lowering a down line off the stern of the dive boat. The first diver goes down with the hand-held magnetometer to search around the down line. We use a proton hand-held magnetometer made by Quantro Sensing. The operator wears an earphone that changes in tone as the head of the magnetometer goes over ferrous metal. We call ours "Baby." At a cost of three thousand dollars, it gets treated with the care a mother has for her newborn. After the diver has swept around the down line, the second diver goes down with the search line and clips it off to the diver with the magnetometer. The diver with the magnetometer now moves off the extent of line let out by the second diver. The first diver then swims a circle, sweeping back and forth with the magnetometer. When the diver finishes the circle, the stationary diver at the down line lets out more line, and the searching diver makes another circle. This continues until the object is found. If the object is sticking up from the bottom, the diver unclips the search line and attaches it to the object (somehow). The finder then returns to the down line, and the two divers attach the other end of the line to the down line, swim back to the anomaly, and do whatever recording is appropriate. If the object found by the magnetometer is buried beneath the bottom, the searching diver uses a probe to pinpoint the object, plunging it down into the bottom alongside the object. The diver then unclips the search line and attaches it to the probe. The finder then returns to the down line, and the divers attach the search line to the down line weight. They then return to the surface for the water dredge. Once the object has been uncovered by the dredge, the divers record what is revealed.

On the off chance that the target shipwreck is actually located, then the decision has to be made as to whether there should be a full-blown excavation of the site. The availability of money rules this decision. Completely uncovering a shipwreck, setting up grids, and recording the timbers takes an incredible amount of time and equipment. Then there is the care and feeding of the artifacts found—cleaning, sorting, analyzing, conservation, and storage. Add to this site security, accommodations, per diem, and transportation costs, and an excavation can cost a not-so-small fortune.

Without a doubt the future of underwater archaeology is in electronics. It's in magnetometers and side-scan sonars and sub-bottom profilers that are far more sophisticated than the machines we now have—and it's in devices that have yet to be invented or even conceived. How exciting! Shipwrecks will not only be easier to find, but also easier to identify. This will save not only survey time but also days of ground truthing. Kind of makes up for those dreary hours spent doing the research that will forever remain the first step in finding a shipwreck.

Man Overboard—Not!

We were running out Charleston Harbor, pushed by a strong ebb. Our plan was to relocate the remains of the Union ironclad *Keokuk* with our magnetometer and, if possible, our side-scan sonar. This was in February 2001, and I was driving our offshore survey vessel, a twenty-five-foot C-Hawk with twin 115-horsepower Evinrudes. Turning from the main channel to take the gap in the south jetty that led to the waters off Morris Island, I had some anxious moments as the Humminbird 100SX on the dash read three feet of water for an agonizingly long time. I had cut the corner too close. I knew I would be in trouble if I ran aground, especially on an outgoing tide. I had no doubt the rest of the crew would "suggest" I get out and push us off should I put the C-Hawk hard onto a sandbar. (This had happened before, but it had been summer and the water warmer.)

At last the depth finder found some depth. The bottom fell to five, then six, ten, twelve feet, and soon we were running in the twenties and thirties. I relaxed into the helmsman's chair. With my little faux pas behind us, a bright sunny day and light chop ahead of us, I began looking forward to our day surveying.

In 1998 the Naval Historic Center (NHC), part of the U.S. Navy Department, contracted with SCIAA's Maritime Research Division to conduct remote sensing and diving operations on a limited number of the wrecks in the NHC's inventory. Our survey was limited to the Charleston area, the Port Royal Sound / Beaufort area, the ACE (Ashepoo, Combahee, and Edisto) Basin, and Winyah Bay. The *Keokuk* was one of the vessels in the Charleston area.

As we went through the gap in the south jetty, I looked behind to see if the crew had seen how close I came to running aground. Apparently none had. Turning back, I spotted an unusual-looking commercial fishing vessel, unusual for southern waters, at least. Running ahead of us, it appeared to be about fifty feet in length and had an aft pilothouse, unlike the familiar lowcountry shrimp boats with their pilothouses far forward. Something else seemed unusual: it was towing a small boat on a short line.

Reaching our survey area, I idled the engines as Chris Amer, Jim Spirek, and Joe Beatty set up our remote sensing equipment. The activity aboard the C-Hawk diverted my attention from the strange vessel. As I was watching our magnetometer, side-scan sonar, and GPS navigation computer screens come to life, a panicky call came over the VHF radio.

"Coast Guard Charleston, Coast Guard Charleston. I have a man overboard!" When the Coast Guard immediately responded, the caller said his son was climbing to the cabin top to start a generator and had fallen off. The father said he heard a scream and saw his son disappear beneath the surface. He went on to describe his location. I quickly realized the call was coming from the fishing vessel I had been watching. Our survey of the *Keokuk* would have to be postponed.

From South Carolina's early days as a colony to modern times, naval vessels of all types have sailed our waters. There were the Royal Navy station ships that visited Carolina when it was an English colony and the Royal Navy frigates and ships of the line that came to keep the colony part of the British Empire during the Revolution. There were the galleys, schooners, and brigs of the South Carolina navy that played their parts in ending that relationship. Jefferson-era gunboats patrolled our waters, protecting coastal and inland navigation. There were the Confederate and Union warships, including the strange new ironclads, and the Confederate blockade runners of the Civil War. And of course there was the famous submarine, the *H. L. Hunley*. In the twentieth century the Charleston Naval Base hosted assorted destroyers, submarines, tenders, and other vessels of the U.S. Navy. Enemy action, bad weather, and tactics of war have resulted in a significant number of these naval vessels remaining in South Carolina waters—as shipwrecks.

The Civil War was the largest contributor to this number. In addition to warships (both Confederate and Union), the list includes blockade runners, troop transports, supply vessels, tugboats, lightships, and the dozens of ships, mostly old New England whalers, sunk by the Union in an attempt to clog the channels in and out of Charleston.

There is the USS *Patapsco*, a Union ironclad that sank just off Fort Sumter, and the USS *Keokuk*, a Union ironclad that sank off Morris Island. There is the USS *Housatonic*, the first ship ever sunk by a submarine, and the USS *Weehawken*, which also sank off Morris Island.

The Confederates scuttled the CSS *Charleston*, a 180-foot Confederate ironclad, in Charleston Harbor to prevent capture. The *Marion*, a side-wheel steamer leased by the Confederate government and used as a transport vessel and for laying mines, hit a mine itself and sank in the mouth of the Ashley River. Also scuttled in Charleston Harbor to prevent capture was the CSS *Palmetto State*, a 150-foot ironclad, and the *Indian Chief*, the Confederate receiving ship.

There is an assortment of blockade runners, including the *Minho* off Bowman's Jetty on Sullivan's Island and the *Mary Bowers* and *Georgiana*, also off Sullivan's Island. The *Ruby*, a 177-foot side-wheel steamer, was run ashore on the bar off Folly Island near Lighthouse Inlet and scuttled.

This is just to name a few. The Civil War is what we like to call the state's first artificial reef program.

The U.S. Navy, through its Naval Historical Center, maintains a database containing ninety-six entries of shipwrecks in or near South Carolina waters that were naval or military vessels of one sort or another. Under federal law the U.S. Navy claims forty-six of these wrecks. These forty-six vessels fall into one of four categories. Either they were (1) the property of the U.S. Navy, (2) purchased or chartered by the U.S. Navy, (3) previously a U.S. Navy ship, or (4) part of the Continental navy. Excluded from this list, but included in the navy's overall database, are Confederate navy ships, blockade runners, U.S. Army transports, foreign flag warships, and South Carolina State Navy vessels.

Ten shipwrecks fall into the first category: the *Ferret*, *Gunboat no. 157*, the *Dai Ching*, the *Harvest Moon*, the *Housatonic*, the *Keokuk*, the *Patapsco*, the *Kingfisher*, the *Weehawken*, and the *Hector*. Thirty-four of the shipwrecks in the database meet the second criteria, including the *Marcia*, the *Robert B. Howlett*, the *YP-481*, and the thirty-one vessels of the first and second stone fleets. One shipwreck—the *Stono*, formerly the USS *Isaac Smith*—meets the third criteria, and one vessel, the *Queen of France*, fits into the last category.

Vessels That Were U.S. Navy Property

The USS *Ferret* was an eight-gun schooner purchased by the navy at Charleston in 1812 for $3,500. Employed in coastal protection, it was on its way to Charleston from Port Royal for supplies on February 2, 1814, when it ran aground during a gale and was lost off Stono Inlet. Fortunately its fifty-three officers and crew succeeded in getting ashore safely.

Gunboat no. 157 was one of the famous Jefferson gunboats. In 1803, acting at the urging of President Thomas Jefferson, the Congress passed legislation authorizing the construction of gunboats to protect American coastal waterways. These gunboats never received formal names. They were known simply by their numbers. Number 9 and numbers 156 through 165 were constructed in South Carolina shipyards. These locally made gunboats were built to similar plans: 60 feet long and 16½ feet wide. On May 18, 1811, *Gunboat no. 157* left Charleston heavily laden with food stores for the other gunboats on patrol off Georgia. Under the command of Lt. John Kerr, its crew of twenty-two soon found themselves in dire trouble as the vessel missed stays coming out the south channel. They drifted upon the south breakers off Morris Island and quickly broke up in the high surf. Nearby fishing boats managed to rescue only nine of its crew.

The USS *Dai Ching* was purchased by the navy on April 12, 1863, at a cost of $117,575. It was 170 feet long, with a width of 29 feet 4 inches, and weighed 520 tons. It twin steam engines were geared to a single propeller. For armament it carried four twenty-four-pounders, two twenty-pounders, and one one-hundred-pounder. In January 1865 the *Dai Ching* was patrolling up the Combahee River, along with the Union tugboat *Clover,* when it came under fire from Confederate batteries at Tar Bluff. Attempting to turn around in the narrow river, it ran up on the riverbank. The *Dai Ching*'s captain, Lt. Cdr. J. C. Chaplin, requested assistance from the tugboat. After nearly getting stranded itself, however, and having the first line sent to it break, the *Clover* took off downriver, leaving the *Dai Ching* stranded with the tide falling and Confederate shells raining down on it. It was struck more than thirty times. Its decks were shot through in six or seven places, with one shot striking below the waterline. All of its cannons except the hundred-pounder soon ran out of shells, and it wasn't long before the hundred-pounder was hit by a shell and put out of commission. The crew, realizing the hopelessness of the situation, set fire to the ship and abandoned it.

The USS *Harvest Moon* was a 193-foot long, 546-ton, side-wheel steamer built in Portland, Maine, in 1863. It carried four twenty-four-pound howitzers, one twenty-pound Parrott rifle, and one twelve-pound rifle. It was sent to Charleston in February 1864 for duty with the Union blockading fleet. Upon its arrival Adm. John A. Dahlgren, commander of the fleet, made it his flagship. On February 29, 1865, it was steaming through Winyah Bay heading for sea and Charleston when it struck a mine. Its pilot ran it into the mudflats, where it sank within five minutes.

The USS *Housatonic* had a wooden hull 215 feet long, 38 feet wide, displacing 1,540 tons. Its two steam engines generated an estimated 1,150 horsepower, giving it a top speed of fourteen knots. The three-masted sloop-of-war mounted two eleven-inch pivot guns, four nine-inch broadside guns, and two rifled guns mounted fore and aft. On the night of February 17, 1864, while on blockade duty outside Charleston Harbor, it had the honor of becoming the first vessel in history to be sunk by a submarine when the *H. L. Hunley* rammed a spar torpedo into its hull and detonated it.

The USS *Keokuk* was a 159-foot long, 677-ton, double-turreted iron-clad launched at New York on December 6, 1862. Commissioned in March 1863, it was armed with two eleven-inch Dahlgren smooth-bore cannons and ordered to join the South Atlantic Blockading Squadron at Port Royal, South Carolina. It was soon in battle, taking part in the Union attack on Charleston in April 1863. Attempting to enter Charleston Harbor on April 7, it came under the guns of Fort Sumter. Riddled with ninety direct hits, many of which were at or below the waterline, it withdrew and anchored off Morris Island, where its crew spent the night trying to keep it afloat. On the next day, with seas rising, it took on too much water and sank.

The USS *Patapsco* was a 190-foot long, 1,875-ton, single-turreted ironclad launched at Wilmington, Delaware, on December 27, 1862, at a cost of four hundred thousand dollars. After its commissioning on January 2, 1863, the *Patapsco* was assigned to the South Atlantic Blockading Squadron. It mounted a Dahlgren 15-inch rifled cannon and a 150-pound Parrott rifle. Two twelve-pounders were later added to its armament. Its side armor was said to have been five inches thick, with its turret armor eleven inches thick. While covering several picket boats that were dragging for submerged Confederate mines near the mouth of Charleston Harbor, the *Patapsco* hit a mine and sank in less than one minute, taking sixty-two of its crew with it.

The USS *Kingfisher* was a 121-foot, 451-ton, wooden sailing vessel commissioned into the navy in October 1861. It was fitted with four eight-inch Dahlgren cannons, one twenty-pounder, and one twelve-pounder. On March 28, 1864, it grounded on Combahee Bank, filled with water, and sank. All attempts to free the stranded vessel failed. It was stripped and abandoned on April 5.

The USS *Weehawken* was an enlarged and improved version of the original *Monitor*. While it was anchored off Morris Island on December 6, 1863, as part of the blockading fleet, a gale hit, and the *Weehawken* began taking on water. It sank five minutes after signaling its distress, taking its crew of thirty-one with it.

The *Hector* was a 403-foot navy collier commissioned on October 22, 1909. On July 15, 1916, it encountered a gale off the Carolina coast, was driven ashore off Cape Romain, and sank three days later.

Vessels Purchased or Chartered by the U.S. Navy

The *Marcia,* a 343-ton bark, was a merchant ship of Portland, Maine. The U.S. Navy purchased it in 1861 as part of the second Stone Fleet. On January 7, 1862, it was lost on the Port Royal bar when it struck bottom and sank.

The *Robert B. Howlett* was used by the U.S. Navy as a lightship off Charleston during 1865. On December 9, it struck the northern bar and went to pieces. Very little other specific information is known about the vessel.

The *YP-481* was a wooden-hulled, forty-eight-foot long patrol vessel built in 1939. The navy purchased it in July 1942 and placed it in service at Charleston. In April 1943 the *YP-481* ran aground at the mouth of Charleston Harbor. It was removed and beached at a place called "Section Base," according to navy records. Declaring it unfit for service, the navy decommissioned the patrol boat in 1943. Since the location of "Section Base" is unknown, the fate of the vessel is unknown.

In April 1861 a Union blockade of Southern ports was established. The Union blockading fleet found it difficult to accomplish the task, however. Lacking sufficient warships to patrol the entrances to the harbors, the Union ships had little success in stopping the flow of goods in and out of the Confederate ports, including Charleston. So the Yankees came up with what they thought was a brilliant plan. They would sink old ships across the channels into the Southern harbors. In December 1861 the Union navy sank seventeen old New England whalers, relics of the vanishing whale oil industry, in Charleston's main channel through the bar. To provide ballast for their trip south and to aid in their sinking, these vessels had been loaded with blocks of granite. As a result they were known as the "Stone Fleet." In January 1862 the blockaders sank another fourteen old whalers in Maffitt's Channel, a favorite route of blockade runners as it ran close to Sullivan's Island and thus as far away from the Union warships as possible. The vessels in this subsequent sinking were known, obviously enough, as the "second Stone Fleet." The effects of the stone fleets were negligible. The rigging and upper structures of the whalers were soon torn apart and washed away in the strong currents, and the hulls quickly vanished into the sand.

Vessels Previously a U.S. Navy Ship

Only one vessel is in this category: the *Stono,* a 171-foot long Confederate blockade runner. The U.S. Navy purchased the three-masted steamer in 1861, mounted it with eleven guns, and named it the *Isaac Smith.* While patrolling on the Stono River in 1863, it was attacked by Confederate forces and taken as a prize. Soon after its capture, the Confederates repaired its damage, outfitted it as a blockade runner, and named it the *Stono.* On June 5, 1863, while attempting to run out of Charleston, it encountered the USS *Wissahicken,* which chased it back over the bar, where it wrecked on Bowman's Jetty.

Vessels Part of the Continental Navy

Again there is only one vessel in this category. The *Queen of France* was built at the port of Nantes, France, as the privateer *La Brune.* Marie Antoinette, then queen of France, purchased *La Brune* in 1777 and in turn sold it to America. In honor of the queen, the twenty-eight-gun frigate was renamed *Queen of France.* It was sent to Charleston in late 1779 as part of Commodore Whipple's fleet of Continental navy ships to help in the city's defense against the British, who were at that time amassing an invasion force. While in Charleston Harbor, the *Queen of France* was declared unfit for sea service. So, in March 1780 it and eight South Carolina State Navy vessels were stripped of their armament and stores, fitted with spiked obstructions on their decks, lashed together, and intentionally sunk as an obstruction at the mouth of the Cooper River between Shutes Folly and the foot of Gillon Street.

These forty-six shipwrecks form the final inventory of U.S. naval shipwrecks in South Carolina waters. Our limited survey of these vessels centered on three shipwrecks in the Charleston area (the USS *Weehawken,* USS *Patapsco,* and USS *Keokuk*), one shipwreck in the Combahee River (the USS *Dai Ching*), one shipwreck in the Ashepoo River (the USS *Boston*), one shipwreck in Winyah Bay (the USS *Harvest Moon*), and several wrecks in the Beaufort area, including an effort to locate the USS *George Washington* in Whale Branch River. You may have noticed that neither the USS *Boston* nor the USS *George Washington* is included in the navy's list of forty-six. Both vessels were U.S. Army vessels. This means they are now the property of the General Services Administration (GSA) and therefore not on the navy list. They both were involved with combined operations with the Union navy during the Civil War, though, and we weren't going to let a little matter of ownership deter us from being interested in their whereabouts and present condition. Our survey began in 1999. As usual we planned to spend periods of several weeks each year on the survey.

Because of problems with our remote sensing equipment, we did not actually start the survey on time. After several months of frustration trying to solve problems with data acquisition, a reinstallation of the computer software and the upgrading of several hardware components seemed to fix the malfunctions. The survey began with the three shipwrecks in and near Charleston Harbor.

Charleston area

In February 2001 we spent three days conducting remote sensing operations on the USS *Patapsco* and USS *Keokuk*. The *Patapsco* was first. We had three separate sets of coordinates for the location. All three locations were just east of Fort Sumter. One set of coordinates came from the state archaeological site files. One came from an 1870 nautical chart. A remote sensing survey of the harbor by Tidewater Atlantic Research for the U.S. Army Corps of Engineers provided the third location. Plotting the three locations showed us that the SCIAA site file coordinates were probably wrong. Since the numbers plotted out to be smack dab in the middle of the shipping channel—an area dredged innumerable times since the Civil War—we essentially discarded this site. We set up a 450-by-150-meter block (just under seventeen acres) over the other two locations and began our search. We ran ten lanes, fifteen meters apart, over the block with no luck. Neither the magnetometer nor the side scan recorded the wreck. On the second day, we extended the block, adding a 100-by-400-meter area (about ten acres) to the original block. This time we acquired the wreck with both the magnetometer and side-scan sonar. The side-scan images show that about a hundred feet of the wreck is exposed, lying along a southeast-northwest axis. The hull protrudes from the bottom from between seven and eighteen inches and disappears into the bottom at both ends. The magnetometer indicated that pieces of the wreck lie some distance from the hull. This is probably owing to salvage operations on the wreck, conducted during 1871–72 by Dr. Benjamin Maillefert. These operations removed the ship's deck, deck structures, and machinery (including the boiler, turret, and pilothouse), leaving the wreck, according to Maillefert's notes, in a distorted condition.

After finding and recording the *Patapsco,* our next objective was the USS *Keokuk,* off Morris Island. So on February 23 we were on our way to the *Keokuk*'s location when we heard the "Man Overboard" call from the strange trawler. Soon helicopters from the Coast Guard and Charleston County Sheriff's Department arrived on the scene, and boats from the Department of Natural Resources, the Charleston County Sheriff's Department, and the Charleston City Police, along with a U.S. Navy dive team, were on the way. We radioed the Coast Guard, identified ourselves, and told them our location and the equipment we were carrying. After noting where the other vessels were looking, we informed the Coast Guard we would conduct a visual and side-scan search close in to Morris Island, while other vessels searched offshore and down current from the incident scene.

After several hours of searching, with the futile search activities winding down and no swimmer or body found (for good reason, as it turned out), we returned to our search for the *Keokuk*. Again we had two sets of coordinates from which to work. One was the same 1870 chart, and the other was from a survey of the wreck conducted in 1980–81 by the National Underwater Marine Agency (NUMA). NUMA is Clive Cussler's group, the same group that found the *Hunley* in 1995. We set up a block over the two sites and began our search. After running lanes over the entire block, we learned one thing—the *Keokuk* was at neither location. We subsequently learned there had been no drowning, either. Two days after the incident, investigators with the Charleston County Sheriff's Department went to talk to the father and learned he had returned to Massachusetts. According to newspaper accounts, the detectives got suspicious and decided to talk with the victim's wife. Workers near the wife's Hollywood home told the investigators that the woman was not home. The police saw a door to the home open and decided to investigate, thinking there might be a burglary in progress. They entered the home only to find the missing man hiding in his bathroom. Apparently the couple hoped to collect on two million dollars in life insurance policies. Authorities charged the couple, along with the man's father, with conspiracy to defraud insurance companies.

We returned to the *Keokuk* site on July 11, 2001, with new locational coordinates provided by Ralph Wilbanks, who had made a more recent NUMA survey of the area. This time we had no trouble finding the *Keokuk*'s remains. The magnetometer revealed that the wreck lies spread out over an area measuring approximately two hundred yards square. The greatest area of magnetic disturbance ran along a northeast-southwest line for a distance of about 162 feet. This fits nicely with the *Keokuk*'s length of 159 feet. The side-scan sonar showed that none of the remains rose above the bottom. As with the *Patapsco*, the *Keokuk* had been salvaged after the war. In a heroic effort, Confederate forces removed two large eleven-inch Dahlgrens and the turret from the hull. In 1873 Maillefert continued the job by removing more of the hull, lowering the wreck so that its top was no closer than fifteen feet below the surface.

Eight months after the loss of the *Keokuk,* the USS *Weehawken* foundered after taking on water while at anchor. We conducted our remote sensing survey of the *Weehawken* site on August 6, 2001. Again using coordinates supplied by Ralph Wilbanks, we easily found the *Weehawken,* or at least its remains, about 1.75 miles north-northeast of the remains of the *Keokuk.* The magnetometer showed that the wreck site spread out over an area of a little more than seven acres, with the large parts of the wreck in about a quarter of that area. The side-scan sonar showed a smooth bottom, meaning the wreck is buried beneath the sediments. As he did with the *Patapsco* and *Keokuk,* Maillefert salvaged some of the remains of the *Weehawken* in 1873. He removed the engines, both Dahlgren guns, portions of the turret and pilothouse, and a forty-foot section of the ship's stern. He also removed portions of the hull and decking, lowering the wreck down to a height of twenty feet at low tide. This demolition could easily have caused the wide dispersal of the wreck remains.

Beaufort area

Meanwhile we began our survey in the Port Royal area. We focused our survey on six areas—Skull Creek, Station Creek, Bay Point, Gaskin Bank, Whale Branch River, and Hilton Head Island. We selected Skull Creek for the presence of a likely Civil War–era shipwreck. Station Creek caught our interest as the site of a Union naval repair facility featuring floating workshops. Bay Point was the site of a naval coal depot with a large T-dock. Gaskin Bank was chosen as the site where the merchant ship *Marcia* was lost. Finding the remains of the USS *George Washington* was our aim in surveying Whale Branch River. Last on our list was the east side of Hilton Head Island, the location of a T-dock complex used to supply the Union forces on the island and to service the South Atlantic Blockading Squadron.

Hilton Head Island

In March 2001 and April 2002, we surveyed two areas of Port Royal Sound adjacent to the southeast corner of Hilton Head Island. One area was chosen for the presence of a T-dock located there during the Civil War. This dock, more than one thousand feet long, included a rail line to transport supplies from arriving ships to the Union encampment on the island. The second site consisted of snags reported to us by local shrimpers.

Fifty-two magnetic anomalies were recorded in the first survey area, eleven of which were in the location of the T-dock. Two medium-sized anomalies ran parallel to the position of the dock. These may have been associated with the rail line on the dock, perhaps remnants of track. Two small anomalies were found within the location of the dock, three were recorded south of the dock, and another four small anomalies were located just north of the dock. These small anomalies are probably debris from moored ships.

Only two anomalies were recorded in the general area of the reported snags, neither of which was near the location of the snags. The decision was made not to investigate these further.

Skull Creek

Skull Creek is a narrow, winding waterway on the north side of Hilton Head Island, connecting Chechessee River and Calibogue Sound. It is also part of the Intracoastal Waterway. In 1985, while conducting a side-scan sonar survey of the area in response to the proposed construction of a marina, SCIAA archaeologists discovered a pile of rocks in the creek. After a quick reconnaissance dive, the archaeologists determined the pile of rocks was indeed a ballast pile associated with a shipwreck. A large wooden pole found near the ballast pile was taken to be a ship's spar or mast. The archaeologists also collected some eighteen artifacts— mostly copper fasteners, an iron nail, and a wood fragment with bronze tacks—from the area surrounding the ballast pile. These items indicated a somewhat large date range—from about 1750 to 1850. The site was not visited again until we returned in March 2001. Meanwhile archival research and archaeologists' penchant for speculation came up with three possibilities for the wreck. One was that the wreck was the Martins Industry Shoal Lightship, which was burned and sunk by the Confederates prior to the arrival of the Yankees in 1862 to prevent its capture. It was also suggested that the wreck could be a Confederate vessel sunk to block the inland passage to Savannah. Another possibility was that it was one of the old New England whalers intended to block Charleston Harbor, but, proving unseaworthy, it sank before it could be taken to Charleston.

We dived the site in September 2001. The ballast pile was easy to find in about twenty feet of water despite limited visibility and seemingly unlimited current. We discovered that the ballast pile consisted of large quarried granite. Using a hand-held metal detector around the wreck

site, we found a number of iron and copper fasteners and other components. The mast or spar turned out to be a telephone pole, probably used
at one time as a post for a channel marker. Creosote oozing from the
pole was a dead giveaway. Overall we obtained very little information. We
returned in May 2003. This time we made a complete site plan of the
area, concentrating on accurately mapping in the ballast pile. We were
unable to determine whether this wreck was the Martins Industry Shoal
Lightship or another vessel. We probably will never know.

Station Creek

Station Creek comes off Port Royal Sound at the junction with the
Beaufort River. As it winds through the marsh, it narrows, becoming
barely navigable before opening up to connect with Trenchards Inlet,
forming St. Phillips Island. It offers easy access from Port Royal Sound
and shelter from the weather that often whips the sound. After the fall
of Port Royal in 1861, the Union forces took advantage of those two
attributes to turn Station Creek into a repair facility for their ships. Flag
officer Samuel Dupont took two of the whalers from the second Stone
Fleet for this purpose. These were the 340-ton bark *Edward* and the
366-ton ship *India*. Covering the upper decks with buildinglike structures, Dupont turned the *India* into a blacksmith's shop and the *Edward*
into a machine shop. The facilities included brass, iron, and copper
foundries. The Yankees also built carpenter shops, barracks, mess rooms,
and storerooms into the ships. In January 1863 Union ironclads began
arriving at Station Creek. This new type of warship had special needs.

To satisfy these needs, the repair station even had its own divers to
check the undersides of the ironclads for damage and to clean the hulls.
It seems Station Creek was a full-service facility. The lead diver's name
was Waters. Reportedly he was a large man of Herculean strength. The
other sailors were in awe of his ability to work underwater for five or six
hours at a time. One day, as the story goes, the diver was scraping the
bottom of a monitor when a small boat from a nearby plantation came
alongside the facility. In it a local man had a load of watermelons he
hoped to sell to the sailors. He was busy selling his produce when what
must have appeared to be some sort of monster rose to the surface. The
alarmed watermelon seller was gaping at the diver as if he were the devil,
when the diver reached into the boat, snatched a watermelon, and sank
back into his watery realm, leaving the water boiling with his bubbles.
The man hastily seized his oars and was off in a flash, never to return.

In March 2001 we surveyed a block off the mouth of Station Creek
(block 1) and a long block just inside the creek (block 2). We recorded

sixty-six anomalies with the magnetometer in block 1 and another thirty-five in block 2. After postprocessing the data, two of the anomalies in block 1 and three in block 2 were determined to be significant enough to ground truth, that is, dive. We returned in 2003 to do just that.

We used our four-inch water dredge to remove the bottom sediments. One anomaly in block 1, buried below two feet of sand in eight feet of water, turned out to be an object resembling a gas station fluorescent light post from the 1950s. At the second location in block 1, we exposed two planks measuring four inches by twelve inches under about four feet of sand. The two planks, apparently pine, joined edge to edge at an angle. We never got down to the source of the magnetic anomaly, but the presence of iron and wooden planking suggests a potential shipwreck. Unfortunately time, or rather lack of, prevented further investigation of the site.

The first anomaly investigated in block 2 turned out to be an LMO (large metallic object), probably iron stock for the foundries aboard the two converted whalers. The second anomaly turned out to be the remains of a small modern boat trailer. The third turned out to be a large pile of rocks. Could this be the remains of one of the whalers, perhaps its ballast? We measured the extent of the rock pile and found it to be 92.8 feet long. Its width ranged from 29.5 feet to 39.4 feet. Investigating the rock pile further, we came across several artifacts, including copper drift pins, a wooden pulley sheave, flint cobbles, and several bottles dating to the Civil War period. We also noted a large amount of iron strewn around the site. Then, poking out from under the pile in one area, we found a small section of ship remains, including the eroded ends of three frames, hull planking covered with copper sheathing, and ceiling planking. The frames measured roughly nine inches square. This was indeed a shipwreck. The remains have been added to the state archaeological site records and named the Station Creek Wreck. (No doubt you will have noticed that when it comes to naming shipwreck sites, archaeologists are masters of the obvious.)

Bay Point

Bay Point lies across Port Royal Sound from Hilton Head Island. Prior to the arrival of the Union forces in November 1861, the Confederates had a fort, Fort Beauregard, on the point. They also built a T-dock more than five hundred feet out into deep water to supply the fort. As did the later Union T-dock on Hilton Head Island, this one also had a rail line for facilitating the movement of supplies. The purpose of our survey of the area was to locate the remains of this dock, having gleaned an approximate location from an 1873 nautical chart of the area. In March and April 2001, while also surveying the nearby Station Creek, we conducted a magnetometer survey of the shore along Bay Point. In all we recorded 125 magnetic anomalies. We recorded 5 large anomalies, 4 small, and 1 medium-sized in the presumed vicinity of the T-dock. None was deemed worthy of further investigation. Two other anomalies, however, merited ground truthing. We returned to the area on May 28, 2003, to do just that. Jim Spirek and I dived on the two objects. The two sites were less than fifty yards apart and more than one hundred yards from shore.

The first anomaly we investigated was in about six feet of water and sat in a shallow, scoured-out area. Despite absolutely no visibility, we quickly located the object. Jim moved one way around it while I went the other way, both of us feeling our way along. It soon became obvious that the object was about fifteen feet long and six or seven feet wide and consisted of a number of connected metallic parts. It took several minutes for me to come up with an idea of its identity. I came to the surface, which meant little more than standing up. Jim was there, too. I asked him what he thought, reluctant to say what I thought we had discovered. He said he thought it was a vehicle of some sort. Relieved that he had come to same conclusion I had, I said it felt like a Ford Model A truck. (My teenage habit of reading hot rod magazines had finally paid off.) Reinforced in our conclusion, we went back down. As we moved along the vehicle we could feel the fenders and wheels, an engine block, the dive shaft, and what was clearly the cargo bed, all still attached to a frame. After describing what we had found back on the dive boat, we spent our lunch break speculating on just how a Ford Model A truck had become an artificial reef more than one hundred yards from shore.

I also teamed with Jim to investigate the second anomaly. This one we had to locate with an underwater metal detector as it was buried beneath the coarse bottom sand. We set up our water dredge and quickly found the object about one foot down. This one also turned out to be part of a vehicle, consisting of part of a car frame. This one was more modern, as was obvious from the lower seat belt connection still attached to the frame.

Gaskin Bank

The merchant ship *Marcia,* a 343-ton bark, struck bottom four miles off Hilton Head Island and sank on January 7, 1862. The area off Hilton Head Island where the *Marcia* was lost is called Gaskin Bank.

In March and May 2003, we surveyed the bank with our magnetometer. Water depths measured from ten to thirty feet. Twenty-two magnetic anomalies were recorded. None was of the strength or duration to indicate a wooden shipwreck.

Whale Branch River

Whale Branch River is merely a ribbon of swift water connecting the Broad and Coosaw rivers. On April 10, 1863, while at anchor in Whale Branch, the USS *George Washington,* a U.S. Army steamer, came under fire from a Confederate battery on the north side of the river. Severely damaged by the artillery fire, the *Washington* caught fire and was abandoned by its crew. A short time later, according to the records, the remains of the steamship were towed to a nearby location out of range of the Confederate artillery. Unfortunately this nearby location was not identified.

In February 2003 we surveyed several miles of Whale Branch with our magnetometer, looking for the vessel's remains. In all we located 384 magnetic anomalies in the survey area. Only one of these was determined worthy of further investigation. In September 2003 we returned to the area to identify this one anomaly. Jim Spirek and volunteer Jack Melton discovered that the target was a large conglomeration of iron rods and crab traps. Under about fifteen feet of water, the conglomeration protruded about two feet above the bottom. We left without being closer to identifying the location of the *George Washington* than we were before the survey.

Winyah Bay

The USS *Harvest Moon* in Winyah Bay was the easiest to locate. Its location is noted in the state archaeological site files. It's clearly marked on navigational charts, and its smokestack sticks up in the air like a navigational beacon at all but the highest tide. Our first chore, as on the other surveys, was to run our remote sensing gear over the area. Our survey of the *Harvest Moon,* conducted in March and April 2003, was made more interesting by the water depth around the wreck. At low tide there was a total of about six inches of water above the mud covering the *Harvest Moon.* This meant that our work was limited to periods of mid to high tide. The magnetometer and sonar survey centered on the smokestack. In all we covered some 58,820 square meters (a little more than 14.5 acres). The magnetometer delineated a wreck site of approximately 250 feet by 200 feet, with the long axis running north-northwest to south-southeast.

The only object recorded by the sonar was the smokestack, or rather the remains of the smokestack. The salvage records note that the smokestack was removed. About sixty-seven inches of smokestack stick up above the mud of Winyah Bay, however. The smokestack consists of two tubes, one inside the other. The outer tube has a diameter of fifty-eight inches. The inner tube's diameter is forty-four inches. Smoke would come out the inner tube, while fresh air would be drawn in through the area between the two tubes. At the mud line, a flange on the stack indicates where it would have passed through the top of the uppermost deck.

To judge better the integrity of the wreck, we decided to probe the area. The Union navy undertook extensive salvage of the stricken ship almost as soon as it settled on the bottom, removing machinery, supplies, and other items. The salvage operation would have had little care for the integrity of the ship in its work removing the machinery.

To investigate the site further, we used our hydraulic probe. Constructed of high-tech components—ordinary garden hose and ten-foot sections of one-inch galvanized pipe—the probe allows us to determine the type and depth of cultural materials that rest below the bottom. We attach the garden hose to our dredge pump and screw on however many lengths of pipe are deemed necessary. To probe the *Harvest Moon* we used two ten-foot sections of pipe. Pumping water through the hose and pipe provides the digging force needed to sink the end of the pipe into the bottom sediments. After some practice, determining whether the probe strikes wood, metal, or some other substance becomes surprisingly easy. We found that the best way to perform our probing was to have someone run the pump located in our johnboat while someone else probed off the bow of the C-Hawk. The C-Hawk provides a stable platform for the person wrestling with the probe. We put the pump in the johnboat, since the small boat was easily bailed out. For some reason we had a hard time keeping the various hose and pipe connections from spraying water all over the pump and probe operators. Perhaps it was because the hose has been in use for more than ten years. After going through four rolls of duct tape, we decided it was easier just to wear foul-weather gear when probing or operating the pump.

We probed 109 locations at measured distances along lines crossing the centerline of the vessel as determined by our magnetometer readings. Twenty-four of the probes encountered wood. Another 24 struck iron. Five encountered something, but the prober was unable to determine its type. Fifty-six probes encounter no resistance down to 20 feet below the bottom. Wood indicates the ship's decks. The iron would be

Joe Beatty (left) and Jim Spirek wrestle with the hydraulic probe over the remains of the USS *Harvest Moon* in Winyah Bay. On February 29, 1865, it was steaming through Winyah Bay heading for sea and Charleston when it struck a mine. SCIAA photograph by Christopher Amer

the vessel's steam machinery. The salvage records do not mention the removal of the boiler or any of the associated machinery. The remains of the smokestack corroborate this. Since the *Harvest Moon* had two decks above the main deck, the distance from the flange (now at the top of the mud) down to the main deck should be about 14 feet. The most consistent depth of our probe down to wood was 13.5 feet, indicating that the top two decks were removed or have disintegrated over time. The depth of the iron contacts ranged from 1 to 12.4 feet. The pattern of the contacts indicated that indeed the hull remains lie along an axis running north-northwest to south-southeast as was indicated by our magnetometer. However, 109 probes—requiring four and a half days of wet, backbreaking work—proved too few to give us a good outline of the hull remains. Perhaps another 300 or so should do it.

Ashepoo and Combahee Rivers

The Ashepoo and Combahee rivers, along with the Edisto River, form a large drainage area between Charleston and Beaufort known as the ACE Basin. During the Civil War the area was the site of several skirmishes between Union and Confederate forces. Most of these skirmishes involved the Union's attempt to sever Confederate rail lines, and most of them proved unsuccessful. Two of the vessels involved in these actions were the USS *Boston* and the USS *Dai Ching*.

As mentioned earlier the *Dai Ching* was patrolling up the Combahee River in January 1865 when it came under fire from Confederate batteries. Attempting to turn around in the narrow river, it ran up on the riverbank. The crew set fire to the ship and abandoned it. On February 10–11, 2003, we conducted both magnetometer and side-scan surveys for the *Dai Ching*. We centered our survey on the location recorded in a 1975 archaeological site file report. The only things our magnetometer recorded after surveying a two-kilometer stretch of the river were several large anomalies close together some 275 yards upstream from the location reported in the site file. The side scan recorded no identifiable objects in the survey area. It was determined that the large magnetic anomalies were the remains of a vessel. To test this we probed the area of the anomalies with our water probe. To outline the target area we put buoys at the upstream and downstream limits of the anomalies, leaving a distance of approximately forty yards between buoys. We probed in fourteen locations between the buoys. Most of the probes struck wood at a distance of six to eight feet below the bottom. In the upstream area we also located a large metal structure about eight feet below bottom. The wood would undoubtedly be decking, while the metal could be engine components. With limited time we were unable to do more, but the magnetometer readings and our probing indicate we indeed located a shipwreck.

The *Dai Ching* also played a part in the loss of the USS *Boston*. Built in 1850 as a coastal passenger liner, the side-wheel steamer *Boston* was 225 feet long and 28 feet wide. In 1861 the U.S. Army purchased it and converted it into a troop transport. On the night of May 24, 1864, the *Dai Ching,* along with the *Boston* and the *Edwin Lewis,* was sent up the Ashepoo River to disembark elements of the Ninth U.S. Colored Troop at the junction of Mosquito Creek. The plan was to flank the Confederate forces and attack the railroad bridges. The *Boston* missed Mosquito Creek, however, sailing seven or eight miles past before discovering the mistake. On the way back downriver, it ran aground. All attempts to get it off failed, and the next morning the Confederates opened fire, hitting the grounded ship repeatedly. The decision was made to abandon the *Boston,* and while the *Dai Ching* provided cover, the *Boston* was set afire to prevent its capture. Thirteen of the Union forces were killed, wounded, or captured in the action, and eighty-three horses burned to death.

In 1866 a group of individuals under contract with the U.S. Army salvaged the *Boston's* engine. Further salvage of the wreck was conducted in the early 1980s under license from SCIAA. Artifacts recovered included brass uniform buttons, sword fragments, uniforms, personal items, and a large number of horse tack and accessories.

Our survey of the *Boston* was conducted on February 12, 2003. Although we had the exact location of the shipwreck, surveying the site proved difficult because of a lack of water over the wreck. The remains of the *Boston's* bow lie embedded in the downstream end of a sandbar. At low tide the bar is high and dry, while at high tide only a few feet of water cover the sand. We waited until high tide to perform our survey, not only so that we could get across the bar but also so we wouldn't strike any portion of the wreck sticking up off the bottom. The side-scan "picture" indicates that a significant amount of the ship's lower structure remains visible, rising as much as three feet above the bottom. The magnetometer indicates that there are parts of the ship scattered in an area of 4,800 square meters (a little more than an acre). This scatter is no doubt due to the Confederate shelling and the two salvage events.

The Naval Wreck Survey project officially concluded with the publication of the final report in April 2004. So what did we learn from all this historic record researching, remote sensing, and ground truthing? As a result of our survey and research, we refined our locational knowledge of several important shipwrecks. We added to our understanding of several known sites. We located a new shipwreck—the Station Creek Vessel—and conducted a preliminary survey of the site. We surveyed more than five square miles of South Carolina waters. We even found what might be a Ford Model A truck. Did we further the cause of maritime archaeology? You decide. After all, your tax money funded the project.

What caught my attention while reading about each vessel we investigated was how these warships and related craft became shipwrecks. The majority of the wrecks in the navy database were lost through deliberate scuttling, a statistic skewed by the inclusion of the first and second stone fleets. What is interesting is that the next most common reason for loss was through accidental grounding. Action with an enemy came in third. The fact that more ships were lost through striking bottom than through warfare reminds us that navigating our coastal waters can be dangerous and lead to disaster. I had that lesson reinforced when I came close to running aground going out Charleston Harbor that day in February 2001 on our way to survey the *Keokuk*.

Navigating our coastal waters led to another type of disaster for the fisherman and his family who tried to fake his drowning. The man received a thirty-month prison sentence. His wife was given five years probation, which included six months in a halfway house. The father also received five years probation.

"Never Sausage an Artifact"

The headline in the *Hilton Head Island Packet* read, "Never Sausage an Artifact." Below the headline was a picture of Chris Amer holding an empty, dented, and slightly crushed Vienna sausage can, its labeling worn from spending years (or perhaps only months) in the mud beneath Chechessee Creek. In the photo Chris is grinning like a Budweiser-guzzling redneck holding free tickets to the Daytona 500.

Chris Amer holds a Vienna sausage can found during a survey of Callawassie Island. Photograph by Jack Karr; reprinted with permission of the *Hilton Head Island Packet*

Chris shook his head on reading the headline and seeing the photo. It was not the image he hoped to convey as the state underwater archaeologist and head of SCIAA's Maritime Research Division. "I didn't think they would use that," he said, slightly embarrassed and seemingly unaware of standard journalistic practice. Considering that we had just spent two weeks diving around Callawassie Island in Beaufort County and that this was the most interesting find, he should have expected nothing less from the reporter. We, too, were disappointed and somewhat surprised by the lack of cultural remains. Considering the rich maritime history of Callawassie and the surrounding area, we should be finding prehistoric dugout canoes, colonial plantation vessels, oyster boats, antebellum barges used to transport rice and cotton; heck, even an abandoned aluminum johnboat would have been nice. Besides the sausage can, though, the most interesting find had been a metal boat trailer.

Native Americans plied the waters around Callawassie at least as early as the seventh century and probably long before that. Evidence for this comes from archaeological investigations of a prehistoric mound located in pinewoods on the northeastern end of the island. Recent radiocarbon dating of the site reveals continual occupation from about A.D. 665 to 1665. No doubt Native Americans used these waters far earlier than that. The dugout canoe recovered by Joe Porcelli in the Cooper River provides proof that the natives were using lowcountry waterways at least 3,800 years ago. Closer to Callawassie Island, prehistoric canoes have been found on Hilton Head Island, on Parris Island, and in the Beaufort, Combahee, Salkehatchie, and Edisto rivers.

All sorts of historic vessels also used the waters near Callawassie Island. With the sixteenth-century settlements on nearby Parris Island, the Spanish and French colonists are sure to have explored the adjacent waterways, perhaps even foraging on this neighboring island. The early English colonists who settled the area in the later part of the seventeenth century and early eighteenth century surely investigated these waters. As the area grew and plantations sprang up on the islands, a variety of watercraft, from oar to sail to steam-powered, have worked and played in the waters around Callawassie Island. During the Civil War both the Confederates and the Yankees came to the island in boats to forage. Surely some of these colonial, antebellum, and Civil War vessels must remain in these waters, the victims of storms, rough seas, overloading, or some other form of carelessness. So where were they?

Callawassie Island is located in the northwest corner of Beaufort County. The Colleton River runs along the 880-acre island's south and west sides. The Chechessee River runs along the north of the island. Callawassie Creek comes off the Colleton River on the south side of the island and runs along its east side. The first European owner of the Callawassie was James Cochran, who received a land grant for the island in 1711. Cochran used the island to raise cattle, and his brother, John, probably operated a store on the island, trading with the Yemassee, whose capital, Altamaha, was on the mainland only a mile from Callawassie. Although profitable, John Cochran's business with the Yemassee ended somewhat abruptly when the local tribe revolted in 1715 and killed him, his wife, and four children. The island remained in the Cochran family until 1756 when it was sold to Daniel Heyward. Heyward and his descendants cultivated indigo and, later, cotton on the island. Control of the island came into the hands of James Hamilton Jr. in 1813 when he married Elizabeth Matthews Heyward. The Hamiltons moved to the island and built a house there in 1815. A year later Hamilton built a tabby sugar mill in the north part of the island.

When constructed, the sugar mill, perhaps the only one of its kind built in South Carolina, consisted of a curing shed, a boiling house, and animal-driven cane crushing machinery. Archaeologists with the Chicora Foundation investigated the ruins of this sugar mill in 1990. The boiling house and curing shed each measured approximately forty by twenty-five feet. They were built in a T pattern, with the end wall of the boiling house separated from the side wall of the curing shed by about five feet. The cane crushing machinery stood on a tabby foundation. We visited the site prior to our survey.

The location of the walls and interior features of the boiling house are still plainly visible. Two of its walls remain mostly intact. Little other than the foundation remains of the curing shed. The tabby foundation for the cane crushing machinery is still there as well, taking up a twenty-one-by-fifteen-foot area. While we were on our visit, we also noticed that the site overlooks a narrow tidal channel connecting Colleton River and Chechessee Creek. This would have been an excellent means of bringing cargo vessels, small flats and bateaux, close to the mill.

In 1819 Hamilton sold the property to John A. Cuthburt. Ownership of the island went through various private hands until 1947. From 1947 until 1981, a variety of timber corporations, private concerns, and even a public utility owned the island with the idea of exploiting its natural resources. None of these plans came to fruition. In 1981 the Three Fountainview Corporation bought Callawassie with the intent of developing the island into a gated, upscale housing community. Three Fountainview Corporation soon found itself overwhelmed by the size of the project and sold the property in 1985. The new owners carried on with the original plans, however, leading to the idyllic housing community we see on the island today.

Professor Clarence B. Moore of the Academy of Natural Sciences of Philadelphia conducted the first archaeological investigation of the island in 1897. Moore was six years into a twenty-seven-year survey of coastal Native American sites from Florida to South Carolina. He kept his focus on the coast for reasons of convenience—he used his stern-wheel steamboat, the *Gopher,* as his base of operations. Commenting on Moore's activities, one contemporary newspaper account described the *Gopher* as "beautiful and commodious" and carrying a crew of eighteen. Moore was solely interested in the island's mound site, already somewhat flattened from farming. At the time the mound measured forty-eight feet across and a little more than three feet tall. Moore excavated the northern half of the mound, finding the remains of eleven burials—nine humans and two dogs. Of the human remains, three were female, three were of undetermined sex, two were male, and one was a child of undetermined sex. There were no artifacts found with the graves. In fact, the graves aside, Moore took little interest in the Callawassie mound or in any of the other South Carolina sites he visited. "On the whole," he concludes in his report, "it would seem probable the South Carolina coast has little to offer from an archaeological standpoint."

Nevertheless SCIAA archaeologist James L. Michie, along with assistant archeologist Tommy Charles, conducted a reconnaissance survey of the island in 1981. The Three Fountainview Corporation initiated the project as part of its plans to develop the island. Michie and Charles recorded eighty-eight archaeological sites, including the mound investigated by Moore. Eighty-three were prehistoric and five were historic. All but two of the prehistoric sites, these being the mound and one site containing a few pottery shards, consisted of oyster shell layers or oyster shell middens. The five historic sites included three tabby ruins and two house sites.

The abundance of oyster shell sites indicates extensive use of the local waterways by the Native Americans who inhabited the island. Moreover an analysis of the faunal remains unearthed at the mound indicates that the area's abundant fish populations were a mainstay of the inhabitants' diet. From 1994 to 1995, Chris Espenshade and Bobby Southerlin of Brockington and Associates, a private archaeological outfit, conducted extensive excavations at the Callawassie mound and recovered more than five thousand bone fragments. While the analysis of these bones reveals that white-tailed deer was a favorite menu item for the inhabitants, fish—from catfish, bass, bluefish, and jack to sheepshead, Atlantic croaker, black drum, and mullet—was often one of the menu's "specials." This seafood industry would have meant the use of the neighboring waterways in dugout canoes.

We began our search for Callawassie's maritime heritage in July 2004. The project was funded by the residents of the island, many of whom came out with us from time to time to watch our operations and graciously fed us in their homes in the evening. The most notable of these were Bill and Kathy Behan and Jim and Evelyn Scott. Bill and Shanna Sullivan, owners of Tabby Point, allowed us the use of their home and guesthouse as a lunch stop.

Our crew consisted of Chris Amer, Jim Spirek, Joe Beatty, and me. Joe and I alternated between driving the boat, our C-Hawk, and tending the remote sensing gear (a job we call being the "fish monkey"), while Chris and Jim operated the magnetometer, side-scan sonar, and navigation computers. Our goal was to circumnavigate the island, if possible. We surveyed stretches of the Colleton River, all of Callawassie Creek, and much of Chechessee Creek. During the two weeks of pulling our mag and sonar fish, water depths ran from twenty feet to about twenty inches. Uncounted times we found ourselves powering over shallow mud bars or oyster beds, our twin 115-horsepower Evinrude outboards trimmed up as far as possible. We surveyed unnamed waterways off the rivers and creeks, any navigable stream that led near the island. We also surveyed a few near the island that were not so navigable, including many that narrowed and finally ended. Often, unable to turn around, the marsh grass brushing against the cabin windows on both sides, we had to stop, retrieve the magnetometer and sonar fish, and reverse out of the stream. We did complete the circumnavigation, mostly. A couple hundred yards of marsh between the end of Callawassie Creek and a small creek off Chechessee Creek prevented a complete 360-degree survey.

In all we recorded 243 magnetic anomalies, most of which were identified as crab traps by their magnetic signature and telltale square sonar image. One immense anomaly, located just off the old oyster processing plant at Bailey's Landing on the Colleton River, produced a sonar picture revealing a large culvert pipe. The remaining anomalies remained to the investigated.

We returned to the island in May 2005. This time we brought the C-Hawk, with brand-new 115-horsepower four-stroke saltwater Mercury outboards, and our twenty-eight-foot pontoon boat to use as a dive platform. Thirty of the 243 anomalies recorded in 2004, we decided, were worth further investigation. This meant ground truthing, or getting in the water and physically finding the anomaly and determining its identity. In shallow water we would jump overboard and, using our J. W. Fisher Pulse 8 metal detector and a metal probe, poke around until we found the object. In deeper water we donned our scuba gear and located the target by doing circle searches with the metal detector and probe. Sometimes we came across the object protruding above the bottom, but more often the anomalies were located after identifying the location with the metal detector and pinpointing the object with the probe. Digging by hand most often revealed the objective. Only once did we use the water dredge to find a deeply buried target.

On the first day of the project, as I maneuvered the C-Hawk into the shallow waters between Callawassie Island and one of the marsh islands in the Colleton River, I put the C-Hawk hard aground. Even our new Mercs could not pull us off. Not wanting to damage our new engines, I shut them off and tilted them up to keep the water intakes from clogging with mud. Unfortunately the tide was still falling. I looked at my watch; there was only about forty-five minutes before low tide. Joe was following along behind us in the pontoon boat. He wisely backed off when he saw us plow into the mud, deciding to anchor the pontoon in deeper water and wait. Chris and Jim got out of the boat to poke around the island on foot for several of the target anomalies while I stayed behind. I watched the water slowly recede. Sure enough, about forty-five minutes later, the C-Hawk was high and dry, but the tide had turned. Waiting for the water to float the C-Hawk was agonizing, but finally we were free to begin our diving operations. Assisting us with the diving chores were Jason Burns, the Georgia state underwater archaeologist; Dr. Paul Work, an associate professor at the Georgia Institute of Technology; and Arnold Postell, a diving safety officer at the South Carolina Aquarium.

The first anomaly we investigated turned out to be a screw-down device like those electric companies use for guide wires on telephone poles. The one object we water dredged was found buried several feet below the bottom. It turned out to be another of the ubiquitous crab traps. One anomaly was revealed to be a rectangular metal object with a rod through the middle. We held a lengthy discussion concerning the identity of the item. Diagnosis: rectangular metal object with rod through middle. Most of the other anomalies turned out to be crab traps, and several were apparently buried beyond the detection range of our metal detector. And of course there was the boat trailer.

We also conducted a low-tide shoreline survey of the island. At Tabby Point we observed the remains of an old landing or wharf. The remains consisted of several timbers set perpendicular to the water's edge. Tabby Point is one of only two deepwater-land interfaces on the island and the site of considerable tabby ruins—hence the name Tabby Point. Jim Michie and his crew visited this site in 1981. In his report Michie notes that "the rectangular [tabby] structure is incomplete. Two of the interior walls have collapsed, and various sections of the outer walls are missing. Other portions have eroded severely. A testing program on the north and out of the structure did not provide any artifacts from the original occupation."

This original occupation would have been in the early 1800s. What are now severely eroded portions of the site were thought to be the home of James Hamilton Jr. and his family, who built a house and moved to the island in 1815. These ruins are now in the front yard of the home of Bill and Shanna Sullivan and form an integral part of a landscaped garden with wooden walkways. For three weeks in January 2006, at the invitation of the Sullivans, SCIAA archaeologists Stanley South, Chester DePratter, and Michael Stoner conducted test excavations at the tabby site. According to Stan South, the goal of the project was to transit-map the ruins to provide a plan drawing, to measure and record the standing wall profiles, and to excavate test squares and shovel tests in and around the ruins.

They found that the remaining walls of the ruins indicate a structure forty feet square. The remains stood eight feet high in places and slightly above ground in others. Two parallel interior walls divide the structure into three rectangular rooms. Michael Stoner excavated fifty test holes and found three ceramic fragments. These shards dated from the mid–nineteenth century but did not indicate a domestic household. According to South the structure was perhaps an office and storage facility for bales of cotton and sugar mill products awaiting transport to market. This begs the question of where the Hamilton home was. Perhaps it was located near the sugar mill. We may never know. Such is the nature of archaeological research. Sometimes what we find is not what we expected. Or as with our underwater investigations, we find nothing at all.

We found not a single vessel. Not a single dugout canoe. Not one barge. No plantation craft. No fishing vessels. Not even one Viking ship. All right, we really did not expect to find a Viking ship in South Carolina. But darn it, we should have found something. Our magnetometer can detect nails (large ones, anyway), and our side-scan sonar can "see" objects as small as car batteries. If something was there, we would have found it. Nevertheless we added one more page to the archaeological history of Callawassie Island. And if the residents of the island ever want to build a museum dedicated to the island's history, we have an empty, dented, and slightly crushed Vienna sausage can they can have for display.

Sexy Wrecks

All shipwrecks are significant. This is a given in maritime archaeology. No matter its age or type, whether it's prehistoric or historic, the remains of these long-lost vessels hold the potential for answering important questions about our past. It is a concept drilled into the skulls of undergraduate archaeology students pursuing the nautical side of that science. An upland riverine boat may provide insight into how the early inhabitants of the upstate coped with their particular environment. A Revolutionary War gunboat may help document the tactics used by the British to combat a rebellious indigenous population. An abandoned nineteenth-century steam tugboat can reveal techniques used to lengthen the longevity of a heavily used working craft.

Archaeologists will tell you that each of these submerged resources is a piece in the puzzle of our cultural heritage. Each deserves our attention and care. Each deserves to be studied and protected. In the world of maritime archaeology, however, some shipwrecks are more important than others. It's just a fact of life. These are the vessels that have some special historical significance. They are tied to some event or are somehow unique. They are one-of-a-kind wrecks. As such they spark the public imagination like no others. They are the wrecks archaeologists actively seek. They get the most publicity. They attract the largest grants. These are the "sexy wrecks."

The Confederate submarine *H. L. Hunley* comes to mind as a sexy wreck. Being the first submarine to sink another warship makes it unique. Its story stirred public interest like no other archaeological event in history. Okay, that might be an exaggeration, but the number of newspaper stories, television specials, made-for-TV movies, and nonfiction books about the submarine's history and raising sure put it in the running. More money has been spent raising and conserving this one small shipwreck than on any other in South Carolina history. Years after its raising, the public comes in droves to see it in its conservation tank. This is a one-of-a-kind wreck. This is a sexy wreck.

Two sexy wrecks in South Carolina waters that have yet to be found are the French corsair *Le Prince*, lost in Port Royal Sound in 1577, and the Spanish cargo ship of the Lucas Vázquez de Ayllón expedition, believed to have gone down near Winyah Bay in 1526. *Le Prince* would be the first French vessel of the sixteenth century ever found in North America. Ayllón's ship would be one of the oldest Spanish ships found in the New World. Presently the oldest known Spanish ships found in America are the wrecks of the *Santa María de Yciar*, the *San Estéban*, and the *Espíritu Santo*. These three cargo vessels went ashore in a storm on Padre Island, Texas, on April 29, 1554. The *Nuestra Señora de Atocha*, famously recovered by Mel Fisher, went down on September 6, 1622. While not carrying gold and riches back to Spain, Ayllón's ship could give us a unique glimpse into the first Spanish attempt at colonization in North America. The Maritime Research Division at SCIAA is actively seeking these two sexy wrecks.

The Search for *Le Prince*

In January 1577, after several months raiding Spanish ships in the Caribbean, the French corsair *Le Prince*, a heavily armed galleon, attempted to enter Port Royal Sound. *Le Prince* was there to raid the Spanish settlement of Santa Elena on what is now Parris Island. The crew of the corsair never got its chance at the Spanish booty. Unknown to them, Santa Elena had been abandoned several years earlier. Even more unfortunate for them, they ran aground "within a mile of the entrance to the river," according to the Spanish records of the time. *Le Prince* was a total loss, yet its crew of approximately 180 made their way to shore. Using a bronze cannon and several harquebuses from the wreck, they hastily built a fort. Within weeks the local Native Americans attacked the French survivors, killing all but forty. The victorious natives enslaved the remaining French, scattering them among local villages. The Spanish, learning of the captive French from their native allies, conducted a search for the hapless *Le Prince* crew members, capturing or killing every one.

About *Le Prince*, little is known. As a three-hundred-ton galleon, it most likely would have been about one hundred feet in length, four masted, square rigged on its forward three masts and lateen rigged on the aft mizzenmast. It would have had a high, rounded stern with an aft castle running half its length. At the bow a raised forecastle would have

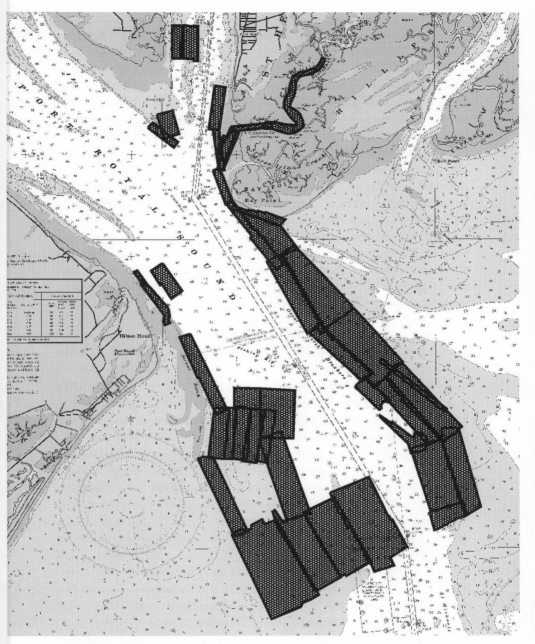

Dark blocks showing areas of Port Royal Sound surveyed during search for *Le Prince*, a French corsair wrecked in 1577. SCIAA graphic by Jim Spirek

supported a built-up bowsprit. The term *corsair* related more to the ship's function as a privateer than to its hull and rigging configuration.

Our magnetometer search of Port Royal Sound for *Le Prince* began in February 2000. It was an inauspicious start. Our magnetometer malfunctioned on the first day. Actually it ceased functioning altogether. Unable to get it working, we broke camp, so to speak, and returned to our offices. Other commitments and delays in getting the magnetometer repaired caused us to postpone the start of the survey until 2001. We returned to Port Royal Sound in March of that year for four weeks. The entire Maritime Research Division was on hand. Jim Spirek, as principal investigator, was in charge. Alternating equipment-operating duties with him was Chris Amer and Lynn Harris. Joe Beatty and I were driving the boat. While there we stayed at the South Carolina Department of Natural Resources' Waddell Mariculture Center, located at Victoria Bluff on the Colleton River. The State Ports Authority transferred this twelve-hundred-acre piece of woodland to the Department of Natural Resources (DNR) in 1979. By 1984 the DNR completed research facilities on the property, including a ten-thousand-square-foot lab building, several greenhouses, outdoor tanks, huge ponds, and a house on the river for visiting scientists. The two-story, plantation-style house has an eat-in kitchen, a living room with TV, a large conference room, and five bedrooms—a single, two doubles, and two that accommodate five persons each in barracks-style splendor. The nearby H. E. Trask Public Boat Landing makes Waddell even more convenient. Trailering our twenty-five-foot C-Hawk survey boat for long distances before the caffeine kicks in is no way to start the day.

We began the survey in the most likely area for a shipwreck—the shoals surrounding the entrance to the sound. Water depths ranged from forty feet to a propeller-polishing two feet. Running at a speed between six and seven knots, we traveled 409 linear miles in grid patterns consisting of lanes twenty meters apart. We covered 3.26 square miles of our target area. In all we took 202,373 magnetic readings, recording 526 magnetic anomalies. After manipulating the collected data, using proprietary computer software to smooth the effects of the sun on the magnetometer, Jim Spirek announced that 4 of the magnetic anomalies could be shipwreck sites and another 38 appeared to be large single objects. This gave us forty-two potential targets.

In late June 2001, we conducted another week of surveying in Port Royal Sound. This time our intent was to gather further information on the forty-two targets we recorded earlier that year. Our plan was to run the magnetometer over each site from different directions to refine the readings. At the same time, we would tow the side-scan sonar fish to see if anything of the object or shipwreck appeared above the bottom and, if it did, perhaps to determine what it was. Again equipment problems shattered our plans. At first we made great progress. After successfully refining seven anomalies on the first day, three of which were possible shipwrecks, we started on the eighth when the side-scan sonar cable parted and we lost the sonar fish. Being an outrageously expensive piece of equipment to replace, not to mention the embarrassment of returning to Columbia saying we had lost it, we decided to conduct a search for the missing sensor. Luckily Jim discovered that a conference of side-scan sonar operators was going on that very week in Savannah. Using all the charm he could muster, he managed to persuade the owner of a unit like ours to lend us his sensor so we could find ours. After two days of searching, we recorded a sonar picture of what could be our fish. Jim and Joe Beatty donned scuba gear to investigate.

They conducted circle searches off a down line. Joe was holding the "dummy end" of the search line at the down line while Jim performed ever-expanding circles around him. Those of us on the dive boat watched the bubbles—Joe's stationary bubbles near the down line and Jim's trail of bubbles as he made his search. After several circuits Jim stopped, and a large rush of bubbles exploded to the surface. We figured either Jim found the lost sensor or his regulator was malfunctioning and free-flowing air out of his tank. Either way we knew he would surface in a very short amount of time. Seconds later Jim popped to the surface, hoisting the lost fish into the air. Letting his regulator drop from his mouth, he was all smiles. His glee no doubt arose from the fact that it would have been his duty, as principal investigator, to explain how we had lost the expensive sonar sensor in the first place. Joe surfaced seconds later. "I knew you had found it," he said nonchalantly to Jim. "I could hear you yelling."

We spent the remaining two days refining targets with the magnetometer only. In all we refined twenty-four targets—seven with both the magnetometer and side-scan sonar and the rest with magnetometer only.

In September we returned with scuba gear, hydraulic probes, and water dredges for a week of ground truthing as many of the anomalies as possible. In addition to Maritime Research Division staff, on hand to assist us were Ronnie Rodgers of the Georgia Division of Historic Preservation and Charles Hughson, an expert diver and underwater archaeological technician from Pensacola, Florida. Owing to bad weather and those ever-present equipment problems, we were able to investigate only one anomaly. This turned out to be a rectangular iron object sticking a foot and a half out of the bottom and measuring about five feet wide and twelve feet long. Old shrimp nets shrouded it, making measurements difficult. Determining what exactly it was proved impossible in the zero visibility. It was obviously not a sixteenth-century wreck, though; we ended our investigation, recording the relic officially as an "LMO" or "large metal object."

In addition to the other problems, another event affected the project. After a day of diving, Joe Beatty and I took the C-Hawk to a gas station on Highway 278 in Bluffton for refueling. It was late in the afternoon. I was pumping gas into the vessel's ninety-gallon tank when a man near the store started shouting something about the end of the world. I shrugged when Joe asked what I thought that was about. Some crazy guy, I said, guessing. The customer across from us looked at us askance. "Haven't you heard what happened?" he asked. It was September 11, 2001. That evening we discussed whether we should cancel the project and head back to our offices. In light of the day's horrific events, our endeavors seemed somehow unimportant. It was as if the steam had gone out of our project. We wondered if we should postpone our activities. Nevertheless we unanimously voted to continue, not realizing how the terrorist attack would directly affect us.

When bad weather hampered our plans to go offshore a couple days later, we decided to do some remote sensing in an area inside the sound. This area was just off Parris Island Spit in the Broad River. Joe Beatty was driving the boat when a small boat came out to block our path. When the boat would not move out of the way, Joe figured they were anglers over their favorite spot. We decided to move over to another lane. The boat moved over with us, again blocking our survey lane. Deciding to approach the boat, Joe was startled to discover that it was crewed by United States Marines armed with M-16 rifles. Because of the terrorist attacks, the Marines had declared a one-mile exclusion zone around Parris Island, and our survey block was within this zone. While the C-Hawk, with all our remote sensing gear, looked a bit odd, we did not think it looked threatening. Nevertheless we left the area and ended this portion of the project.

We made two excursions to Port Royal Sound in 2002, spending a week surveying each time. Again we stayed at Waddell Mariculture Center. We enjoyed excellent weather both times, which facilitated our operations. Concentrating our efforts on the Great North Breakers and Joiners Bank, we increased our survey coverage to 8.4 square miles. We recorded another 353 magnetic anomalies, several of which Jim Spirek determined needed further investigation.

Our 2003 field season searching for *Le Prince* consisted of two surveying sessions, one in March and the other in August, and one of ground truthing in September. We conducted the surveying on Gaskin Bank off Hilton Head Island and again on the Great North Breakers, adding another 6.5 square miles to the total area covered. In September we dived on only one anomaly in the target area, the rest of the one-week undertaking being devoted to the navy survey. Nevertheless the one anomaly proved difficult. Our side scan revealed no bottom relief over the anomaly; our magnetometer recorded a complex magnetic signature, however, indicating the presence of multiple metallic objects. Using our hydraulic probe with a ten-foot section of galvanized pipe attached to the end of the hose, we investigated the area of the magnetometer contact. After several probes into the bottom sediments, we finally thumped into an object about four feet down. Dredging down to it, we discovered two planks connected along their sides at an angle. So where was the metal that triggered off our magnetometer? After reacquiring the target, getting divers geared up and in the water, circle searching with a metal detector for the anomaly, setting up the probe, probing, setting up the dredge, and dredging, it was late in the day. We had no time to dredge further around the two planks, so we packed up and left (a bit frustrated), ending our survey for the year.

We returned to Port Royal Sound for three weeks of surveying in August 2004. We "mowed the lawn" over another 3.2 square miles of survey area, adding several intriguing anomalies to our list for ground truthing. After three weeks of continuous use, however, our old Evinrudes on the C-Hawk began to give out. We thought it prudent to cancel our planned one week of diving, hoping to return in 2005 with new engines and the funds to uncover those anomalies. We indeed put new engines on the C-Hawk, a pair of new 115-horsepower four-stroke saltwater Mercury outboards, but we didn't return to Port Royal Sound. A lack of available funding has put our search for *Le Prince* on hold, having covered about 21 square miles out of a target area of 26 square miles.

The Search for Ayllón's Flagship

In July 1526 Lucas Vázquez de Ayllón, a wealthy Spanish lawyer and high-level functionary on the Caribbean island of Hispaniola, left that island with six (some say five, some seven) boatloads of settlers and supplies in an attempt to settle a land the Spanish called Chicora. Aboard the vessels were five hundred settlers, more than one hundred crew members, a number of black slaves, three Dominican friars, eighty-nine horses, and a number of cattle, sheep, and pigs. The fleet also carried a quantity of supplies, including 3,036 tons of bread, 1,000 bushels of corn, and 16,332 liters of olive oil, plus the tools to build a new settlement. Facts regarding the types, sizes, capacities, or even the names of the vessels making up Ayllón's fleet are scarce and contradictory, but we can conclude they were of good size to hold all those settlers, crew members, animals, and supplies.

On August 9, 1526, they came to the mouth of what they called the Jordan River. Crossing the bar to enter the river, Ayllón's flagship (or "Capitana") ran aground. Everyone got off the vessel, but the ship and its entire cargo were lost.

Ayllón and company soon discovered that the area they had chosen was unsuitable for colonization. Ayllón immediately sent scouts along the coast in both directions to find a more habitable location. While the scouts were abroad, he tasked the settlers with making a vessel to replace the flagship. Spanish records state that the new vessel was a *gabarra*. This was a type of small open boat. It had one mast but also the capability of being rowed. Ayllón had the vessel made from oak and pine and named it *La Gavarra*. Its construction took most of August and possibly some of September to complete. This may well have been the first instance of European boatbuilding in North America.

The scouting parties returned with news that indeed a more suitable location was available. The women and sick were loaded into the ships while those remaining made their way by land. Arriving at the new location, they established a settlement called San Miguel de Gualdape. After less than a year, many of the settlers, including Ayllón himself, had died of sickness. Dissension and mutiny in the ranks followed, and the enterprise soon folded. The remainder of the would-be Spanish settlers (now totaling about 150) beat feet back to Hispaniola.

What intrigues archaeologists about this minor moment in history is that no one knows exactly where Ayllón's Capitana went aground nor where San Miguel de Gualdape was located. As a result there is no shortage of speculation about the ship's whereabouts. Two prevailing theories exist. One theory holds that the Jordan River is present-day Cape Fear River in North Carolina and the site of San Miguel de Gualdape is somewhere on Waccamaw Neck near Georgetown. The other theory says that the Jordan River is really either the South Santee River or Winyah Bay and that San Miguel is on Sapelo Island, Georgia. Despite this disparity in theories, there have been some minor archaeological searches for San Miguel de Gualdape. All have failed. Finding the site of the short-lived Spanish settlement could make an archaeologist's career.

It is the stuff archaeologists daydream about: The excavation they would lead! The books they would write! The notoriety they would gain!

In the fall of 1990, Jim Michie, an institute archaeologist and associate director of the Waccamaw Center for Historical and Cultural Studies at Coastal Carolina College, conducted a search for San Miguel de Gualdape on Hobcaw Barony. His thinking was that if the first theory held true, that the settlement was on Waccamaw Neck, it would probably be on high ground with access to navigable waters. The only place that fit these requirements on Waccamaw Neck was the area of Hobcaw Barony from just north of the Hobcaw House south to Frazier's Point, Barnes Ridge, and Denny's Corner. Michie ran transects every 100 feet from the marsh/high ground interface inland for a distance of 240 feet. He and his crew dug test holes along these transect at intervals of 30 feet to a depth of 20 inches. They found oyster shell middens, colonial period settlements, plantation components, a small Civil War fortification, and prehistoric Native American occupations. But no evidence of a Spanish presence. Michie also conducted an underwater survey in the channel near this high ground. For the survey he enlisted Hampton Shuping, finder of the Brown's Ferry Vessel, and a group of volunteer divers. The divers found a light scatter of nineteenth- and twentieth-century materials and a small number of prehistoric artifacts. But no Spanish artifacts.

Testing the second theory, that Winyah Bay was Ayllón's Jordan River, Jim Michie conducted a shoreline survey of the beaches and dune area from North Island down to the South Santee River during August and October 1991. His idea was that if Ayllón's Capitana went down anywhere near the entrance the Winyah Bay, then some artifacts from the shipwreck should be washing up on the nearby beaches. Presumably the olive oil would be in large earthenware jars of the period. This type of earthenware was fragile. Shards should have washed ashore. He zigzagged across miles of dunes and beach areas and found not a single relevant Spanish artifact. In fact he found few artifacts of any kind.

Does this mean neither theory is correct? Perhaps Jordan River is some other river, and San Miguel de Gualdape is somewhere else altogether. It's possible. But the reason these theories have persisted is that the best evidence fits their premises, despite coming to such different conclusions as to the specific locations. Besides, there's an old archaeological saying that absence of evidence is not evidence of absence.

Naturally our interest is Ayllón's flagship. Since Cape Fear River is not in South Carolina, a minor technicality in our view, surveying there for the Capitana was out of the question. So we decided on Winyah Bay as the site of the lost Spanish ship. According to the Spanish records, the vessel was a *nao*. Usually sixty-five to eighty feet in length, *nao*s were developed in the Mediterranean during the fifteenth century. The only difference between a *nao* and a galleon would have been the amount of armament aboard. The galleon would be heavily armed, while the *nao* would have lighter armament, with more space being devoted to passengers and cargo. Columbus's *Santa María* was a *nao*.

On February 18, 2005, the Maritime Research Division received a grant of $6,640 to conduct an archaeological survey to locate and identify the remains of the flagship. The grant came from the Archaeological Research Trust (ART), which is the fund-raising arm of the institute.

The project plan called for three weeks of remote sensing with our magnetometer, side-scan sonar, and GPS unit and one week of ground truthing. The three weeks of remote sensing began in August 2005. While we conducted the survey, we stayed at Hobcaw Barony just north of Georgetown. Hobcaw Barony is a 17,500-acre wildlife refuge on the Waccamaw Neck. In the early part of the twentieth century, Bernard M. Baruch purchased eleven of the old rice plantations on Waccamaw Neck to form Hobcaw Barony. Baruch was a Wall Street financier and adviser to seven presidents, from Woodrow Wilson to Dwight D. Eisenhower. He used the barony as a winter hunting retreat, entertaining such dignitaries as Franklin Delano Roosevelt and Winston Churchill. In 1943 Baruch deeded all of Hobcaw Barony to his daughter Belle. In her will Belle made the barony available to academic researchers through the Belle W. Baruch Foundation. In the late 1960s, the foundation established long-term agreements with the University of South Carolina and Clemson University. Today the barony houses the Baruch Marine Field Laboratory of the Belle W. Baruch Institute for Marine and Coastal Sciences, which is a research institute of the University of South Carolina, as well as Clemson University's Belle W. Baruch Institute of Coastal Ecology and Forest Science. As an adjunct to the field lab facilities, the University of South Carolina maintains the Kimbel Living and Learning Center, which includes a conference center and one eight-bedroom "dorm," two four-bedroom "dorms," and two two-bedroom "cottages" for visiting scientists. For the 2005 project, as well as those in subsequent years, these dorms and cabins have been home.

Unfortunately we had to abandon the project after a week and a half due to equipment problems. We were unable to continue it until August 2006, returning to Georgetown for four straight weeks of remote sensing in offshore blocks just south of the Winyah Bay entrance. When heavy seas kept us from going offshore, we turned our attention to several areas inside Winyah Bay. We judged the seas by how bad we got beat up going out through the jetties. When the seas, already confused by bouncing back and forth between the jetties as they fought to get into the bay, combined with a strong outgoing current, we found ourselves battling waves that broke over the cabin of our C-Hawk. By the end of the four grueling weeks of ten-hour days, including several during which we probably should not have defied the heavy seas, we had covered 5.8 square miles of ocean and bay, and several potential shipwrecks were located, both offshore and inside Winyah Bay.

After two weeks back at our offices, recuperating and preparing for diving operations, we returned to Georgetown for two weeks in September 2006. Our goal was to ground truth as many of the anomalies we recorded in August as possible. A prestigious array of marine scientists and divers assisted us. We were fortunate to have Dr. M. Scott Harris, an associate professor of marine science at Coastal Carolina University; Dr. Paul Work of Georgia Tech University; and Arnold Postell, a dive safety officer and senior biologist at the South Carolina Aquarium. Steve Luff, an adjunct instructor at Coastal Carolina University and a scuba instructor, and Jay Hubbell and Ted Churchill, both volunteer team leaders at the South Carolina Aquarium, dived with us at various times during the two weeks.

The two proverbial gremlins of bad weather and equipment problems joined us on the first day. When we arrived at South Island Ferry Public Boat Landing, strong winds and heavy seas greeted us—the effects of Hurricane Florence, which at that moment was ravaging Bermuda. Nonetheless we decided to see if we could dive on one of the anomalies we recorded inside Winyah Bay. As soon as we started the Honda generator powering our remote sensing gear, however, oil began pouring out of it. We agreed to scrap the day. To chase away the gremlins, we rented a generator while a local Honda dealer repaired ours. With the rented generator running our remote sensing equipment, we surveyed a section of the North Santee River, the site of a reported sunken blockade runner. After a day of towing the equipment, we decided there was no blockade runner in the bay, at least not where it was reported to be.

The next day, with heavy winds and heavy seas still making going offshore untenable, we dived on several anomalies recorded inside Winyah Bay. Two were on the west side of the bay, just off the Yawkey Wildlife Center. Another was on the east side behind North Island, between some unnamed islands and the North Island Lighthouse. The two anomalies on the west side turned out to be mooring blocks of some kind. The one on the east side was a crab trap mixed with some small pipes.

Finally fair weather arrived, allowing us to work offshore. We dived three sites. Two turned out to be LMOs. One was possibly an old boiler or tank of some sort, and one was several pieces of pipe three to four feet in diameter. But one turned out to be a shipwreck of a wooden vessel. About ninety feet of the vessel is exposed above the sandy bottom. Copper sheathing showed that it was not Ayllón's Capitana or any other pre-nineteenth-century vessel. At first there was some thought that the remains could be the *Sir Robert Peel,* a blockade runner scuttled by its captain to avoid capture by Union forces as it attempted to enter Winyah Bay in 1863. There just was not enough machinery, however, to indicate a blockade runner. More likely the wreck is the U.S. Army transport steamer *Osceola,* which sank off Georgetown in 1861. Built in 1848, the *Osceola* was wooden hulled, 120 feet long, and schooner rigged. It was fitted with a steam engine and boiler to drive a seven-foot iron propeller. The historic records indicate the *Osceola* was also copper sheathed.

The gremlins returned during the second week of diving. We decided to leave the landing, head south, and go out to sea through the entrance to the North Santee River. This allowed us to avoid the mountainous seas in the jetties, especially since we had the seventeen-foot McKee with us as chase/pump boat. Joe Beatty captained the McKee. As we charged out into the coastal waters on the C-Hawk, we kept an eye on Joe. If he was shaking his head, we knew the seas were too rough for the smaller boat, and we turned around, going to plan B for the day.

We did manage a few days offshore. On Wednesday Chris Amer and Scott Harris dug up a nineteenth-century "admiralty anchor." Six feet long and made of iron, the anchor had stationary arms with balls, one bent down. While exposing the anchor, the divers found an object of "amorphous metal" at four feet down. The pair also dug up a towing cable consisting of a long cable looped back on itself and bound together in several places.

We dismissed our finds, knowing they were not from the sixteenth century. So what exactly are we looking for? What aspects of any shipwreck we find would indicate a Spanish *nao?* What sort of artifacts would indicate an early-sixteenth-century wreck, specifically a Spanish ship of exploration? Logically it would be carrying the tools necessary to create a sizable settlement, along with enough foodstuffs to sustain the settlers until they could forage, trade for, or cultivate food. Presumably it would have crates of axes, hammer, nails, and other metal tools that our magnetometer would pick up. There would be anchors and perhaps a cannon or two.

Like our 2006 schedule, our 2007 plans called for four weeks of surveying and two of ground truthing. We spread the four weeks of the survey portion from May through the beginning of July. The first two survey weeks passed with little to note. During the third week, we were surveying an offshore block when we recorded a large magnetometer hit. Jim Spirek, who was running the remote sensing equipment that week, suspected that the anomaly was a large shipwreck, perhaps the location of the *Sir Robert Peel*. When plotted onto a navigational chart of the area, the magnetometer hit matched nicely with a symbol for a submerged shipwreck site, what is referred to fondly as a "football" because of its shape. This was surprising, since we have found that the wreck symbols on navigational charts seldom correspond to the actual location of shipwrecks. Even the chart maker, the National Oceanic and Atmospheric Administration, recognizes this by putting a double letter designation near many, if not most, of their submerged wreck symbols. These designations include the ever-popular *PA*, standing for *Position Approximate*, and my favorite, *ED*, for *Existence Doubtful*.

During the fourth week of the survey, we conducted perhaps the most dangerous aspect of our survey, running our magnetometer and side-scan sonar along the outside of the jetties. Keep in mind that the jetties are composed of rocks—large, jagged rocks. At low tide the waves crash against them, shooting geysers of water high into the air. At high tide the currents swirl across the submerged rocks, making it difficult to pinpoint their exact locations as they lurk just below the surface. I'm not sure which is worse, envisioning being smashed against the rocks by the waves at low tide or imagining the bottom of our C-Hawk being ripped out as the current tried to push us over the piercing tops of the jetty rocks. The payoff was recording a large magnetic anomaly about fifteen feet off the south jetty. We also surveyed north of the jetties, recording several promising magnetic anomalies.

Unfortunately equipment problems cut short the fourth week of our survey. While trailering the C-Hawk back to Hobcaw Barony at the end of the third day, one of the leaf springs on the boat trailer broke. By chance this occurred on Highway 17 right in front of Nautica Marine Center. We dragged the boat and trailer into their lot and left it for them to fix. The next day, while the good folks at Nautica fixed the trailer, we worked on equipment and generally loafed. We picked up the repaired trailer at 2 P.M. but decided this was too late to do any surveying that day. Then the next morning, as we were at South Island Ferry Boat

Landing, readying the C-Hawk for our last day of surveying, we discovered that the steering on the boat was not working properly. Actually it was not working at all. This was the last straw, so we cancelled the day's surveying and headed back to our offices.

We began the two weeks of diving on Monday, July 30. On hand was the entire Maritime Research Division staff, including Chris Amer, Jim Spirek, Lora Holland, Joe Beatty, and me. At different times during the two weeks, we had two volunteers. These were Dr. M. Scott Harris, who had dived with us in 2006, and Emily Jateff, who had taken a break from her duties as lab manager at Brockington and Associates, a private archaeological firm in Mount Pleasant, to dive with us.

On the first day, Chris and Jim dived on a large magnetic anomaly about one mile south of the jetties and about one mile off the beach in six to nine feet of water. The side-scan sonar had detected a small object protruding from the bottom. After a futile search for any visible signs of the anomaly, the divers used our hand-held magnetometer and found the magnetic anomaly's location beneath the bottom sediments. Probing into the bottom sediments, they came across a cylindrical "pipe" six inches or so in diameter about a foot down. Removing the sand covering the object with the water dredge, they discovered a long iron "spar" about twenty feet long. At one end the spar split into a Y. The other end sloped down into the sediments. At a depth of six feet below the bottom, the divers terminated the dig. After much speculation as to the identity of the object, we decided to remain stumped.

On Wednesday we dived the football—the location of the shipwreck symbol on the chart where we had recorded a large magnetic anomaly during the third week of surveying. We thought it could be the blockade runner *Sir Robert Peel*. Jim Spirek and Scott Harris were the divers. Whether what they found was the *Sir Robert Peel* is speculation, but it is a shipwreck with all the right aspects of a blockade runner. Jim and Scott found a boiler, six feet in diameter, ten feet long, and sticking up five feet from the sand. Nearby an exposed propeller shaft, six inches in diameter and twenty feet long, ended with a three-blade propeller about six feet in diameter with blades eighteen inches across. Several other unknown metal objects, covered with tubeworms, littered the area.

On the last day of the first week, we decided to dive on several magnetic anomalies we recorded in North Santee Bay back in 2006. None of the anomalies alone indicated a wreck, but their proximity to each other said that on whole they might. We knew that on February 24, 1863, the blockade runner *Queen of the Wave*, a British steamer, ran ashore trying to enter the North Santee River. The next morning the

USS *Conemaugh* arrived and found that the blockade runner's crew had set it on fire and abandoned it. Waiting another day, the captain of the *Conemaugh* sent an armed boat to salvage the wreck, but found that seven members of a local Confederate light artillery unit were on board. The Union sailors captured the Confederates and returned to the *Conemaugh*. The fire only partially destroyed the wreck, but bad weather prevented the Union ship from salvaging any of the cargo. On March 6 the *Conemaugh* returned to the scene to see if the crew could refloat the *Queen of the Wave,* but found that it had been broken in two by the recent bad weather. Nevertheless the Yankees salvaged as much of the wreck as possible. Items from the cargo included sheets of tin, bales of calico cloth, reams of printing paper, bottles of quinine and morphine, and fifteen pounds of opium. They also took the *Queen of the Wave*'s boat and davits, its binnacle, two anchors, and its compass. The Union sailors completed their work on the ill-fated blockade runner by blowing it up.

The anomalies we recorded in the North Santee were in shallow water near the beach of South Island. Large clumps of oysters mixed in with the bottom mud, and the search went slowly for the two divers, Jim Spirek and Lora Holland. Using Baby, our handheld proton magnetometer, the two divers managed to find the first anomaly among the oysters. It turned out to be an unknown domed metal object about two feet in diameter with a rope attached. We listed it as an LMO.

The trickiest day of diving came on Monday, August 6. We wanted to dive the anomaly just below the south jetty. For this dive we wanted a south wind and little current. This Monday promised to be the closest to our desired weather that week, our last week of the 2007 survey. The anomaly had a large magnetic signature and showed plenty of relief off the bottom. Normally this would have been an ideal dive. With such a large magnetic signature, it promised to be a shipwreck. With abundant relief it would be easy to find. The problem was that the side-scan sonar picture showed the anomaly rested only fifteen feet south of a large pile of sharp-edged rocks forming the southern jetty. In our favor the wind was coming from the south. Normally we anchor into the wind, allowing for any current, so that the stern of the C-Hawk settles on top of the anomaly. On most sites the direction of the wind does not matter, but on this site it did. To anchor into the wind, it needed to be southerly. If it were from the east or west, any cross current could sweep us across the jetty. If from the north, we would have had to toss the anchor on the rocks, with little possibility of retrieving it. As was our custom, we lowered our eighty-five-pound lead weight off the stern as a down line.

Over the years this weight has taken on the name "the clunk." I think this is from the sound it makes as it strikes the boat on being retrieved.

Chris and Lora dived on this one. As suspected the anomaly turned out to be a wreck, with a massive amount of associated machinery. The main portion was thirty-six feet long and about twenty feet wide, rising off the bottom as much as ten feet. Its piston engine indicated a disappointingly modern wreck. Scattered pieces of machinery surrounded the main site. "Possible dredge vessel," Chris wrote in his field notes. As luck would have it, the clunk caught on the wreck. As the divers related it, the clunk slid between two pieces of the wreck and down into a hole from which it could only be retrieved by complicated twisting and lifting maneuvers. After much twisting and lifting (and probably grunting), the maneuvers proved impossible for the two divers. We decided to buoy the weight and leave it for future recovery. We returned to the site on Wednesday. Using a lift bag to counter the clunk's eighty-five pounds of lead and a crowbar to twist the weight, the divers easily retrieved it.

That afternoon we went inside Winyah Bay to dive a possible shipwreck just off the main channel in eleven feet of water. This anomaly was tantalizingly close to a shipwreck symbol on the NOAA navigational chart. The "shipwreck" turned out to be a large, A-frame contraption with rungs between the legs of the frame. Our best guess was that the object was part of a shrimp boat's outrigger.

On Friday, the last day of diving, we returned to North Santee Bay to uncover the remaining two anomalies we thought might be the *Queen of the Wave*. Our first chore was to run the magnetometer over the area to relocate the anomalies. We knew they were close to the beach of South Island. We discovered how close on our first run when we found there was only two feet of water covering the bottom. To keep the engines from grounding us, I tilted them up as far as I could and still have steerage. Nevertheless the skegs on the bottom of the outboards scraped along the hard sand bottom, and I had to power up to make it through. On a subsequent pass, we had the sonar out to see if there was any relief to the anomalies. I was sure there was none, as I was certain we would have found them with the bottom of the C-Hawk's hull. The sonar run allowed us to stay further off as the sonar could "see" a good distance to the side. We saw no objects sticking up out of the bottom sand, but we could clearly see the twin lines where our outboards' skegs dragged through the hard sand bottom.

Jim Spirek and Scott Harris got into the water, again using Baby to pinpoint the anomalies. The second anomaly—the domed metal object found earlier was the first—turned out to be a pile of cement blocks and metal objects of undetermined shape and purpose. The third anomaly was a small Danforth anchor. Nearby was an eighteen-inch section of railroad track. Usually a find as unusual as a piece of railroad track would illicit all kinds of speculation as to what it was doing on the bottom of North Santee Bay. It was Friday, however. It was the last day of the project for 2007. It was probably used as an anchor.

Will we ever find *Le Prince* or Ayllón's Capitana? Much can happen to a shipwreck ravaged by the marine environment in more than four hundred years. There could be no remains left at all. There could be so few remains that our instruments fail to register their presence in any way that we would interpret as a possible shipwreck.

In addition time creates entirely new landmasses and deletes others. Sandbars move. Channels change. In the case of the Capitana, there is now an island, called appropriately Sand Island, where we think the entrance to Winyah Bay was in the sixteenth century. The Capitana may lie under dry land rather than underwater.

Finding *Le Prince* and Ayllón's Capitana could take years. We may not find either wreck. The thrill of discovery may await the next generation of archaeologists. On the other hand, the wrecks may never be found. Nevertheless if that should happen, the work we are now doing, the weeks and weeks of surveying and diving, will not have been for nothing. During our search for *Le Prince*, we have found a previously unknown ironclad in Port Royal Sound. Off Winyah Bay we located the remains of two other long-lost vessels. And we have eliminated miles and miles of sea bottom as the final resting place of these two sexy wrecks.

Bibliography

The Lewisfield—No, Two Cannon—No, Little Landing Wreck Site

Albright, Alan. "Field Notes." Field notebook, Maritime Research Division, South Carolina Institute of Archaeology and Anthropology, Columbia, 1986.

———. "Two Cannon Project Research Design." Photocopy, Maritime Research Division, South Carolina Institute of Archaeology and Anthropology, Columbia, 1987.

Allen, Debra, and Hans Knoop. "British Armed Vessel Discovered in Cooper River." USC News press release, January 1986. Information Services, University of South Carolina, Columbia.

Amer, Christopher, Bruce F. Thompson, and Ruth Trocolli. "Little Landing Survey." Photocopy, Maritime Research Division, South Carolina Institute of Archaeology and Anthropology, Columbia, n.d.

Cross, J. Russell. *Historic Ramblin's through Berkeley.* Columbia, S.C.: R. L. Bryan, 1985.

Hogg, O. F. G. *Artillery: Its Origin, Heyday, and Decline.* London: Archon, 1970.

Irving, John B. *A Day on Cooper River.* 2nd ed. Columbia, S.C.: St. John's Hunting Club, 1932.

Johnson, Joseph. *Traditions and Reminiscences Chiefly of the American Revolution in the South.* Charleston, S.C.: Walker & James, 1851. Reprint, Spartanburg, S.C.: Reprint Company, 1972.

McCray, Edward. *The History of South Carolina in the Revolution, 1780–1783.* New York: Russell & Russell, 1902.

Noël Hume, Ivor. *A Guide to Artifacts of Colonial America.* New York: Knopf, 1985.

Orvin, Maxwell Clayton. *Historic Berkeley County, South Carolina, 1671–1900.* Charleston, S.C.: Comprint, 1973.

Padfield, Peter. *Guns at Sea.* London: Evelyn, 1973.

Peterson, Harold L. *The Book of the Continental Soldier.* Harrisburg, Pa.: Stackpole, 1968.

Seidel, John L. "China Glaze Wares on Sites from the American Revolution: Pearl-ware before Wedgwood?" *Historic Archaeology: Journal of the Society for Historical Archaeology* 24, no. 1 (1990): 82–95.

Thompson, Bruce F. "Little Landing Survey." In *Underwater Archaeology Proceedings from the Society for Historical Archaeology Conference,* edited by John D. Broadwater, 125–31. Tucson, Ariz.: Society for Historical Archaeology, 1991.

Wilkinson-Latham, Robert. *British Artillery on Land and Sea, 1790–1820.* Newton Abbot, U.K.: David & Charles, 1973.

Mud Sucks

Amer, Christopher F., Joseph Beatty III, Lynn B. Harris, Carleton Naylor, James D. Spirek, and Mark K. Ragan. *A Management Plan for Known and Potential United States Navy Shipwrecks in South Carolina.* Columbia: Maritime Research Division, South Carolina Institute of Archaeology and Anthropology, 2004.

Bennett, Robert B., Jr. "The Santee Canal, 1785–1939." Master's thesis, University of South Carolina, 1988.

Charles, Tommy, and James O. Mills. *An Archeological Reconnaissance Survey of the Proposed Santee Canal Sanctuary, Berkeley County, South Carolina.* Research Manuscript Series 202. Columbia: South Carolina Institute of Archaeology and Anthropology, 1986.

Coker, P. C., III. *Charleston's Maritime Heritage, 1670–1865: An Illustrated History.* Charleston, S.C.: CokerCraft, 1987.

Cross, J. Russell. *Historic Ramblin's through Berkeley.* Columbia, S.C.: R. L. Bryan, 1985.

Crowson, E. T. "The Santee-Cooper: A Pioneering Effort in South Carolina Canaling." *South Carolina Magazine* 35, no. 8 (1971): 6–9, 14–20.

Leland, J. "The Santee Canal." *Sandlapper: The Magazine of South Carolina* 3, no. 3 (1970): 8–13.

Newell, Mark M. *The Santee Canal Sanctuary, Part II: Preliminary Archaeological Investigations of a Portion of the Old Santee Canal and Biggin Creek, Berkeley County, South Carolina.* Cultural Resource Management Publication 6. Columbia: Underwater Antiquities Management Program of the South Carolina Institute of Archaeology and Anthropology, 1989.

Orvin, Maxwell Clayton. *Historic Berkeley County, South Carolina, 1671–1900.* Charleston, S.C.: Comprint, 1973.

Porcher, F. A. *The History of the Santee Canal.* Charleston: South Carolina Historical Society, 1903.

Savage, Henry, Jr. *River of the Carolinas: The Santee.* Chapel Hill: University of North Carolina Press, 1956.

Simmons, Joe J., III, and Mark M. Newell. *The Santee Canal Sanctuary, Part I: Preliminary Archaeological Surveys of a Portion of the Old Santee Canal, the Biggin Creek Vessel and the Mouth of Biggin Creek, Berkeley County, South Carolina.* Columbia: Underwater Antiquities Management Program of the South Carolina Institute of Archaeology and Anthropology, 1989.

Webber, Mabel L., ed. "Col. Senf's Account of the Santee Canal." *South Carolina Historical Magazine* 28 (January 1927): 8–21; 28 (April 1927): 112–31.

The Day the Johnboat Went up the Mountain

Anderson, David G. "The Mississippian in South Carolina." In *Studies in South Carolina Archaeology: Essays in Honor of Robert L. Stephenson,* edited by Albert C. Goodyear III and Glen T. Hanson, 101–32. Columbia: South Carolina Institute of Archaeology and Anthropology, 1989.

Ashley-Montague, M. F. "A Seventeenth Century Account of Burial Customs among the Indians of South Carolina." *American Anthropologist* 42, no. 1 (1940): 177–78.

Blanding, William. "Description of the Mulberry Site." In "Archeological Investigations at the Mulberry Site," ed. Leland Ferguson, special issue, *Institute of Archeology and Anthropology Notebook* 6, nos. 3 & 4 (1974): 61–62.

Caldwell, Joseph R. "Study of the Mulberry Pottery." In "Archeological Investigations at the Mulberry Site," ed. Leland Ferguson, special issue, *Institute of Archeology and Anthropology Notebook* 6, nos. 3 & 4 (1974): 88–98.

Deetz, James. *Invitation to Archaeology.* Garden City, N.Y.: Natural History Press, 1967.

DePratter, Chester B. "Cofitachequi: Ethnohistorical and Archaeological Evidence." In *Studies in South Carolina Archaeology: Essays in Honor of Robert L. Stephenson,* edited by Albert C. Goodyear III and Glen T. Hanson, 133–56. Columbia: South Carolina Institute of Archaeology and Anthropology, 1989.

———. "Explorations in Interior South Carolina by Hernando De Soto (1540) and Juan Pardo (1566–1568)." *South Carolina Institute of Archaeology and Anthropology Notebook* 19 (1987): 1–5.

———. *Late Prehistoric and Early Historic Chiefdoms in the Southeastern United States.* New York: Garland, 1991.

DePratter, Chester B., and Christopher Amer. *Underwater Investigations at the Mulberry Site (38KE12) and Adjacent Portions of the Wateree River.* Columbia: South Carolina Institute of Archaeology and Anthropology, 1988.

Ferguson, Leland Greer. "South Appalachian Mississippian." Ph.D. dissertation, University of North Carolina, 1971.

Grimes, Kimberly M. "Dietary Choices at the Mulberry Mound Site." Master's thesis, University of South Carolina, 1986.

Hudson, Charles. *The Juan Pardo Expeditions: Explorations of the Carolinas and Tennessee, 1566–1568.* Washington, D.C.: Smithsonian Institution Press, 1990.

Judge, Christopher. "Aboriginal Pottery Vessel Function in South Appalachian Mississippi Society: A Case Study from the Mulberry Site (38KE12)." Master's thesis, University of South Carolina, 1987.

Kelly, A. R. "Excavation History at the Mulberry Plantation." In "Archeological Investigations at the Mulberry Site," ed. Leland Ferguson, special issue, *Institute of Archeology and Anthropology Notebook* 6, nos. 3 & 4 (1974): 67–87.

Lawson, John. *A New Voyage to Carolina.* London, 1709. Reprint, edited with an introduction and notes by Hugh Talmage Lefler. Chapel Hill: University of North Carolina Press, 1967.

Lowery, Woodbury. *The Spanish Settlements within the Present Limits of the United States, 1513–1561.* New York: Putnam, 1901.

Quattlebaum, Paul. *The Land Called Chicora: The Carolinas under Spanish Rule with French Intrusions, 1520–1670.* Gainesville: University of Florida Press, 1956.

Savage, Henry, Jr. *River of the Carolinas: The Santee.* Chapel Hill: University of North Carolina Press, 1956.

Shetrone, Henry Clyde. *The Mound-Builders.* New York: Appleton, 1930.

Squier, E. G., and E. H. Davis. *Ancient Monuments of the Mississippi Valley.* Smithsonian Contributions to Knowledge 1. Washington, D.C.: Smithsonian Institution, 1847.

Stuart, George. "Analysis of the Mulberry Site." In "Archeological Investigations at the Mulberry Site," ed. Leland Ferguson, special issue, *Institute of Archeology and Anthropology Notebook* 6, nos. 3 & 4 (1974): 100–110.

———. "Description of the Mulberry Site and Excavations." In "Archeological Investigations at the Mulberry Site," ed. Leland Ferguson, special issue, *Institute of Archeology and Anthropology Notebook* 6, nos. 3 & 4 (1974): 98–100.

Thomas, Cyrus. "Henry Reynolds' Excavations at the Mulberry Site." In "Archeological Investigations at the Mulberry Site," ed. Leland Ferguson, special issue, *Institute of Archeology and Anthropology Notebook* 6, nos. 3 & 4 (1974): 63–67.

Wagner, Gail E. "Losing Late Prehistory at Mulberry Mounds." In *Site Destruction in Georgia and the Carolinas,* edited by David G. Anderson and Virginia Horak, 10–17. Atlanta: National Park Service, 1993.

Hobcaw Shipyard

Amer, Christopher F., and Carleton A. Naylor. "Pritchard's Shipyard: Investigation at South Carolina's Largest Colonial Shipyard." In *Mount Pleasant's Archaeological Heritage,* edited by Amy Thompson McCandless, 36–49. Mount Pleasant, S.C.: Town of Mount Pleasant, 1996.

Clowse, Converse D. *Economic Beginnings in Colonial South Carolina, 1670–1730.* Columbia: University of South Carolina Press, 1971.

———. *Measuring Charleston's Overseas Commerce, 1717–1767: Statistics from the Port's Naval Lists.* Washington, D.C.: University Press of America, 1981.

———. "Shipowning and Shipbuilding in Colonial South Carolina." *American Neptune* 44, no. 4 (1984): 221–44.

Goldenberg, Joseph A. *Shipbuilding in Colonial America.* Charlottesville: University Press of Virginia, 1976.

Hamer, Philip M., and George C. Rogers, eds. *The Papers of Henry Laurens.* Vol. 2, *Nov. 1, 1755–Dec. 31, 1758.* Columbia: University of South Carolina Press, 1970.

Langley, Clara A., abstractor. *South Carolina Deed Abstracts, 1719–1772.* Vol. 1. Greenville, S.C.: Southern Historical Press, 1983.

———. *South Carolina Deed Abstracts, 1719–1772*. Vol. 2, *1740–1755, Books V–PP*. Easley, S.C.: Southern Historical Press, 1984.

———. *South Carolina Deed Abstracts, 1719–1772*. Vol. 3, *1755–1768, Books QQ–H-3*. Greenville, S.C.: Southern Historical Press, 1983.

———. *South Carolina Deed Abstracts, 1719–1772*. Vol. 4, *1767–1773, Books I-3–E-4*. Easley, S.C.: Southern Historical Press, 1984.

Lloyd's Register of Shipping. 132 volumes. Reprint, London: Gregg, 1965–1968. Especially volume for 1764.

Milling, Chapman J., ed. *Colonial South Carolina: Two Contemporary Descriptions, by James Glen and George Milligen-Johnston*. Columbia: University of South Carolina Press, 1951.

Moore, Carolina T., comp. and ed. *Records of the Secretary of the Province of South Carolina, 1692–1721*. Columbia, S.C.: R. L. Bryan, 1978.

Morby, Sarah J. "Pritchard's Shipyard: A Landscape Analysis of South Carolina's Largest Colonial and Antebellum Shipyard." Master's thesis, University of South Carolina, 2000.

Olsberg, Nicholas. "Ship Registers in the South Carolina Archives, 1734–1780." *South Carolina Historical and Genealogical Magazine* 74, no. 3 (1973): 189–299.

Plat EC-532. Register of Mesne Conveyance Office, Charleston County, S.C., 1998.

Pritchard, Paul. Will of November 10, 1791. *Records of Wills, Inventories, and Miscellaneous Records for Charleston County, South Carolina, 1671–1868*, 24-C: 963.

Rogers, George C., Jr., and David R. Chesnutt, eds. *The Papers of Henry Laurens*. Vol. 5, *Sept. 1–July 31, 1768*. Columbia: University of South Carolina Press, 1976.

———. *The Papers of Henry Laurens*. Vol. 6, *Aug. 1, 1768–July 31, 1769*. Columbia: University of South Carolina Press, 1978.

———. *The Papers of Henry Laurens*. Vol. 7, *Aug. 1, 1769–Oct. 9, 1771*. Columbia: University of South Carolina Press, 1979.

———. *The Papers of Henry Laurens*. Vol. 8, *Oct. 10, 1771–April 19, 1773*. Columbia: University of South Carolina Press, 1980.

Salley, A. S., Jr., ed. *Journal of the Commissioners of the Navy of South Carolina, October 9, 1776–March 1, 1779*. Columbia: Historical Commission of South Carolina, 1912.

———. *Journal of the Commissioners of the Navy of South Carolina, July 22, 1779–March 23, 1780*. Columbia: Historical Commission of South Carolina, 1913.

———. *Warrants for Lands in South Carolina, 1672–1711*. Columbia: University of South Carolina Press for the South Carolina Department of Archives and History, 1973.

Sayen, John J., Jr. "Oared Fighting Ships of the South Carolina Navy, 1776–1780." *South Carolina Historical Magazine* 87, no. 4 (1986): 213–37.

South Carolina and American General Gazette, November 27, 1770, 3.

South Carolina Gazette, April 27, 1767, 1; November 29, 1770, 3; October 25, 1773, 3.

Webber, Mabel L."The Bond Family of Hobcaw Plantation, Christ Church Parish." *South Carolina Historical and Genealogical Magazine* 25, no. 1 (1924): 1–22.

———. "Extracts from the Journal of Mrs. Ann Manigault, 1754–1781." *South Carolina Historical and Genealogical Magazine* 21, no. 1 (1920): 10–23.

———. "Josiah Smith's Diary, 1780–1781." *South Carolina Historical and Genealogical Magazine* 34, no. 4 (1933): 194–210.

Dredging for the First Americans

Adovasio, J. M. *The First Americans: In Pursuit of Archaeology's Greatest Mystery.* New York: Random House, 2002.

Collins, Jan. "Revolutionizing First American Thinking?" *American Archaeology* 9, no. 4 (2005/2006): 12–17.

Dewar, Elaine. *Bones: Discovering the First Americans.* New York: Carroll & Graf, 2002.

Goodyear, Albert C. "Allendale Research Project." *Council of South Carolina Professional Archaeologists Newsletter* 16, nos. 3 & 4 (1995): 1, 8–11.

———. "Backhoes, BBQs, and B Horizons: The 2002 Allendale Paleoindian Expedition." *Legacy* 7, no. 2 (2002) / 8, no. 1 (2003): 22–29.

———. "The Early Holocene Occupation of the Southeastern United States: A Geoarchaeological Summary." In *Ice Age People of North America: Environments, Origins, and Adaptations,* edited by Robson Bonnichsen and Karen L. Turnmire, 432–81. Corvallis: Oregon State University Press for the Center for the Study of the First Americans, 1999.

———. "The Return of the 1997 Allendale Paleoindian Expedition." *Legacy* 2, no. 2 (1997): 4–7.

———. "The Return of the 1998 Allendale Paleoindian Expedition: The Search for Some Even Earlier South Carolinians." *Legacy* 3, no. 2 (1998): 8–10.

———. "Summary of the Allendale Paleoindian Expedition—2003 and 2004 Field Seasons." *Legacy* 9, nos. 1 & 2 (2005): 4–11.

———. "Topper Site in the *New York Times.*" *Legacy* 9, nos. 1 & 2 (2005): 1, 11.

Goodyear, Albert C., and Alan B. Albright. "Underwater Archaeology of a Paleo-Indian (10,000–8,000 B.C.) Chert Quarry on Smiths Lake Creek." Unpublished technical report for Carolina Venture Fund Committee, October 21, 1985.

Lepper, Bradley T., and Robson Bonnichsen, eds. *New Perspectives on the First Americans.* College Station: Texas A&M University Press, 2004.

South Carolina Institute of Archaeology and Anthropology Annual Reports. Columbia: South Carolina Institute of Archaeology and Anthropology, 1983–1997.

Tibbetts, John H. "Ancient Tools? Searching for the First Americans." *Coastal Heritage* 19, no. 4 (2005): 3–12.

The Upside-Down Wreck

Amer, Christopher F., Suzanne C. Linder, Mark M. Newell, and William Barr. *The Ingram Vessel 38CT204: Intensive Survey and Excavation of an Upland River-craft at Cheraw, South Carolina.* Columbia: South Carolina Institute of Archaeology and Anthropology, 1995.

Baylor, Thomas G. "Inventory of Ordnance and Ordnance Stores Captured by the Army of the Tennessee in Cheraw, S.C., March 3, 1865." In *The War of the Rebellion: A Compilation of the Official Records of the Union and Confederate Armies,* series 1, vol. 47, pt. 1, 182–83. Washington, D.C.: Government Printing Office, 1895.

Charleston Courier, January 17, 1825, 2; March 15, 1841, 2; April 3, 1841, 2; May 23, 1842, 2; April 1, 1843, 2; November 23, 1853, 2.

Charleston Mercury, November 22, 1853, 2; November 23, 1853, 2.

Cheraw Intelligencer, June 5, 1823; June 19, 1823, 1.

Gregg, Alexander. *History of the Old Cheraws.* Columbia, S.C.: State Company, 1925.

Linder, Suzanne Cameron. "A River in Time: A Cultural Study of the Yadkin / Pee Dee River System to 1825." Ph.D. dissertation, University of South Carolina, 1993.

McCrady, Edward. *The History of South Carolina.* New York: Russell & Russell, 1902.

Mills, Robert. *Mills' Atlas of South Carolina.* Reprint, Lexington, S.C.: Sandlapper Store, 1979.

Nelson, Larry E. "Sherman at Cheraw." *South Carolina Historical Magazine* 100, no. 4 (1999): 328–54.

———. *Sherman's March through the Upper Pee Dee Region of South Carolina.* Florence, S.C.: Pee Dee Heritage Center, 2001.

Noël Hume, Ivor. *A Guide to Artifacts of Colonial America.* New York: Knopf, 1985.

South Carolina Hobby Diver License Files. Sport Diver Archaeology Management Program, Maritime Research Division Field Office, South Carolina Institute of Archaeology and Anthropology, Charleston, 1969– .

South Carolina Statewide Archaeological Site Inventory files. South Carolina Institute of Archaeology and Anthropology, University of South Carolina, Columbia, 1963– .

Stanley Consultants. *Great Pee Dee River Basin Navigability Study.* Report no. 11. Charleston, S.C.: U.S. Army Corps of Engineers, Charleston District, 1977.

Wilbanks, Ralph. "A Preliminary Report on the Mepkin Abbey Wreck, Cooper River, South Carolina: An Early 19th-Century River Trading Vessel." In *Underwater Archaeology: The Challenge before Us; Proceedings of the Twelfth Conference on Underwater Archaeology,* edited by Gordon P. Watts Jr., 151–57. San Marino, Cal.: Fathom Eight.

Salvage License #32

Bonds, John B. "Opening the Bar: First Dredging at Charleston, 1853–1859." *South Carolina Historical Magazine* 98, no. 3 (1997): 230–50.

Burton, E. Milby. *The Siege of Charleston, 1861–1865*. Columbia: University of South Carolina Press, 1970.

Charleston Daily Courier, November 1, 1862, 1; November 5, 1862, 3; November 6, 1862, 4.

Charleston Mercury, January 31, 1863, 2; February 2, 1863, 2; June 8, 1863, 2; August 10, 1864, 2.

Davis, John L. "Abstract Log of the U.S.S. *Wissahickon,* Lieutenant-Commander Davis, U.S. Navy, Commanding." In *Official Records of the Union and Confederate Navies in the War of the Rebellion,* series 1, vol. 14, 240–41. Washington, D.C.: Government Printing Office, 1901.

Edwards, William B. *Civil War Guns.* Harrisburg, Pa.: Stackpole, 1962.

Gillmore, Q. A. "Annual Report upon the Improvement of Rivers and Harbors on the Coast of South Carolina, Georgia, and the Atlantic Coast of Florida." Appendix T of *The Annual Report of the Chief of Engineers for 1874.* Washington, D.C.: Government Printing Office, 1874.

———. "Annual Report upon the Improvement of Rivers and Harbors on the Coast of South Carolina, Georgia, and the Atlantic Coast of Florida." Appendix U of *The Annual Report of the Chief of Engineers for 1875.* Washington, D.C.: Government Printing Office, 1875.

Naval War Records Office. "Report of Captain Green, U.S. Navy, of the Breach of Blockade by the Steamer *Minho,* October 20, 1862." In *Official Records of the Union and Confederate Navies in the War of the Rebellion,* series 1, vol. 13, 396–97. Washington, D.C.: Government Printing Office, 1901.

———. "Report of Captain Green, U.S. Navy, Regarding the Destruction of a Blockade Runner Aground off Fort Moultrie." In *Official Records of the Union and Confederate Navies in the War of the Rebellion,* series 1, vol. 15, 624–25. Washington, D.C.: Government Printing Office, 1902.

———. "U.S.S. *Isaac Smith.*" In *Official Records of the Union and Confederate Navies in the War of the Rebellion,* series 2, vol. 1, pt. 1 (Statistical Data of Union and Confederate Ships), 109. Washington, D.C.: Government Printing Office, 1921.

Salvage License #32 files. Maritime Research Division, South Carolina Institute of Archaeology and Anthropology, Columbia, 1985–1991. Contains license and renewal applications, minutes of public hearings, letters between parties, SCIAA staff memos, salvage activity reports, and report of criminal investigation.

Scharf, J. Thomas. *History of the Confederate States Navy.* New York: Rogers & Sherwood, 1887; New York: Gramercy, 1996.

Tower, Howard B. Jr. "Civil War Wreck Salvaged: *Minho* Gives Up Military Relics." *Treasure Found* 15, no. 1 (1989): 28–33, 61.

Wise, Stephen R. *Lifeline of the Confederacy: Blockade Running during the Civil War.* Columbia: University of South Carolina Press, 1988.

The Wreck of the SS *William Lawrence*

Fike, Richard E. *The Bottle Book: A Comprehensive Guide to Historic, Embossed Medicine Bottles.* Salt Lake City: Peregrine Smith, 1987.

Harris, Lynn. "SS *William Lawrence.*" 1995. Photocopy, Maritime Research Division, South Carolina Institute of Archaeology and Anthropology, Columbia.

Hawkins, Falcon B. *Order.* Filed in reference to Civil Action #2:87-3409-1. United States District Court for the District of South Carolina, Charleston Division in Admiralty, December 20, 1989.

———. *Order Granting Temporary Injunction.* Filed in reference to Civil Action #2:87-3409-1. United States District Court for the District of South Carolina, Charleston Division in Admiralty, April 5, 1988.

Huggins, Phillip Kenneth. *The South Carolina Dispensary: A Bottle Collector's Atlas and History of the System.* Columbia, S.C.: Sandlapper, 1971.

McTeer, J. E. *Adventure in the Woods and Waters of the Low Country.* Beaufort, S.C.: Beaufort Book, 1972.

Savannah Morning News, February 14, 1899, 8; February 15, 1899, 6, 8; February 16, 1899, 8; February 17, 1899, 8; February 18, 1899, 6; February 20, 1899, 8; February 21, 1899, 9; February 22, 1899, 8; February 23, 1899, 8.

U.S. Congress. *Pure Food and Drug Act of 1906.* U.S. Statutes at Large, 59th Cong., 1st sess., chap. 3915, pp. 768–72. http://coursesa.matrix.msu.edu/~hst203/documents/pure.html (accessed April 19, 2006).

Hobby Divers

Albright, Alan B. "The Law and the Amateur in Resource Management." In *Studies in South Carolina Archaeology: Essays in Honor of Robert L. Stephenson,* edited by Albert C. Goodyear III and Glen T. Hanson, 253–60. Columbia: South Carolina Institute of Archaeology and Anthropology, 1989.

Brewer, David M. "The Continuing Importance of the Contributions of Sport Divers to South Carolina History." Unpublished manuscript, South Carolina Institute of Archaeology and Anthropology, Columbia, 1986.

Harris, Lynn. *The Waccamaw–Richmond Hill Waterfront Project 1991: Laurel Hill Barge No. 2.* Research Manuscript Series 214. Columbia: South Carolina Institute of Archaeology and Anthropology, Underwater Archaeology Division, 1991.

Harris, Lynn, Jimmy Moss, and Carl Naylor. *The Cooper River Survey: An Underwater Reconnaissance of the West Branch.* Research Manuscript Series 218. Columbia: South Carolina Institute of Archaeology and Anthropology, Underwater Archaeology Division, 1993.

Pecorelli, Harry, III. "Archaeological Investigation of the B&B Wreck (38BK1672) An Eighteenth-Century Plantation-Built Vessel, Charleston, South Carolina." Master's thesis, East Carolina University, 2003.

Ruddy, Drew. *Willtown Bluff: An Avocational Underwater Archaeological Report.* Columbia: South Carolina Institute of Archaeology and Anthropology, 2000.

South Carolina Hobby Diver License Files. Sport Diver Archaeology Management Program, Maritime Research Division Field Office, South Carolina Institute of Archaeology and Anthropology, Charleston, 1969– .

South Carolina Statewide Archaeological Site Inventory Files. South Carolina Institute of Archaeology and Anthropology, University of South Carolina, Columbia, 1963– .

South Carolina Underwater Antiquities Act of 1991 (as amended 2002). *Code of Laws of South Carolina,* chap. 7, title 54, art. 5.

Spence, E. Lee. "Wreck of the Confederate Mystery Ship *Georgiana,* 1863." *Ship-Wrecks* 1, no. 1 (1990): 35–56.

Stephenson, Robert L. "The South Carolina Underwater Salvage Law of 1968 as Amended in 1969 Together with the Uniform Rules and Regulations Prescribed to Carry Out the Law." Unpublished manuscript, Institute of Archeology and Anthropology, University of South Carolina, Columbia, 1970.

Tower, Howard B., Jr. "Civil War Wreck Salvaged: *Minho* Gives Up Military Relics." *Treasure Found* 15, no. 1 (1989): 28–33, 61.

Joe and the Alligator

Calder, Dale R., and Margaret Callison Pridgen. *Guide to Common Jellyfish of South Carolina.* Charleston: S.C. Sea Grant Consortium and Clemson University, 1985.

Cech, Rich, and Guy Tudor. *Butterflies of the East Coast.* Princeton: Princeton University Press, 2005.

Newell, Mark M. *Intensive Underwater Archaeological Survey of a Section of the Historic Waterfront District City of Conway, S.C.* With an appendix by Christopher F. Amer. Cultural Resource Management Series 12. Columbia: Underwater Archaeology Division, South Carolina Institute of Archaeology and Anthropology, 1991.

Brown's Ferry Vessel Arrives in Georgetown

Albright, Alan B., and J. Richard Steffy. "The Brown's Ferry Vessel, South Carolina: Preliminary Report." *International Journal of Nautical Archaeology and Underwater Exploration* 8, no. 2 (1979): 121–42.

"Brown's Ferry Vessel to Be Restored." *New South Carolina State Gazette* 12, no. 3 (1979): 1, 3.

Cauthen, Andrew. "Merchant Ship Taken to Georgetown's Rice Museum." *Myrtle Beach Sun News,* July 29, 1992, 1A, 5A.

Chapelle, Howard I. *The History of The American Sailing Navy: The Ships and Their Development.* New York: Norton, 1949; New York: Bonanza, 1988.

Hocker, Fred. "The Place of the Brown's Ferry Vessel in the Evolution of the Flat Bottomed Boat." Report prepared as assignment for Anthropology 615: The History of Wooden Ship Construction, Texas A&M University, May 1985.

Killingbeck, Rochelle. "Brown's Ferry Vessel Lifted into Museum." *Charleston Post and Courier,* July 29, 1992, 1-B, 4-B.

Saunders, Randy. "Brown's Ferry Vessel Comes Home to Roost." *Georgetown Times,* July 30, 1992, 1.

———. "18th Century River Trader to Return Home Tuesday." *Georgetown Times,* July 28, 1992, 1.

Steffy, J. Richard. "Preliminary Report: Hull Construction Features of the Brown's Ferry Vessel." *Institute of Archeology and Anthropology Notebook* 10 (1978): 1–29.

Wilbanks, Ralph L. "A Preliminary Report on the Construction Details of the Brown's Ferry Vessel." *South Carolina Antiquities* 10, no. 1 (1978): 416–21.

Those Darn Dugouts

Alford, Michael B. "Origins of Carolina Split-Dugout Canoes." *International Journal of Nautical Archaeology* 21, no. 3 (1992): 191–203.

Beta Analytic, Inc. "Report of Radiocarbon Dating Analysis." Letter dated May 7, 1999. On file. Charleston Field Office, South Carolina Institute of Archaeology and Anthropology.

Hudson, Charles. *The Southeastern Indians.* Knoxville: University of Tennessee Press, 1976.

Lawson, John. *A New Voyage to Carolina.* London, 1709. Reprint, edited with an introduction and notes by Hugh Talmage Lefler. Chapel Hill: University of North Carolina Press, 1967.

Newsome, Lee Ann, and Barbara A. Purdy. "Florida Canoes: A Maritime Heritage from the Past." *Florida Anthropologist* 43, no. 3 (1990): 164–80.

Smith, Bruce [Associated Press]. "Ancient Canoe Pulled from Cooper River." *Charleston Post and Courier,* July 30, 1997, 1-A, 9-A.

South Carolina Gazette, March 4–11, 1731; February 5–12, 1741; January 25–February 1, 1768; February 1–8, 1768.

South Carolina Statewide Archaeological Site Inventory files. South Carolina Institute of Archaeology and Anthropology, University of South Carolina, Columbia, 1963– .

Wilbanks, Ralph. "A Progress Report on the Small Watercraft Research Project in South Carolina." *Institute of Archeology and Anthropology Notebook* 12, no. 3 & 4 (1980): 17–27.

———. "The Roots Site, a Post-Contact Canoe." Unpublished manuscript, South Carolina Institute of Archaeology and Anthropology, University of South Carolina, Columbia.

Wilbanks, Ralph, and Katherine Singley Dannenburg. "Small Watercraft Research Project Update." *South Carolina Institute of Archaeology and Anthropology Notebook* 17, no. 1 (1985): 1–5.

The *Hunley,* the *Housatonic,* and the *Indian Chief*

Charleston Mercury, August 18, 1864.

Foenander, Terry. "Service aboard the CSS 'Virginia': Memoirs of James Thomas

Brady." U.S. Civil War Navies. http://home.ozconnect.net/tfoen/brady.htm (accessed July 29, 2005).

Harris, Lynn. "Field Notes for August 2, 16, 17, 18, 2002." Field notebook, Maritime Research Division Field Office, South Carolina Institute of Archaeology and Anthropology, Charleston.

Hicks, Brian, and Schuyler Kropf. *Raising the "Hunley": The Remarkable History and Recovery of the Lost Confederate Submarine.* New York: Random House, 2002.

Naval War Records Office. "Information Obtained from the Examination of Deserters from the Enemy." In *Official Records of the Union and Confederate Navies in the War of the Rebellion,* series 1, vol. 15, 227–28. Washington, D.C.: Government Printing Office, 1902.

———. "Order of Captain Ingraham, C.S. Navy, to Lieutenant Dozier, C.S. Navy, Regarding a Change of Command." In *Official Records of the Union and Confederate Navies in the War of the Rebellion,* series 1, vol. 13, 813. Washington, D.C.: Government Printing Office, 1901.

———. "Order of Flag-Officer Tucker, C.S. Navy, to Lieutenant Dozier, C.S. Navy, Regarding the Disposition of the Steamer Moultrie." In *Official Records of the Union and Confederate Navies in the War of the Rebellion,* series 1, vol. 14, 763. Washington, D.C.: Government Printing Office, 1902.

———. "Order of Flag-Officer Tucker, C.S. Navy, to Lieutenant Dozier, C.S. Navy, Regarding the Disposition of the Steamer Moultrie." In *Official Records of the Union and Confederate Navies in the War of the Rebellion,* series 2, vol. 1, 257. Washington, D.C.: Government Printing Office, 1921.

Ragan, Mark F. *The Hunley.* Orangeburg, S.C.: Sandlapper, 2005.

———. "Military Shipwrecks in South Carolina Waters 1740–2000." Unpublished manuscript. On file. Maritime Archaeology Division, South Carolina Institute of Archaeology and Anthropology, Columbia.

Rivers, Henry F. Log Books, 1920–1938. South Carolina Historical Society, Charleston.

Scharf, J. Thomas. *History of the Confederate States Navy.* New York: Rogers & Sherwood, 1887; New York: Gramercy, 1996.

The Mysterious French Cargo Site

Craig, Alan K. *Spanish Colonial Silver Coins in the Florida Collection.* Gainesville: University Press of Florida, 2000.

Deetz, James. *In Small Things Forgotten: The Archeology of Early American Life.* New York: Anchor, 1977.

Hobby Diver License File #3242. Sport Diver Archaeology Management Program, Maritime Research Division Field Office, South Carolina Institute of Archaeology and Anthropology, Charleston.

Nash, Steve. "South Carolina Hobby Diver Quarterly Report for July–September, 1995." Sport Diver Archaeology Management Program, Maritime Research

Division Field Office, South Carolina Institute of Archaeology and Anthropology, Charleston.

Noël Hume, Ivor. *A Guide to Artifacts of Colonial America*. New York: Knopf, 1985.

Peterson, Harold L. *The Book of the Continental Soldier*. Harrisburg, Pa.: Stackpole, 1968.

The Cooper River Anchor Farm

Curryer, Betty Nelson. *Anchors: An Illustrated History*. Annapolis, Md.: Naval Institute Press, 1999.

Davis, Charles G. *American Sailing Ships: Their Plans and History*. New York: Dover, 1984.

Harland, John. *Seamanship in the Age of Sail: An Account of the Shiphandling of the Sailing Man-of-War, 1600–1860, Based on Contemporary Sources*. Annapolis, Md.: Naval Institute Press, 1995.

Harris, Lynn. "Field Notes, February 2, 2000." Field notebook, Maritime Research Division, South Carolina Institute of Archaeology and Anthropology, Charleston.

Mowing the Lawn

Amer, Christopher. "SCIAA Receives State-of-the-Art Marine Remote Sensing Equipment." *Legacy* 3, no. 2 (1998): 28.

Man Overboard—Not!

Albright, Alan B. "The USS *Boston* Project." In *In Search of Our Maritime Past: Proceedings of the Fifteenth Conference of Underwater Archaeology*, edited by Jonathan W. Bream, 14–19. Greenville, N.C.: Program in Maritime History and Underwater Research, East Carolina University, 1984.

Amer, Christopher F., Joseph Beatty III, Lynn B. Harris, Carleton Naylor, James D. Spirek, and Mark K. Ragan. *A Management Plan for Known and Potential United States Navy Shipwrecks in South Carolina*. Columbia: Maritime Research Division, South Carolina Institute of Archaeology and Anthropology, 2004.

Bell, Jack. *Civil War Heavy Explosive Ordnance*. Denton: University of North Texas Press, 2003.

Chapelle, Howard I. *The History of the American Sailing Navy*. New York: Bonanza, 1949.

Devens, Richard Miller. *The Pictorial Book of Anecdotes and Incidents of the War of the Rebellion, Civil, Military, Naval and Domestic . . . from the Time of the Memorable Toast of Andrew Jackson—"The federal union; it must be preserved!" . . . to the Assassination of President Lincoln, and the End of the War. With Famous Words and Deeds of Woman, Sanitary and Hospital Scenes, Prison Experiences, etc.: By Frazer Kirkland [pseudo.]* Hartford, Conn.: Hartford Publishing, 1867.

Dudley, William S., ed. *The Naval War of 1812: A Documentary History.* Vol. 1, *1812.* Washington, D.C.: Naval Historical Center, Department of the Navy, 1985.

———. *The Naval War of 1812: A Documentary History.* Vol. 2, *1813.* Washington, D.C.: Naval Historical Center, Department of the Navy, 1992.

Frazier, Herb. "Fake Drowning Nets Prison Time, Probation for 3 from Fishing Family." *Charleston Post and Courier,* March 14, 2003, 1B, 6B.

Hunter, Alvah F. *A Year on a Monitor and the Destruction of Fort Sumter.* Columbia: University of South Carolina Press, 1987.

Smith, Glenn. "Fisherman Believed Drowned Is Charged with Insurance Fraud." *Charleston Post and Courier,* March 3, 2001, 1A, 9A.

———. "Fisherman's Father Faces Hoax Charge." *Charleston Post and Courier,* March 8, 2001, 3B.

Tucker, Spencer C. *The Jeffersonian Gunboat Navy.* Columbia: University of South Carolina Press, 1993.

Walker, Tyrone. "Fisherman's Wife: Despair Led to Hoax." *Charleston Post and Courier,* March 4, 2001, 1B, 6B.

"Never Sausage an Artifact"

Behan, William A. *A Short History of Callawassie Island, South Carolina: The Lives and Times of Its Owners and Residents, 1711–1985.* New York: iUniverse, 2004.

Flathmann, Jessica. "Never Sausage an Artifact." *Hilton Head Island Packet,* June 4, 2005.

Larson, Lewis, ed. *The Georgia and South Carolina Coastal Expeditions of Clarence Bloomfield Moore.* Tuscaloosa: University of Alabama Press, 1998.

Michie, James L. *An Archeological Investigation of the Cultural Resources of Callawassie Island, Beaufort County, South Carolina.* Research Manuscript Series 176. Columbia: Institute of Archeology and Anthropology [University of South Carolina], 1982.

Reid, Dawn M. "Beyond Subsistence: Prehistoric Lifeways on the South Carolina Coast as Reflected by Zooarchaeological Analysis." *South Carolina Antiquities* 38, nos. 1 & 2 (2006): 1–19.

South, Stanley. "Archaeologically Testing a Tabby Ruin on Callawassie Island, South Carolina." *Legacy* 10, no. 1 (2006): 1, 20.

South Carolina Statewide Archaeological Site Inventory files. South Carolina Institute of Archaeology and Anthropology, University of South Carolina, Columbia, 1963– .

Spirek, James. "Callawassie Island Submerged Archaeological Prospecting Survey: Ground-Truthing Results." *Legacy* 10, no. 2 (2006): 1, 4–5.

———. "An Incomplete Circumnavigation: The Callawassie Island Submerged Archaeological Prospecting Survey—Brief Report." *Legacy* 9, no. 1/2 (2005): 32.

Trinkley, Michael, ed. *Further Investigations of Prehistoric and Historic Lifeways on Callawassie and Spring Islands, Beaufort County, South Carolina.* Research Series 23. Columbia, S.C.: Chicora Foundation, 1991.

Sexy Wrecks

Amer, Christopher. "Ayllón Project Field Notes." Field notebook, Maritime Research Division, South Carolina Institute of Archaeology and Anthropology, Columbia, 2007.

Arnold, J. Barto, III, and Robert Weddle. *The Nautical Archeology of Padre Island: The Spanish Shipwrecks of 1554.* New York: Academic Press, 1978.

Doran, Edwin, Jr., and Michael F. Doran. "Appendix E: A Reconstruction of the Padre Island Ship." In *The Nautical Archeology of Padre Island: The Spanish Shipwrecks of 1554,* edited by J. Barto Arnold III and Robert Weddle, 375–84. New York: Academic Press, 1978.

Hoffman, Paul E. *A New Andalucia and a Way to the Orient: The American Southeast during the Sixteenth Century.* Baton Rouge: Louisiana State University Press, 1990.

Lowery, Woodbury. *The Spanish Settlements within the Present Limits of the United States, 1513–1561.* New York: Russell & Russell, 1959.

Michie, James L. *A Reconnaissance Search for Evidence of the Capitana: Lucas Vazquez de Ayllón's 1526 Flagship.* Research Manuscript Series 3. Conway: Waccamaw Center for Historical and Cultural Studies, University of South Carolina–Coastal Carolina College, 1993.

———. *The Search for San Miguel de Gualdape.* Research Manuscript Series 1. Conway: Waccamaw Center for Historical and Cultural Studies, University of South Carolina–Coastal Carolina College, 1991.

Miller, Mary E. *Baroness of Hobcaw: The Life of Belle W. Baruch.* Columbia: University of South Carolina Press, 2006.

Morison, Samuel Eliot. *The European Discovery of America.* Vol 1, *The Northern Voyages,* A.D. *500–1600.* New York: Oxford University Press, 1971.

National Oceanographic and Atmospheric Administration. *Winyah Bay.* Navigational Chart #11523. Washington, D.C.: U.S. Commerce Department, 1985.

Naval War Records Office. *Official Records of the Union and Confederate Navies in the War of the Rebellion.* Series 1, vol. 13, *South Atlantic Blockading Squadron (May 14, 1861–April 7, 1863).* Washington, D.C.: Government Printing Office, 1901.

Pope, Peter. "Ships and Navigation in Atlantic Canada in the 16th Century." Final Report for the Nova Scotia Department of Tourism and Culture, March 27, 1992. http://www.matthew.co.uk/history/navigation2.html (accessed August 24, 2005).

Quattlebaum, Paul. *The Land Called Chicora: The Carolinas under Spanish Rule with French Intrusions, 1520–1670.* Gainesville: University of Florida Press, 1956.

Spirek, James. *Port Royal Sound Survey, Search for "Le Prince": Progress Report, 2 August 2001.* Columbia: South Carolina Institute of Archaeology and Anthropology, 2001.

———. "A Search for *Le Prince*: Underwater Archaeological Prospecting in the French Archives." *Legacy* 3, no. 3 (1998): 10–13.

Index

ACE Basin, 187, 204
Adovasio, James, 70
airlift/airlifting, 10, 13–15, 19, 40, 73–74
Albright, Alan, 2; at Allendale Chert Quarry, 72–73; and Brown's Ferry Vessel, 140–43; and canoes, 151, 154; at Lewisfield, 6–7, 9–10, 14–16; and salvage license #32, 92, 94–96, 98–100, at Santee Canal, 28
Allendale, S.C., 71, 74
Allendale Chert Quarry, 3, 71, 73–74, 77
Ameika, Mike, 165
Amer, Christopher, 3, 136–37; at Allendale Chert Quarry, 74, 77; and Ayllón project, 226, 228, 230; and Brown's Ferry Vessel, 139; at Callawassie Island, 207–8, 211–12; at Hobcaw Shipyard, 67; and SS Lawrence, 109; and Le Prince project, 218; at Lewisfield, 16; and Mulberry mound project, 49–50; and Naval Historic Center survey, 188; and salvage license #32, 98–107; at Santee Canal, 35; and the Upside-Down Wreck, 81–82, 84
Arbuthnot, Admiral Marriott, 64
Archaeological Research Trust (ART), 125, 152, 224

Archaeological Society of South Carolina (ASSC), 72, 84, 153
Arctic, CSS, 161
Ard, Don, 5–6, 13, 15, 17
artifacts, 161; from Allendale Chert Quarry, 70, 72–75, 77–78; anchors, 173, 180; from Ayllón project, 223, 226; from USS Boston, 205; British cartridge box, 20; from Brown's Ferry Vessel, 139, 141–42, 148; from Callawassie Island, 210, 213; curation of, 2, 185; from French Cargo site, 167–72; collected by hobby divers, 3, 116, 118–23, 125, 131–32; from Hobcaw Shipyard, 65–67; illegally obtained, 149, 156–57; from SS Lawrence, 108, 110, 112; from Lewisfield project, 5, 11, 13–14, 19–21; from Mulberry mound project, 42, 47, 49, 50, 53–54; and salvage license #32, 91–92, 94–95, 98–105; from Santee Canal project, 27–29, 36–38, 40–41; from Skull Creek wreck site, 197; from Station Creek, 199; from the Upside-Down Wreck, 80–81, 83, 86. See also bar shot; bottles; buttons; cannon; chert; Clovis points; coins; Enfield rifles, English wine bottles; gunflints; ceramics, historic; mica; minié ball;

About the Author

After spending four years in the U.S. Navy, CARL NAYLOR worked as a South Carolina newspaper journalist before turning to his third career as a scuba-diving instructor in 1985. Two years later he joined the staff of the South Carolina Institute of Archaeology and Anthropology, where he is diving supervisor and archaeologist assistant for its Maritime Research Division. He is an instructor for the institute's underwater archaeology field-training course and acts as captain for its research vessels. Naylor lives on James Island near Charleston.